The Theology of
Battlestar Galactica

The Theology of
Battlestar Galactica

American Christianity
in the 2004–2009
Television Series

KEVIN J. WETMORE, JR.

McFarland & Company, Inc., Publishers
Jefferson, North Carolina, and London

LIBRARY OF CONGRESS CATALOGUING-IN-PUBLICATION DATA

Wetmore, Kevin J., Jr., 1969–
    The theology of Battlestar Galactica : American Christianity
in the 2004–2009 television series / Kevin J. Wetmore, Jr.
      p.   cm.
    Includes bibliographical references and indexes.

    ISBN 978-0-7864-6550-7
    softcover : acid free paper ∞

    1. Battlestar Galactica (Television program : 2003)
    2. Battlestar Galactica (Television program : 2004–2009)
    3. Television broadcasting — Religious aspects — Christianity.
    4. Television broadcasting — United States.   I. Title.
PN1992.77.B354W48 2012
791.45'72 — dc23   2012011446

BRITISH LIBRARY CATALOGUING DATA ARE AVAILABLE

Front cover: The cast of *Battlestar Galactica*, Season 4, 2007–2008
(SCI FI Channel/Photofest); Cover design by David K. Landis
(Shake It Loose Graphics)

Manufactured in the United States of America

McFarland & Company, Inc., Publishers
  Box 611, Jefferson, North Carolina 28640
    www.mcfarlandpub.com

This one is dedicated to
the Rev. Jeffrey Siker —
teacher, mentor and friend.

Table of Contents

Acknowledgments   ix

Introduction   1

I. Created Theologies   17

1. A Systematic Theology of Human Religion / The Human Understanding of God   19

2. A Systematic Theology of Cylon Religion / The Cylon Understanding of God   38

3. A Systematic Theology of the Baltar Cult / The Baltar Cult Understanding of God   55

II. Real-World Echoes   67

4. Gospels, Sins and Salvation: The Use of Christian Terminology in *BSG*   68

5. "In His Own Image He Created Them": Creation and Falls   79

6. Exile and the Remnant: Religion of the Planetless   93

7. The Role of Prophets   109

8. Starbuck Died, Starbuck Is Risen, Starbuck Will Come Again: Messiahs and Resurrection in *BSG*   125

 9. Cylon Messiah, Human Judas: Baltar, Betrayal
     and Redemption 139

10. From Patmos to Caprica: Battlestar Apocalyptica 153

Conclusion: The Plan 169

Epilogue: The Theology of *Caprica*; or, Why Parents
     Don't Always Look Like Their Children 174

Appendix I: Episode List by Season 191
Appendix II: Glossary 195
Bibliography 199
Index of Scriptural Quotations 205
General Index 207

Acknowledgments

Thanks are due to my many fine teachers of religion and theology: Fr. Kenneth Frisbie, David Tracy, Fred Clothey, David Sanchez, Daniel Smith-Christopher, Father Jim Fredericks, Thomas Rausch, S.J., Tracy Sayuki Tiemeier, Charlotte Radler, and Jonathan Rothchild. Special thanks to Jeff Siker who read and commented on an earlier version of this project.

Many thanks to my colleagues at Loyola Marymount University, especially Dan Weingarten, Grant Garinger, S.J., Katharine Noon, Mark Seldis, Jim Holmes and Neno Pervan. Thanks as well to the administration and support staff in the Department of Theatre Arts and Dance, the College of Communication and Fine Arts and the Bellarmine College of Liberal Arts.

The author would also like to thank the creators, cast and crew of *BSG*, especially Graham "Colonel Fisk" Beckel.

Thanks to my family: Kevin Sr., Eleanor, Lisa, John, Sean, Tom, Eileen and Toni.

Lastly, thanks to Anthony Miller for watching them all with me and entertaining endless conjectures, to Cody Kopp for also entertaining endless conjectures and offering his own in return, to Kimberly Garmoe, for supplying some sources, and to Lacy Hornick for putting up with me during the watching of the show, the reading of the many sources, the writing of the manuscript and the endless thinking-out-loud sessions.

Introduction

Diane Winston, in her introduction to *Small Screen, Big Picture,* remarkably postulates that "television has superseded church insofar as it is a virtual meeting place where Americans across racial, ethnic, economic and religious lines can find instructive and inspirational narratives" (2009: 2). While this statement might raise eyebrows in some theological quarters, I must confess that many Friday nights from 2005 to 2009 were a religious experience for me. With each new episode of the reimagined *Battlestar Galactica* (*BSG*) on the Sci-Fi network, I found "instructive and inspirational narratives," in Winston's terms. The television program inspired thought, conversation, reflection and insight in a manner religion often claims for itself.

Stewart M. Hoover, in *Religion in the Media Age,* observes that religion and media now "occupy the same spaces, serve many of the same purposes, and invigorate the same practices in late modernity" (2006: 9). Both religion and media are meaning-making practices that include meaning-making narratives and contain identity-making practices. While not conceding entirely to Hoover's lack of distinction between religion and media, I do concede that there is frequent overlap between religion and popular media (*The Passion of the Christ, Left Behind, The Chronicles of Narnia, Seventh Heaven, Touched by an Angel,* etc.), and a growing body of literature on film and popular culture addresses their intersections and interactions with theology. Especially for younger generations, "popular culture is a major meaning-making system," in the words of Tom Beaudoin, and more and more Americans are "living

religiously through popular culture" (1998: xiv, 25). As a member of
Generation X, I must agree that popular culture texts are meaning-
making texts that frequently shape my own religious and theological
understandings in a manner that scripture does not always do. Popular
culture mediates the narratives of scriptures in new ways, riffs on scriptural themes, and translates, manifests and echoes Biblical theologies
in ways that are oftentimes more accessible than the original scriptures
are today.

From the writings of Robert Jewett (1993), who places the epistles
of Paul in dialogue with contemporary films; to Christopher Deacy
(2001), who finds meditations on redemption in film noir cinema and
the movies of Martin Scorsese that are insightful for Christians; to Timothy J. Gorringe, who writes that "culture ... is concerned with the spiritual, ethical and intellectual significance of the material world.... It is,
therefore, of fundamental theological concern" (2004: 3); it is apparent
that film and television do not need to be overtly religious in order to
have a perceived theological content and value.

Popular media often manifest and reflect the material culture, narrative culture and intellectual culture of popular religion (the minister
as a character, the crucifix on the wall, the use of recognizable phrases
such as "prodigal son," "turn the other cheek" or "Armageddon") without
necessarily constructing an explicitly religious narrative. Yet what
Christopher Deacy and Gaye Williams Ortiz note of films, that they "do
not need to be explicitly Christian in their context or form to be theologically significant" (2008: 11)(indeed, they are often more effective
when they are not overtly Christian), I here write about television programs.

The reimagined television series *Battlestar Galactica* (*BSG*), which
ran on the Sci-Fi network from 2005 to 2009 with a total of 84 episodes,
including the original miniseries and two television films (*Razor* and
The Plan), is an example of "theologically significant" narrative.
Together, these episodes tell a narrative arc from the destruction of
humanity at the hands of the mechanical Cylons to the finding of a new
world upon which human and Cylon can live together in peace. There
is also the implication in the narrative for both human and Cylon that
there is a teleological plan on the part of some divinity(ies) to bring
about this new world.

BSG begins with the destruction of the majority of humanity and
ends with the finding of a new planetary home, the rejection of technol-

ogy by the surviving humans and a coda stating that this planetary home is our world 150,000 years in the past. We should note that *BSG* is an overtly apocalyptic narrative that is ultimately concerned with salvation. The world ends (actually 12 worlds end), and a surviving remnant of humanity (itself a Biblical motif) must wait for literally a New Earth. Both the Colonials (humans) and the Cylons (who are self-aware, sentient, cybernetic organisms, some of which outwardly resemble humans ["skinjobs"] and some of which are mechanical ["toasters"]) are concerned with "salvation," although what each group or even individual characters mean by this is fluid and not fixed. In addition to apocalypse and salvation, *BSG* is repeatedly concerned with prophesy, creation, sin, exile, resurrection, and betrayal. In short, it is a narrative that is rife with theological concern, is pregnant with religious meaning, and contains many echoes of the concerns, concepts and beliefs of American Christianity.

I fully concede that "American Christianity" is both a problematic term and an umbrella category; it covers hundreds of different faith traditions. When engaging in placing the theologies of *BSG* in dialogue with a generic "American Christianity," I also concede that the latter is in some ways as much a created and composite theology as the former, as I am drawing on numerous traditions. The need to compare *BSG* with this generalized American Christianity, however, is mandated by the wide variety of American Christianity, by the program itself, and by the overall religiosity of the United States. "The United States is the most religious of any major industrialized country," writes Doyle McManus, "a larger percentage of Americans attend a weekly religious service than Iranians—and Iran is a theocracy" (2011: A28). The United States is a deeply religious nation, steeped in the varieties of Christianity, and its popular culture reflects this reality.

In this study, I propose to examine *Battlestar Galactica* as a theological text that makes explicit and implicit statements about the nature of faith and reality. I also rely upon what Gordon Lynch terms "a broad definition of theology — namely, "the process of seeking normative answers to questions of truth, goodness, evil, suffering, redemption, and beauty in the context of particular social and cultural situations" (2005: 26). The series featured an ongoing debate between monotheism and polytheism and characters debating prophesy, visions, ethics, and the true nature of reality from a variety of faith positions. The show constructed two societies in conflict, each shaped by a variety of religious experiences and faith levels from atheist to fundamentalist.

The show and its creators overtly reference the religious nature of *BSG* in the DVD commentary, blog posts, interviews with journalists and even the advertisements for the program. A 2008 marketing campaign for *BSG* featured a parody of DaVinci's *The Last Supper* with the characters from the show in the positions from the painting. As Diane Winston analyzed, "That Jesus's place is held by a sexy robot in a slinky red dress, whose religious exhortations resemble Jerry Falwell's, exemplifies the interpenetration of religion, entertainment and sexuality that composes the contemporary sacred gaze" (2009: 6). It also exemplifies the religious element of *BSG*—real world references to a real world, with its own constructed identity, that transcends the medium.

Speculative Fiction and Theology

BSG, as a work of speculative fiction, is part of a long series of religiously influenced or oriented texts within the genre. Speculative fiction's origins are literary, beginning with Jules Verne, Edgar Allan Poe and H.G. Wells, combining the advent of literary naturalism and the short story with the emerging science of the late eighteenth century. The term "speculative fiction" was coined by Robert Heinlein as a synonym for science fiction, but one that recognized that the genre included not just science-based fiction but also tales of fantasy, the supernatural, superheroes, alternate history, and post-apocalyptic, utopian and dystopian worlds.

A generation after the literary genre began, the cinema began, and that medium from very early in its development seized upon its ability to represent the impossible or not yet possible (the miraculous?). Among the first films produced were Georges Méliès' famed *La lune à un mètre* (A Trip to the Moon, 1898), *Le voyage dans la lune* (Voyage to the Moon, 1902) and *Frankenstein* (1910, produced by Thomas Edison!).

The use of scripture in speculative fiction began in the pulp period (1920s through the 1950s). One of the more prominent motifs was Adam and Eve, in which human (or other) astronauts would land on a planet that simulated (or was) Eden. Early masters also turned to the New Testament for inspiration. Examples include Arthur C. Clarke's "The Star," in which a Jesuit astronaut discovers that a star—which had gone supernova in order to guide the astronomers from the East to the birth of Jesus (Matthew 2:1–10)—had had a planet with an ancient civilization that was destroyed so that the birth of Jesus might be heralded on Earth.

Or Ray Bradbury's *The Martian Chronicles,* in which a priest dreams of Christ and an indigenous Martian caught up in the dream must reenact the crucifixion. Or Bradbury's remarkable poem "Christus Apollo," which asks the question: if intelligent life were discovered elsewhere in the universe, did God also incarnate among them to atone for and save them from their sins? C.S. Lewis, of course, used speculative fiction to engage and explore Christian theology in his Ransom Trilogy (*Out of the Silent Planet, Perelandra* and *That Hideous Strength*), as well as in the seven volumes of *The Chronicles of Narnia.* Ursula Le Guin plays with theology in many of her works, most notably in *The Dispossessed.* Mary Doria Russell incorporates a great deal of theological exploration in her twin speculative fiction novels *The Sparrow* and *Children of God,* which imagine the implications of a Jesuit mission to a newly discovered planet with two sentient species.

Lastly, what is the bestselling *Left Behind* series, if not literally speculative fiction based on dispensationalist theories of the book of Revelation? I would argue the Left Behind series is Christian speculative fiction — employing the same tropes as Howard, Heinlein, Bester, Clark and Asimov, not to mention the more action-driven science fiction of reactionary American apocalyptic speculative fiction such as the "Survivalist" series of Jerry Ahern, the "Doomsday Warrior" series of Ryder Stacy or the "Endworld" series of David L. Robbins. All of these, like *Left Behind,* focus on a small group of diverse individuals surviving through the end of the world over the course of a series of novels. *Left Behind* is, in fact, Christian pulp sci fi. Speculative fiction has offered an opportunity for unique theological flights of fancy.

Conversely, as Gabriel McKee notes, "science fiction is a form of faith, even a form of mysticism, that seeks to help us understand not only who we are, but who we will become" (2007a: xiii). The major themes in speculative fiction, involving as it does imagining the future, changes in technology, encounters with non-humans, and the end of the world, make it an excellent genre to examine what it means to be human, to reflect upon the true nature of reality and to allow consideration of moral or ethical issues outside of their current and contemporary contexts. Just as John of Patmos shows a future to give hope to Christians in crisis in the first century C.E., to warn them of the dangers of pagan culture, and to give a model for understanding the world, so, too, does speculative fiction imagine the future to give hope, to give warnings and to give models for understanding the world.

Models of theological analysis of speculative fiction in popular culture (Paffenroth 2006, Grimes 2007, and Staub 2005, for example) tend to fall into two models. The first attempts to shoehorn the narrative of the popular culture text (*Star Wars, Matrix,* etc.) to fit a Gospel message. The purpose in doing so is what Gordon Lynch terms "a missiological response to popular culture" (2005: 21). In *The Force of Star Wars,* for example, Frank Allnutt sees the Force as God, Obi-Wan Kenobi as Jesus Christ, Vader as the False Prophet and the Emperor as Satan. Allnutt argues that *Star Wars* serves as an elaborate metaphor for the history and future of Christians, particularly as seen through Revelation. Then *The Empire Strikes Back* came out, and his schema (which did not really fit to begin with) completely fell apart.* Allnutt reads *Star Wars* through the Gospels and finds it to reflect what he already believes.

In the second model, the Gospels are read through culture. Dick Staub, for example, describes the "Christian of the Jedi persuasion," seeing Thomas Merton, Theresa of Avila, Paul, G.K. Chesterton and Thomas Aquinas, among others, as "Jedi Christians" (2005: 142, xxi). Likewise, Caleb Grimes sees Yoda as "the Christian Jedi master" whose teachings parallel those of Paul (2007: 5). Whereas Allnutt tries to make *Star Wars* reflect the Gospels, this second model sees the Gospels reflecting *Star Wars.* Grimes offers "the practical application of Jedi principles" for Christians by finding the Gospels in what *Star Wars* actually says (2007: 244). This second model attempts to read popular culture through the Gospels, finding theological similarities, but not conflating the two. In other words, the first method reads *Star Wars* (for example) through the Gospels, and the second method reads the Gospels through *Star Wars.* Neither of these models is particularly satisfactory, and both attempt to conflate two dissimilar sets of texts for the purpose of making *Star Wars* (or whatever popular text they engage) rooted in Biblical principles and therefore acceptable and even useful to Christians.

I propose to follow a third model, not arguing that *BSG* is actually a Christian allegory (as Allnutt did with *Star Wars*) or that it is a text through which we might better understand Christianity in order to be better Christians who also happen to be *Star Wars* fans (as Staub and Grimes do with *Star Wars*), but rather engaging the various faiths

---

*Although, I must confess, I always wondered what Allnutt thought the Ewoks were in his schema. Philippians? Sadducees? The Church at Ephesus? Rahner's "anonymous Christians"?

depicted in *BSG* as imaginary/fictional but real religions. I shall engage in comparative theology in the Fredricksian sense of looking at the religious elements of the faiths of *BSG* and then reading real-world theology through their lenses. This comparison is not merely an academic exercise but, following James L. Fredericks, will attempt to "be helpful to Christian believers today in their efforts to build new forms of social and religious solidarity in a world of considerable religious diversity" (2004: 25). Thus, it is a variation on the Staub approach without attempting to construct *BSG* as a Christian narrative, but rather one that reflects a culture in which Christians predominate.

After constructing a brief systematic theology of the three constructed faiths of *BSG* (human, Cylon, cult of Baltar), I shall then examine real-world echoes of specific elements. In other words, after examining the faiths of *BSG*, I shall engage in an exercise of comparative theology to consider how *BSG* reflects contemporary Christian theology in order to better understand our own traditions. How does *BSG* use its religions to comment on mainstream American religion? How does *BSG* echo and reflect Christian imagery, concepts, language and ideas, and what can *BSG* then tell us, its viewers, about our understanding of the imagery, concepts, language and ideas?

One of the reasons that this approach works best is that the above-mentioned works attempt to transform the *Star Wars* films (or other speculative fictions) into Christian works, which they are not. Similarly, there is no Christian missiological dimension to *BSG*, nothing that covertly or overtly affirms a Christian worldview. To attempt to argue so would be wrong. Likewise, it also seems counterproductive for the person of faith to observe and evaluate *BSG* through the lenses of Niebuhr's "Christ against culture" or "Christ of culture" models, which would find *BSG* lacking, if not morally offensive. As Deacy and Ortiz note, the objective of Christian evaluation of film (or in this case, television) "is not to render moral judgments but to attain greater insight about human experience and destiny" (2008: 41). And certainly, *BSG* has much to offer in terms of reflecting upon destiny, not to mention many topics of great import to Christians: faith, the role of religion in political life, resurrection, salvation, messiahs, ethics, eschatology, apocalypse, the relationship between creation and creator, betrayal, falls, and even living in an interfaith community.

Theology in/and Battlestar Galactica

The original *Battlestar Galactica* was inspired by *Star Wars* but profoundly shaped by the Mormon faith of series creator Glenn A. Larson.*
As James E. Ford observes, its characters and narrative arcs, not to mention many of its concepts, "are carefully situated within a Mormon universe" (Ford 1983: 83). The idea of humanity ruled by a Quorum of Twelve, overseen by a president; the concept that there were 13 tribes of Israel, 12 that stayed in the homeland and one that wandered to a far place (Earth, in the case of *BSG*; North America, in the case of Mormons); the slightly anagrammatic "Kobol" from the Mormon star "Kolob"; and the theology of the evolution of humanity into godlike beings were all derived by Larson from Mormonism (see Ford 1983, Wolfe 2008 and Lorenzon 2009 for extended analyses of *BSG* as Mormon inspired). As others have already demonstrated the Mormon influence on the original (and, in turn, on the reimagined series), I will not engage that topic in this study. Suffice it to say, *BSG* began firmly under a specific theological influence, although the reimagined series moves beyond the Mormon roots into larger theological issues of the American landscape.

Unlike many, if not most, television programs, *Battlestar Galactica* takes religion seriously and takes metaphysics seriously. In an early episode in the first season, "Flesh and Bone," the female pilot Starbuck is charged with interrogating the Cylon Leoben. Much of the episode is an extended conversation about comparative theologies of polytheism and monotheism. Leoben, after telling Starbuck that "our faiths are similar but I look to one god, not many," states the most basic article of his (and all) faith: "This is not all that we are ... I know that I am more than this body, more than this consciousness. A part of me swims in the stream, but in truth I'm standing on the shore — the current never takes me downstream" (1.08). What is this statement, if not a remarkable summary of the idea of the immortality of the soul as both part of the tem-

---

*There are those who might argue that my positing a generalized "American Christianity" in conversation with BSG is problematized by this Mormon influence. As I write this, the media carries analyses of whether or not a Mormon could be elected president because "most evangelicals don't believe Mormons are Christians" (McManus 2011: A28). Despite a different theological understanding of the nature, person and even history of Christ from that of evangelical Christianity, Mormonism claims to be a Christian faith (indeed, the full name of the religion is the Church of Jesus Christ of Latter-day Saints), and there is no reason to doubt it.

porally and spatially located person and yet something also eternal and immortal, linked to the divine?

Even more remarkable, the elements of the invented religions in *BSG* are shown to be rooted in reality. The colonials discover the planet Kobol from their scriptures, prompting President Roslin to remark: "It's real: the scriptures, the myths, the prophets—they're all real!" (1.12). Prophesies come true, angels appear and speak to mortals, conveying God's will, and prayer has efficacy. *BSG* takes religion seriously and explores it in all its aspects. *BSG* also takes theology, distinct from religion, seriously and explores its invented theologies in all their aspects. Within each invented faith tradition, the series shows a variety of religious experiences and levels of belief from atheism to fundamentalism. Among the Cylons, Leoben is a mystic, Cavil an agnostic priest (!) and Six a prophet. Among the humans, Adama is an agnostic atheist, Roslin moves from a cultural worshipper to a prophesied leader, and Baltar moves from agnostic to cult leader and instrument of God. While faith is proven to be correct on many ways, there is still a place for the nonbeliever.

The overall narrative arc concerns two profoundly theological ideas. First, it presents a metahistory of humankind from original earth to present Earth, through Kobol, the Twelve Colonies, the Cylon genocide, and exile. Just as the Bible is a metahistorical text, describing not only the entire history of creation and humanity but also describing God's plan for the future of humanity and creation, so, too, does *BSG* lay out a metanarrative of the past, present and future of humanity. Second, *BSG* presents not just competing faiths but competing understandings of salvation. Both humans and Cylons are interested in "salvation." The Pythia Scroll promises a dying leader "will lead all humanity to salvation," and, in the same episode, Virtual Six informs Baltar that "despite everything, despite all that, He still wants to offer our salvation. Our child will bring that salvation, but only if you accept your role as her father and her guardian" (2.03). Whereas the humans are promised a divinely inspired leader who will lead them to salvation, the Cylons are promised a child, the product of human and divine love, who will bring salvation to both human and Cylons. Behind both the metahistory and the salvation of human- and Cylonkind is a divine plan. Thus, on both the micro and macro levels, *BSG* serves as a collective of theological texts.

BSG features three different invented religions: the polytheistic religion of the humans, the monotheistic faith of the Cylons and the monotheistic (yet still evolving) religion of the Baltar cult. Theological debates frequently occur within the faiths (such as over the ethics of abortion in "The Captain's Hand" [2:17]) and between faiths (such as over God's plan in "Flesh and Bone" [1.08]). No on-screen divinity is ever shown, yet the implication that there is some sort of divine being(s), that said divinity has a plan, and that "angels" that serve as Its messengers exist and communicate some sense of Its will, runs through the entire series.

In the opening minutes of the miniseries, *BSG* begins with a debate about faith in an apocalyptic, eschatological setting. Baltar gave the woman who will be known as the Cylon "Six" access to the planetary defense systems (which also serves to make him, from the very beginning, a Judas figure who hands over humanity to the Cylons). She ensured that the Cylons could attack the humans using nuclear weapons and destroy most of the colonies. Right before the bombs begin to fall, when Baltar claims she helped him in his work because he gave her access to the defense computers, she explains to him not only why all this has happened, but what she believes: that God "wanted" her to help Baltar. Baltar disbelieves, mockingly asking her if God spoke to her, if they had a "chat."

She explains that God does not literally talk to her, but that she knows his will and she finds it troubling that Baltar mocks her faith. He is puzzled by her religious belief, especially as he feels it is not rational but rooted in "mysticism," but is willing to ignore her belief system because she is so sexually attractive (MS). Many scholars, fans and journalists have highlighted the presence of religion in *BSG,* but ultimately the reason one might write about the theology of *Battlestar Galactica* is that it is a show about belief, about the role belief plays in our lives and about the greater structure of reality that belief implies. Baltar, who begins the series as an atheist, ends up leading a monotheistic cult and may, in fact, be a prophet of God. *BSG* is, first and foremost, a show about belief.

As Tom Beaudoin notes, "All theology is to some extent autobiography" (1998: xvii). In my own case, I write as both a theologian interested in popular culture and a *BSG* fan interested in theology. My own background is as a Roman Catholic, Euro-American (of Anglo-Irish descent), male academic whose own research to date has centered on interculturalism, postcolonialism and the intersection between popular and high cultures. My own work in popular culture, speculative fictions, and religion and my own admitted status as a *BSG* fanboy brought me to consider *BSG* as a theological text worthy of academic study. Unlike Jewett, Grimes or Staub, I will not privilege Gospel over *BSG* nor find *BSG* lacking for not being appropriately Christian, since no one has ever claimed it was in any way a Christian text. Yet, as a fan of the show, I also must acknowledge my own position and academic responsibility. As Jeffrey H. Mills writes of *Star Trek*, I must also assert of my own relationship to my object of study:

> There's a certain sense of heightened responsibility that comes with being a fan of something: because the fan knows the object of his love very well, he is able to identify standards of quality that the casual observer may not see [1990: 126].

I therefore acknowledge my responsibility, both as a fan of *BSG* and as a theologian from a Catholic background, to both cultures and also to accept both *BSG* and Christian theology on their own terms and not on the other's. Even invented theologies must be treated respectfully in doing comparative theology.

In the first section, I use faith statements from characters in the show, quotations from their sacred texts, and the represented rituals and practices to construct brief systematic theologies of the created faiths of the show. The first chapter is a systematic theology of Colonial (human) religion. The humans are polytheistic with a series of divinities based on Greco-Roman gods. These divinities are known as "the Lords of Kobol," and they are constructed as pagan divinities in which some individuals believe literally, some metaphorically, and some not at all. Interestingly, however, the humans frequently employ not the language of the votive religion of ancient Greece, but that of Christianity: sin, salvation, angels, etc., including one description of the "sacred scrolls" as "gospels."* All of this terminology will also be examined in the fourth chapter.

More difficult is the construction of a systematic theology of the Cylons, which is presented in the second chapter. Monotheistic but lacking a divine incarnation, they nevertheless evince a theology closer to Christianity than to Judaism. The Cylons believe in a "living God," who is the only God. His commandment is to love and obey him and to

---

*Interestingly, in the miniseries, an actor whose character was watching the destruction of the fleet ad-libbed the line "Jesus!" in response, which was not edited out of the scene. This phrase is the only direct mention of Christianity in the series and, since it was not scripted, can be discounted. But it does demonstrate how even an actor taking the Lord's name in vain will shape the theological content of a television series.

love one another. Humanity was made in his image. But humanity, having sinned, is fallen, and thus God has now adopted the Cylons as his children (which might also be read as a variation on Christian replacement theology—humans seen as the Jews rejecting Christ and thus all humankind becoming the "chosen people"). The Cylons are greatly concerned with sin and salvation. There is also a group of Cylons who might be perceived as mystics. Their prayer at the moment of death is called "The Prayer to the Cloud of Unknowing," whose very name is taken from the anonymous fourteenth-century text *The Cloud of Unknowing,* which encourages the reader to seek God not through knowledge but through love and the apophatic tradition. Love (both divine and human) is central to *BSG*'s theologies.

The third chapter, briefest of the three in the first section, offers a systematic theology of the Baltar cult. In the fourth and final season of the series, one of the central human characters, Gaius Baltar, becomes the leader of a predominantly female human religious community. Previously an atheist, he becomes a prophet of a monotheistic God similar to, but distinguished from, the Cylon god. It is during this season that Baltar makes some of the strongest faith statements presented on the show, especially since they are depicted as being the most accurate of the religious statements seen on the series.

The second section consists of what I am terming "real-world echoes" on and with *BSG.* Rather than following the models outlined and then dismissed previously in this Introduction, I place *BSG* in conversation with elements of contemporary American Christian theology (particularly post–9/11), sometimes but not always relying upon Catholic theology and other times focusing on a general Christian theology as a conversation partner.

Chapter 4, "Gospels, Sins and Salvation: The Use of Christian Terminology in *BSG*," engages the use of specifically Christian language in the theologies of *BSG.* Set in a seeming alternate universe in which Earth is 2,000 years dead (or 20,000 years in the future), and with two major invented theologies (polytheistic human and monotheistic Cylon), the language employed by *BSG* is remarkably Christian. This chapter explores the use of "sin," "salvation," "angels," "Gospel," and other Christian terms and analyzes how they are both similar to and different from the popular American tradition. When a Cylon speaks of "sin," of what is she speaking? When a human talks about "salvation," is it in a true Christian sense, or is the word employed differently?

The next chapter, "'In His Own Image He Created Them'": Creation and Falls" explores the larger use of creation-and-fall narratives within *BSG.* Much in the series is made of the Cylons as human creations. The first words written on the screen of each episode are: "The Cylons were created by man. They rebelled." The series also focuses on the idea of "Falls"; the Cylons posit that after humanity began to sin, God changed His favor to the Cylons. In the prequel series, *Caprica,* the title credits list the series as taking place "58 years before the Fall," which constructs the Cylon attack on the Twelve Colonies (the human homeworlds) as another Fall. In this chapter I explore what *BSG* says about Creations and Falls and compare it with Christian teachings rooted in Genesis.

Following in scriptural order, after Creation come the chosen people and a series of exiles, occupations and enslavements for those people. In chapter 6, "Exile and the Remnant: Religion of the Planetless," following the scholarship of Daniel Smith-Christopher, I engage the Hebrew Bible and *BSG.* After the destruction of the Twelve Colonies, the humans wander the galaxy looking for Earth, the home promised them by the gods. They first return to Kobol, supposedly the home of humanity, then discover that Earth is a nuclear wasteland, destroyed millennia ago. The narrative contains echoes of Israel and its various points of exile, as well as the "remnant"—the part of Israel that survives catastrophe. Building on theories of the remnant, as well as Smith-Christopher's *Religion of the Landless* and *A Biblical Theology of Exile,* this chapter examines *BSG*'s humanity-as-Israel through the lens of Hebrew Bible theology.

Continuing from the previous chapter, chapter 7, "The Role of Prophets," continues exploring the Hebrew Bible echoes in *BSG* through the use of prophets—not those who predict the future but those who speak for divinity. Six, Baltar, D'Anna Biers, Starbuck, Leoben Conoy, the Hybrids and Laura Roslin at one point or another during the series serve as prophets—voices of God (or the gods) who tell the people (whether human or Cylon) the will of God and the need for repentance, a change of behavior, or to obey the will of the Lord.

Chapter 8 represents a fundamental shift of concerns. "Starbuck Died, Starbuck Is Risen, Starbuck Will Come Again: Messiahs and Resurrection in *BSG*" combines two themes: messianism and resurrection. Kara Thrace (call sign: Starbuck) dies while flying over a gas giant planet. Her ship explodes and she perishes (3.17). Two episodes later, she returns, flying in her ship, telling the other pilots she really is Starbuck, and that she has found the way to Earth and humankind's salvation (3.20). In a later episode, on Earth, she finds her own dead body and cremates it (4.11). At the end of the series, she simply vanishes. The Cylons, as well, have a process of "organic memory transfer"—downloading their consciousness (what they call their souls) into an exact duplicate body when their current body perishes, a process they call "resurrection." The ships used to do this are referred to as "resurrection ships." In short, the Cylons have invented bodily resurrection of the dead, which might give us some insight into Christian understandings of what we mean by "resurrection," a central tenet of Christian faith. In this chapter, I explore the use of resurrection (bodily return of the dead, like Starbuck) and "resurrection" (consciousness present in an exact replicate) and explore the echoes of Christianity in *BSG*'s use of messiahs and incarnations.

Gaius Baltar is again the focus of chapter 9, "Cylon Messiah, Human Judas: Baltar, Betrayal and Redemption." Baltar, presented initially as a Judas figure who betrays humanity to the Cylons and yet survives the Cylon genocide to follow a fascinating character arc, rises to become first vice-president and then president of the survivors, he then runs a Vichy-style government when the Cylons capture many of the remaining humans. Found not guilty after a treason trial, he becomes first a prophet, then a healer, and finally, the implication is that he is the voice of God. The suggestion is made toward the end of the series that Baltar is the imperfect vessel through which the divine plan makes its teleological end, not unlike the necessity of Judas's betrayal for the salvation of humankind. No Judas, no Christ. In this chapter I explore the duality of Baltar's roles within Biblical archetypes.

As Revelation closes out the Bible, so too does the final chapter on apocalypse close this study. With the approach of the millennium followed by the apocalyptic events of the attacks on September 11, there was an obvious increase in apocalyptic (and apocalyptically titled) science fiction: *Terminator: Judgment Day, Armageddon,* and *Terminator: Salvation* are but three of many science fiction narratives that use language and images from Revelation to explore and explode the human future. If *Star Trek* in its many incarnations was the dominant science fiction narrative of the late twentieth century, *Battlestar Galactica* is the apocalyptic science fiction narrative of the twenty-first. "From Patmos to Caprica: Battlestar Apocalyptica" examines Revelation, apocalypse(s), planetary destruction and the end of the world. However, though apocalypse has become synonymous with disastrous endings, Revelation actually concerns the new beginning after the devastation. This chapter explores the duality behind the horrible devastation of the Cylon genocide and the literal "New Heaven and New Earth" that the series presents at its finale.

After a brief conclusion on the main topic of the book, an epilogue closes out the volume. Concerning the prequel series, *Caprica*, and subtitled "Why Parents Don't Always Look Like Their Children," this final analysis considers how *Caprica* offers a different theology while also expanding on the one contained in *Battlestar Galactica*. Although the origins of Cylon monotheism are given, the prequel series' focus is on two primary theological topics: the desire to overcome death and develop a form of resurrection not for the individual who has died but so that those left behind will not have to feel loss, and the internal struggles of a fundamentalist group that wants to bring about conversion through acts of terror.

A Note on Sources and Citations

The Scripture quotations contained herein are from the New Revised Standard Version Bible, copyright 1989, Division of Christian Education of the National Council of the Churches of Christ in the U.S. Used by permission. All rights reserved. Citations from episodes of *Battlestar Galactica* are parenthetical, listing season and episode number (4.01 for "He That Believeth in Me," or 3.18 for "The Son Also Rises," for example). An episode list follows the text of this study, before the bibliography. These numbers may be cross-referenced there. I also include a glossary of *BSG* terminology for readers not overly familiar with the program.

I. Created Theologies

The first section of this work consists of three separate fictional systematic theologies: human, Cylon, and Baltar cult — the three religious faiths that constitute the religious world of *BSG*.

Three elements have been used to construct these theologies: first, faith statements by characters on the show. Throughout the entire series, various characters have expressed statements of faith and belief. These statements will be considered in their context, as some characters believe or practice differently from others, and some characters evince sincere faith and believe their faith statements while others cynically exploit their belief systems for their own purposes (which does not necessarily make their faith statements less true; it is just that that character does not genuinely believe the article of faith). More weight will be given to clerical characters, as their statements are usually more informed by "official teachings" of the faith tradition than those characters whose faith is more experiential. When the priestess Elosha makes a faith statement about the Lords of Kobol, she often identifies whether this statement is from the "sacred scrolls" or her own opinion. Again, however, context matters, as certain characters, such as the Cylon minister Brother Cavil, are cynical and self-serving and agnostic at best. Thus, his statements of faith may reflect Cylon belief and practice, may reflect genuine human belief and practice (when he pretends to be a human), or may be false and manipulative.

The second element is the observed rites, rituals, practices and prayers of the different groups. The three faiths differ significantly, reflecting their historic development. The human faith is millennia old, the Cylon faith is only a few decades old, and the faith of the Baltar cult emerges and develops during the run of the series. The humans have temples, organized worship services and traditional prayers. The Cylons have none of these. The Baltar cult listens to long sermons from Baltar, but their rites and rituals seem to still be emerging. Each group's depicted practices also serve as a means to construct their theology.

The third and final element consists of the statements and analyses from secondary sources, whether interviews with show creator Ron Moore or *Official Companion* books or even the online *Battlestar Wiki*. Likewise, there is a growing number of scholarly publications on *BSG*, both original and reimagined, and the observations of these sources have also been used to construct this book's theologies.

These three systematic theologies are as complete as possible, given the nature of the task. All three are invented theologies for a television program, so the creators and writers of the show did not intend to create a fully developed theology for each group with complete rites, rituals, scriptures and concepts. Admittedly, some of what follows is as much anthropology (the academic discipline) as it is theology. My purpose in these first three chapters is to lay out a systematic theology for each faith as completely as possible, bearing in mind the limitations noted and the larger purpose of this work, which is comparative theology.

There also exists a challenge in distinguishing between Cylon theology and Baltar theology, as much of what Baltar teaches comes from Virtual Six. Virtual Six seems initially to be a Cylon and speaking of Cylon belief, but then is revealed to be an angel who has taken the form of a Cylon. Thus, her pronouncements sometimes belong in one theology and sometimes in another. Baltar's belief system is rooted in the one Cylon God but transcends that belief and adds to it. Baltar, for better or worse, is the only character on the program shown to have a direct link to the divine. Others read prophesy and believe it, and others engage mystical experiences, but Baltar has an angel whispering God's plans in his ear.

The methodology employed here is a combination of hermeneutical, analytical and correlation. Hermeneutical method is based on the language and experience of the characters and the belief that "religious language is not only expressive, but also constitutive of religious experience" (Fiorenza 1991: 44). The analytical tools, such as Avery Dulles' models of theology, acknowledge diverse models of understanding the Church, and "that each perspective grasps, in a particular way, a significant and indispensable dimension of the Church while at the same time showing that other perspectives are equally valid" (Fiorenza 1991: 52; see Dulles

1974). Correlation, as outlined by Paul Tillich in his own work on systematic theology, seeks to relate "the interdependence of concepts" with "the interdependence of things and events," as "is found in the correlation between one's ultimate concern and that about which one is ultimately concerned" (Fiorenza 1991: 52–53). Tillich himself writes that there is even correlation between question and answer:

Theology formulates the questions implied in human existence, and theology formulates the answers implied in divine self-manifestation under the guidance of the questions implied in human existence. This is a circle which drives man to a point where question and answer are not separated [1951: 61].

Using Tillich's idea, we may consider the relationship between the language and symbols of ultimate reality as expressed in the three faiths described herein and in that ultimate reality. By employing these different methodologies, it is my hope that three different but interrelated systematic theologies will emerge that present a picture of how *BSG* constructs imagined religions. These theologies will also serve as a springboard for real-world echoes present in them to be discussed in the second part of this study.

1

The Systematic Theology of Human Religion / The Human Understanding of God

Human beings in the world of *BSG* are referred to as "Colonials," reflecting the Twelve Colonies that are the home to humankind at the beginning of the series, although these 12 planets are not the original home of humanity, as the name "colonies" suggests. *BSG* offers a full history of humanity rooted in a polytheistic religion that incorporates technology and space travel.

Because of its polytheism, human religion is communally based, by which I mean the theology is not about a personal relationship with the gods but rather one's relationship to the larger community. One follows the example of the gods and attempts to live in harmony with others. Ritual, prayer, practice and even scripture are based in the idea that the community is the most important element of existence. While the Christian says "Amen," meaning "I believe" or "let it be so," placing focus on the relationship between the individual and God, the Colonial says "So say we all," reflecting the importance of the group.

History of the Colonials

Kobol is a planet that is the ancestral home of humanity. Kobol is the cradle of humanity, where human beings believe gods and humankind lived together in a kind of paradise until the humans left the planet in 13 tribes, one group headed to Earth, the other 12 to the Twelve Colonies (1.10). Kobol was a world very similar to real-world Earth in terms of its geography, terrain and features. Human beings were created there by the gods, and lived with the gods in 13 tribes. The central city of Kobol was, in fact, called "The City of the Gods," and humanity and divinity lived together in a sort of Golden Age, much like the Garden of Eden or the ancient Greek myths.

For reasons never disclosed, the tribes decided to leave Kobol. Four thousand years in the past, the 13th tribe left for a planet called Earth and supposedly left signposts along the way. Two thousand years in the past, again for undisclosed reasons (although later we are told that "commercialism, decadence [and] technology run amuck" resulted in the ruin of Kobol [4.20]), humanity left Kobol as the gods watched in an event called "The Great Exodus." The humans made their way to a new home, each tribe receiving its own planet to colonize. The 12 planets (in the same solar system, named Cyrannus) that support the 12 tribes of Kobol after they leave the homeworld — Aerilon, Aquarion, Canceron, Caprica (the home of the Colonial government), Gemenon, Leonis, Libran, Picon (headquarters of the Colonial fleet), Sagittaron, Scorpia, Tauron, and Virgon — each developed its own culture with variations on the religious faith they had brought from Kobol. Some humans are fundamentalists, who believe in the literal truth of the scrolls (such as those from Gemenon); others are agnostic; others have outright contempt for religion. Tom Zarek, for example, tells Elosha that the scrolls are "more superstition," and Laura Roslin once refers to Adama, whose name is suggestive of the Biblical "Adam," as "Admiral Atheist" (2.06; 4.02).

I. Divinity / The Gods

Humans are polytheistic, worshipping the Lords of Kobol in a faith that is devotional, but oddly not votive, modeled after Greco-Roman religion. Because there is no single divinity, from its very roots the Colonial religion is based upon plurality — the importance of the group. Although Zeus is the "father of the gods" and the most important and powerful of the Lords of Kobol, most prayers are addressed to the gods collectively.

The Lords of Kobol who are named in the series are:

> Zeus, "father of the gods," also called Jupiter [1.03]
> Hera, his wife [2.07]

Apollo, his son, god of the hunt [1.03]

Artemis, his daughter, goddess of the hunt (and therefore patron of pilots) [1.08]

Ares, sometimes also called Mars, his son, god of war [3.01]

Aphrodite, his daughter, goddess of love and sex [1.08]

Athena, his daughter, "goddess of wisdom and war" [3.06]

Aurora, "goddess of the dawn; "she brings the morning star and a fair wind, a fresh start" [3.17]

Poseidon, only mentioned by name once, in passing, but in Greek mythology the god of the ocean [4.01]

Asclepius, god of healing [4.04]

The gods are understood in different ways by different characters on the series. Those from Gemenon accept their existence as literal. Others see them as metaphors or the cultural remnants of something else (as Sharon Agathon* states, Athena was real, but she was not a god — she was something else that we do not understand [2.07]). This ambiguity is captured in a debate between Emily Kowalski, who is dying of cancer, and President Laura Roslin, also dying of cancer, who calls Baltar's god "a fantasy." Emily responds that it is foolish to believe in the literal reality of scripture as well, as no one is handed a fate out of an urn by Zeus before being born. Roslin counters that the myths are metaphors. Emily does not want metaphors, but "answers," and Laura oddly responds that her mother was also not satisfied with the idea that the stories were metaphors and wanted to believe in a literal Aphrodite who would bring her to some sort of paradise after her death (4.06). Thus, some Colonials believe in the literal truth of the Lords of Kobol, while others see them as "metaphors" for larger theological ideas or the embodiment of virtues.

The humans integrate their gods into their lives, sometimes in very unconventional ways. Pilot Lee Adama takes "Apollo" as his call sign; Sharon Agathon's call sign is "Athena." This identification with the Lords of Kobol occasions comment from others. Tom Zarek, who leads a prison-ship revolution against his guards, captures Lee Adama and mocks him for having the name of a god as his call sign, in that Apollo is the son of Zeus. Later, when it is announced that Commander Adama is on the radio, Zarek quips, "Zeus is calling" (1.03). Zarek, who calls

---

*Interestingly, "Agathon," the name shared by both Helo and Sharon, means "good" in Greek. She is the "good" Cylon, but also occupies a unique place in the history of the universe as the mother of the only human/Cylon hybrid. She is "good" in much the same way the Virgin Mary is.

the Colonial religion "superstition," still acknowledges the power of the mythic images (2.06).

Yet, at the same time, the actual, nonmetaphoric existence of the Lords of Kobol may be demonstrated by the artifacts and relics they left behind. Throughout the series, possessions supposedly owned, used or named for the gods are discovered: the Arrow of Apollo, the Tomb of Athena, the Gates of Hera, and the statues of the gods in the Tomb of Athena. While none of these is concrete proof of the existence of the gods, they do demonstrate some greater level of reality behind the Colonial faith that is not merely metaphoric.

While the gods lived with humans on Kobol at one point, their home is referred to as "Olympus" (2.05). It is not clear if Olympus is a real, physical place on Kobol (perhaps at or near the City of the Gods) or is, as Emily Kowalski calls it, "a metaphysical mountain" (4.06). Yet it would seem to indicate the gods occupying real existence on Kobol combined with a larger existence on another plane of being.

The gods are served in different ways, depending on their roles and spheres of influence. Apollo and Artemis seem to be of importance to pilots, as they are gods of hunting, while others pray to Asclepius when they or someone close is ill or injured. The gods themselves seem to have different individual rites and rituals as well, but just as often are worshipped collectively.

Considering that Colonial religion is modeled after ancient Greek religion, it seems that insights into that religion may also prove of value. Robert Garland, in his analysis of ancient Greek religion, argues that polytheism is "by definition" pluralistic, as "god is not one but many" (1994: 1). Thus, one may choose from a variety of means to serve a variety of gods. Unlike monotheism, in which all interactions with the divine are with and through a single deity, polytheism postulates a multitude of gods with different spheres of influence. In monotheism, "God" proposes a set of rules and behaviors to which His followers must adhere. In polytheism, one is answerable to a multitude of gods, sometimes at cross purposes to one another, and therefore the relationship between human and divine is different from in monotheism. Polytheism implies pluralism, even within belief and practice.

Furthermore, Garland argues that Greek religion is "votive in essence," by which he means that the relationship between human and divine is rooted in the exchange of gifts (1994: 1). Humans offer sacrifice so that the gods will grant a boon. Polytheistic ritual is often rooted in this ritual exchange; when one needs something from a god, one offers an appropriate sacrifice to that god. An individual might prefer one deity over another, but one must sacrifice to the appropriate god in order to achieve success within the god's sphere.

The votive aspect is what is missing from *BSG,* where the Colonial religion more closely resembles Christian worship, although the Colonial faith used to be votive and used to entail real sacrifice. In fact, human sacrifice became prevalent right before the Great Exodus and may be one of the reasons for the Great Exodus (2.02). The votive / sacrificial aspect at the root of Colonial religion is discovered when the Colonials discover Kobol. Baltar and Virtual Six find a pile of skulls near the ruins of the city. Six confirms that the skulls are evidence of human sacrifice, that humans killed each other as offerings for the gods. Baltar, who claims to be an atheist, is still dismayed, as Kobol is supposed to be a pre–Fall paradise where humanity and the gods lived peacefully and harmoniously together. He is shattered by the barbaric reality of Kobol and human religion. The sacred scrolls report that as Kobol was being abandoned by the humans, "the body of each tribe's leader was offered to the gods in the tomb of Athena" (2.06).

As the humans abandoned Kobol, Athena threw herself off a mountain and died. The other gods placed her body in a tomb on a mountain ridge and then sealed the tomb so that it could only be unsealed with a relic called the Arrow of Apollo. Upon opening, the tomb of Athena displays a hologram showing the constellations as seen from Earth.

Another significant religious structure is The Temple of the Five, a building on the "algae planet," 4,000 years old, built by the 13th tribe on their way to Earth. The temple is the home of the "Eye of Jupiter" a signpost on the way to Earth that is revealed to be the nova seen at the explosion of the star around which the algae planet rotates. Until that is seen by the Colonials, however, they do not know what the "Eye of Jupiter" is supposed to be. The scrolls contain several references to the Temple of the Five, which has five pillars dedicated to the five priests who are secretly monotheist (3.12). The Temple of the Five, also known as the Temple of Hopes, is written about in the Sacred Scrolls.

In short, the gods used to live with and amongst humanity but now are in some distant location. They are accessible through prayer, and the dead join them in the afterlife, but once humanity leaves Kobol, the gods are no longer seen or experienced in the flesh.

II. Scripture: The Sacred Scrolls

The Colonial holy text is called "the Sacred Scrolls," although they are seen as both literal scrolls and in book form. The Sacred Scrolls were given by the Lords of Kobol to the humans, both telling the story of human history and prophesying the future of humankind. The Sacred Scrolls were written and compiled approximately 2,000 years ago. Adama refers to them as "letters from the gods" (2.07). Series creator Ronald D. Moore refers to them as "the Colonial version of the Bible" (2003: 4). They contain history (the story of humanity and the gods), instructions for living, and prophesies for the future. As the name suggests, the Scrolls are a collection of different texts, but only one, Pythia, is ever named. We might safely assume, however, that since one Scroll is named, the others are as well and the series simply never names the others.

The opening line of the scrolls is: "Life here began out there...," acknowledging not only the divine origins of life but also the galactic nature of human religion (MS).* Colonial faith is aware of space travel and incorporates it into its beliefs with the first line of its scripture. Humanity began "out there," and thus every planet is just another step on the way back to some cosmic home. This is a central tenet of human belief.

The most repeated scriptural citation is: "All of this has happened before and all of this will happen again." Laura Roslin describes this citation thus: "If you believe in the gods, then you believe in the cycle of time: that we are playing our parts in a story that is told again and again and again throughout eternity" (1.12). The humans believe not only in the idea of the eternal return, but also the cyclical nature of reality. Everything from the gods to humans is subject to the repetition of reality.

The Sacred Scrolls narrate the entire history of humanity. How the gods and humans lived together on Kobol, how 4,000 years ago the 13th tribe left and went to a distant planet called Earth (MS). But the scrolls promise that Kobol points the way to Earth (1.10). The scriptures also

---

*This phrase is taken directly from the voiceover of the original series: "There are those who believe that life here began out there, far across the universe, with tribes of humans who may have been the forefathers of the Egyptians, or the Toltecs, or the Mayans. Some believe that there may yet be brothers of man who even now fight to survive somewhere beyond the heavens." This VO evokes both Erich von Daniken's "Chariots of the Gods" theory, which states that ancient divinities could have been extraterrestrials, and Mormon theology.

give instructions on how to find the way to Earth, should humanity ever return to Kobol.

Likewise, the Sacred Scrolls narrate the Great Exodus and its effects. The planet begins to burn, and the people could either leave on ships or pass along a high road on a rocky ridge (2.06). The humans leave and go to the 13 colonies (the Twelve Colonies and Earth). The gods remained behind, and Athena killed herself by throwing herself off a cliff onto some rocks in despair of the exodus of humanity (2.06; 2.07). Her tomb, as noted, serves as another signpost to find Earth and the 13th tribe.

Tangentially, these parts of the Sacred Scrolls are fulfilled during the run of *BSG,* which some, including President Roslin, believe is proof of the veracity of the Sacred Scrolls. As Roslin herself states, "We have found Kobol. We have found the City of the Gods. And when we retrieve the arrow [of Apollo] we will open the Tomb of Athena and we will find the road to Earth" (2.03). Thus, the Sacred Scrolls provide directives on how to return to Kobol and how to reunite with the 13th tribe.

Kobol, like Eden, is a forbidden place, once humanity departs from it (see Genesis 3: 23–24). Elosha proclaims that the scriptures warn that those who go to Kobol will pay "a cost in blood" (2.06). Adama later reads, "And Zeus warned the leaders of the 12 tribes that any return to Kobol would exact a price in blood" (2.07). This warning of the Scrolls is shown to be accurate when the characters do find Kobol. At least a dozen humans, including Elosha, the priestess, are killed while on Kobol (1.13; 2.01; 2.06; 2.07).

The Sacred Scroll known as "Pythia" serves as a form of book of Revelation — it is a series of prophetic visions and statements about the future of humanity. It also supposedly tells about the way to Earth and the fate of the 13th tribe (3.06). Pythia is described by Elosha as "an oracle" (1.10). It prophesies the exile and rebirth of the human race, a dying leader who will lead the people to a new home, and the visions of the leader, primarily a vision of a dozen snakes that will be proof of the truth of scripture (1.10). We also learn that this leader is prophesied to suffer from a disease that will slowly kill him/her and prevent this leader from entering the new land (1.10).*

Pythia also contains a variety of other stories. Baltar, when shot,

---

*Like Moses, Laura Roslin will not enter the promised land to which she leads her people (Numbers 20:12). See chapter 7 for more on this topic.

tells Laura Roslin that there is a story in Pythia about a flood wiping out most of humanity on Kobol (shades of Genesis and the Noah narrative!) (4.09). When Roslin is concerned about receiving help on Kobol from Sharon Agathon, a Cylon, Elosha tells her that Pythia also contains a prophesy of a "lower demon" whose assistance is vital to humanity during the journey to the new home (2.06).

Possibly other unnamed scrolls also contain prophesies about the time of the Cylon genocide, prophesying the division of humanity in space and the deaths of large numbers of people (3.03). Lastly, in a deleted scene, available on DVD, the priest Elosha explains that humanity's exodus from Kobol was motivated because monotheism, prompted by a "jealous god" (again, shades of Moses speaking with YHWH) caused a war when that god demanded he be placed above and before all other gods (suggestive of the first commandment of Exodus) (1.12). It was possibly a religious war that drove humanity from Kobol.

The Sacred Scrolls are referred to frequently as "scripture," and as Francis Schüssler Fiorenza writes of Christian Scripture, they "are not simply sources for theological reflection but themselves are examples of theological reflection" (1991: 7–8). Just as scripture attempts to understand and interpret God, the Christological event, and salvation, so, too, do the Sacred Scrolls attempt to understand and interpret the Lords of Kobol, humanity's place in the cosmos, and the teleological journey it is on.

III. Ritual and Prayer

A. Rituals

In his own analysis of Greek religion, Walter Burkert describes ritual "as a kind of language" by which humans may communicate with the gods (1985: 55). Rituals, rites and prayers may be broken down into the individual and the collective practices of Colonial religion, each with their own language. *BSG* shows both individual and collective prayer, various religious rites and rituals, and ceremonies designed not only to communicate with the gods, but also to remind the humans of their own place in the cosmos and in the community. Much of what we know about Colonial religion comes from funeral rituals. More memorial and funeral services are shown than all other rites and rituals put together.

Colonial religion is a civic religion, now somewhat disconnected from its historic roots. The ceremonies we see aboard the *Galactica* and among the Colonials focus as much on civic identity as religious belief. The memorial service at the end of the miniseries is carried out in front of the flags of the Twelve Colonies. There are no symbols of the gods, no music, no idols or images. There are only the flag-draped coffins and the flags of the colonies. Admittedly, this ceremony is an impromptu one, but the emphasis is on the civic aspect, not the gods. Colonial religion is as much about the community as it is about the divine.

Concerning the Greeks, Burkert claims that in a group context, ritual forms a communal bond that joins the participants into a community (*koinonia*) (1985: 58). He maintains the effect of ritual on the gods was irrelevant to the Greeks. Greek religious ritual is primarily designed not for the benefit of the divine but for the benefit of the community. Colonial group religious rituals seem to follow this idea.

The Colonials also mention three rituals, one of which, marriage, is referred to as a "sacrament" (3.11). Unlike the funeral rituals, which are communal, these rites are individual and focused on transforming the individual, although even these have their communal-affirming aspects. They are dedication, confession and marriage.

Dedication is a ceremony carried out shortly after birth. After a child is born, the parents bring the child to a temple to be "placed in the service" of one or more of the Lords of Kobol. When Galen Tyrol and his wife Cally have a son, they have a Dedication ceremony in which the Sister touches him, saying, "With this mark, we dedicate Nicholas Stephen Tyrol to the service of Ares and Apollo. May he prove worthy of their blessings and those of mighty Zeus. So say we all" (3.01). Much like a baptism, the dedication serves to link the individual with the divine and welcome the infant into the community of believers.

Marriage is a sacrament and a religious ritual for the Colonials as well. Starbuck will not divorce Anders, though she is cheating on him with Lee: marriage is a "sacrament," she tells Lee (3.11). She will commit adultery, but not divorce, because she will not break a vow she made in the sight of the gods (3.11). Again, when one is married, it is not simply a civil action linking two individuals together; it is also a "vow in the sight of the gods," thereby making it a religious ritual with theological consequences. Yet, like all Colonial religion, it is also based in the community.

The only other ritual we witness is "Confession." In *The Plan*, Sam Anders asks if Brother Cavil, a "Man of the Gods," hears confessions.

Cavil agrees to hear Anders' confession. Anders begins, "Bless me, Brother, for I have acted against the example of the gods" (P). Anders tells Cavil his sins, and Cavil responds, "You're absolved in the example of the gods" (P). What is interesting in this exchange is that the one confessing does not state that he or she has wronged the gods in any way; he or she has not sinned in the Christian sense. Instead they have "acted against the example of the gods" and are forgiven "in the example of the gods." Humans do not sin against the gods—they sin against one another. The act of confession becomes a ritual in which one reflects upon how one has sinned against the group and then is absolved in the name of the group.

B. Prayer

Prayer is both individual and communal and serves multiple purposes:

1. Thanking the gods.

The shortest one, frequently heard, is: "Thank the Lords of Kobol" (MS; 1.01; et. al.), a variation on "thank God," obviously. One expresses gratitude to the gods for perceived blessings.

2. Concern for others, especially the dead.

Most of the prayers heard on *BSG,* individual or collective, are for the dead. For example, Starbuck prays as the temporary morgue fills with bodies during the initial attack in the miniseries, asking the Lords of Kobol to take the souls of the dead "into your hands" (MS). The prayer also indicates the importance of the community. When one dies, one leaves the community of the living for the community of the dead, who are in the hands of the gods. Even enemies, even Cylons, are part of this larger community. Interestingly, after Leoben is executed by being thrown out an airlock, Starbuck also prays for him: "Lords of Kobol, hear my prayer. I don't know if he had a soul or not, but if he did, take care of it" (1.08). Colonials pray to the gods for the dead asking that their souls be welcomed into the community

Communally, we are shown in the miniseries a large memorial service led by the priest Elosha. After chanting in an unidentified language, she proclaims a prayer that is focused on the living ("we") and "you" (the Lords of Kobol), asking for eternal life for the dead, asking for mercy and love for the living, reminding the Lords of Kobol of what they have done for the "forefathers" and asking them to lead humanity to a new home, and concluding with the traditional "So say we all" (MS). This prayer demonstrates as well the communal nature of Colonial faith. While there are Christian echoes in this prayer, and acknowledgment of the powers and roles of the gods, the prayer also obviously links the dead with "us" and the forefathers.

Cally Tyrol's funeral features text to be spoken by her husband, Galen: "The Lords of Kobol, as many and varied as mortal men, must bend down and lean low to hear that voice and hear my lament" (4.04). Remarkably, this is the only example of individual grief ("hear *my* lament"), and yet even in this prayer, the communal nature of the gods ("as many and varied as mortal men") reflects the individual within the larger context of the group.

Even in impromptu situations, prayer for the dead is important, especially for the military. When several Colonial marines are killed in a firefight with Cylons on Kobol, Lt. "Crashdown" leads a memorial that similarly both displays the communal nature of faith and focuses on the fact that death eventually comes for all: "Lords of Kobol, take these brave men into your arms. Take the spirits of our fallen friends so that they may share in the everlasting life that awaits us all beyond the veil of tears. So say we all" (2.03). Note the focus on the group: the dead are not identified individually but are "our fallen friends" and "brave men;" the prayer asks that "they may share in the everlasting life;" and the traditional concluding "so say we all." Note as well that "everlasting life" is not for "the elect" or "the saved" but for "us all." For the Colonials, salvation concerns the community, not the individual soul.

3. Protection, Deliverance or Victory:

Prayers are offered to the Lords of Kobol as a request for protection, deliverance or victory against one's enemies. A guard asks Laura Roslin, currently ensconced in the brig, to pray with him during a Cylon attack. They pray for help from the Lords of Kobol; they pray for Laura to lead the people well; they pray for victory over their enemies; yet they also pray to be righteous, to turn away from wickedness, and for salvation (2.01). On New Caprica, before he kills himself in a suicide bombing aimed at killing Baltar and several Colonial police officers, Duck goes to a temple and prays, apologizing to the gods for his mistakes and asking for their protection (3.01). Even when planning on a course of action that will end his life, Duck looks to the gods for protection in carrying out that plan.

4. Healing and as a Last Resort when Hope is Lost

Several characters pray when they fall ill or are injured. Also, prayer is seen as a last option when there are no other options. When Laura's cancer diagnosis is confirmed, "Doc" Cottle, the chief medical officer in the fleet, tells her: "And for what it's worth, I would seriously consider prayer" (1.04). Prayer is therefore both a comfort and a remaining option in negative situations.

There are different methods of prayer. Prayers may be said quickly, improvised based on the situation, or read from the Sacred Scrolls. One may pray as is or one might use icons or small idols: We see Starbuck holding figurines of Apollo and Artemis that she keeps in a pouch in her locker when she prays for Leoben's soul (1.08).

Prayer is thus a comfort to the individual but always oriented toward the larger communal context.

IV. Ecclesiology

Three types of religious figure are seen: Priest, "Brother" and Oracle.

A. Priest

There are both male and female priests in the human religion of *BSG*. Priests lead religious services. They may preside over civic ceremonies, such as the swearing in of a new president or a memorial service (both seen in MS). Priests also serve as counselors and guides. Elosha, the priest who advises President Roslin until she is killed on Kobol, is termed "the fleet's spiritual leader" by David Bassom (2005: 133). A woman of color (played by actress Lorena Gale), Elosha advises, comforts, and leads religious ceremonies.* Gale states that Elosha is the president's "spiritual guide" (quoted in Bassom 2005: 134). Thus, priests serve to meet the individual and collective needs of the people. Priests may marry and have children, which may also be a sign of the importance of the group — that priests are expected to also have families in addition to serving the people (2.19).

---

*Interestingly, Bassom reports Elosha was originally envisioned as "an eighty-year-old wizened male priest (2005: 133). Later, in the pilot of *Caprica*, we see an elderly white male priest leading a funeral service. Thus, it stands that priests are of all ethnicities and genders.

B. "Brother"

Only one "Brother" is shown, "Brother Cavil," who is, in fact, a Cylon. But the fact of his existence, that he is, until his true nature is discovered, welcomed by the human community, of evidence of this class of cleric. Brothers, and presumably "sisters," are also spiritual leaders. Brothers lead prayer, hear confessions, and counsel individuals. The series does not explain the distinction between "priest" and "brother," so they may be the equivalent of monk or perhaps a lay brother, i.e., laity who agree to serve in a religious capacity as well. Given the Colonial dedication to the community, this role would make sense.

C. Oracle

Oracles are mystics and seers who are consulted for advice and prophesy. Unlike the priests, who work with individuals but who also serve a communal function, oracles are only seen working with individuals. We know of at least three. Galen Tyrol's mother was an oracle (2.18). There is an oracle on New Caprica, Selloi (3.03). Starbuck consults the oracle Yolanda Brenn when she has strange dreams (3.17). Oracles tell prophesies and give advice and information. They interpret dreams. They rely upon a number of different means to divine. Most of all, oracles seem to have access to the gods in the here and now. Whereas priests relate the past and talk about prophesies of the future, oracles interpret signs in the present.

When the Cylon Three comes to see the oracle on New Caprica, the oracle has insights and messages not available through natural means. Selloi tells D'Anna Biers that Zeus sees her and sees her pain and her emptiness (3.03). Selloi knows D'Anna no longer knows what she believes in, knows that D'Anna had a dream that troubled her, and has a message for her "from the one you worship," meaning the Cylon god, that Hera is alive, that she will see and hold Hera, but that she will lose everything (3.03). Prophesy is not limited to sacred scrolls—Oracles are mystics who have powers of prophesy and bring messages from the gods.

Oracles seem to be the one aspect of Colonial faith that is not group oriented. Oracles live alone, oracles meet with individuals, not groups, and oracles prophesy and interpret for individuals. Although they speak for the gods, they speak to individuals.

V. Moral Theology and Ethics

Colonial moral theology is rooted, as all Colonial faith is, in the community. One is expected to follow "the example of the gods" (P). When one sins, one sins against the community rather than against the gods. Individuals are expected to behave toward others in ways that support the group.

The Sacred Scrolls also argue for the sanctity of life. Sarah Porter, a Gemenese delegate to the Quorum, offers a view on the right to life when a teenager requests an abortion, calling it "obscene" and "an abomination" that is forbidden by scripture (2.17). While Colonial law guarantees the right to an abortion, Roslin changes this law after the Cylon genocide, but for very different reasons. President Roslin argues that humanity has a moral obligation to reproduce and increase in number, as there are now only 50,000 humans left in the universe, and thus outlaws abortion (2.17). While she is conflicted in doing so, her reasoning is rooted in the moral obligation to the community. The need of humanity's survival is a moral imperative that outweighs individual rights. In issues of ethics, the group is more valuable than the individual, or, to quote another speculative fiction text, "the needs of the many outweigh the needs of the few."*

VI. Eschatology

The dead receive "Life eternal" (MS) in the Elysian Fields (4.06). All human dead, whether good or evil, sinner or saint (so to speak) go to the Elysian Fields. The dead are together with their loved ones, reunited forever, together with the Lords of Kobol (4.06).

BSG shows a good deal of Colonial eschatological belief through funeral rituals. At a funeral for dead pilots carried out by Elosha, the narrative flashes back to the funeral for Zak Adama, Admiral Adama's older son who died in a Viper crash. Both priests speak words that relate the bodies of the dead with the ground and with the universe. We come from the universe; we come from the ground, and to both will we return upon death. This theology is similar to God's curse upon humanity when casting Adam and Eve out of Eden, in which He tells them, "By the sweat of your face you will eat bread, Till you return to the ground, Because from it you were taken; For you are dust, And to dust you shall return"

---

*Spock's statement of moral evaluation from Star Trek II: The Wrath of Kahn.

(Genesis 3:19), which, tangentially, are also the words spoken by Catholic priests on Ash Wednesday, reminding individuals that they, too, will return to the soil someday.

Again, we might note the importance of the community in both of these prayers. Elosha states that the dead are united in the afterlife with those who have died before and that "we" will join them when we die. Death separates the living from the dead, but the living form one community and all the dead form another single community. There is also no "end" in the sense of a linear history when there will be a judgment day and an end of time. The Colonials believe, as noted, in an eternal return: "all this has happened before and all this will happen again."

VII. Variations of Faith

Different groups of Colonials believe in the Colonial faith in different ways. Some of these variations are individual, and some are by Colonial ethnicity. All of them find justification for these beliefs in the Sacred Scrolls. People from Gemenon believe in the literal truth of the scriptures and are morally opposed to abortion (2.03; 2.17). Sagittarons do not believe in medicine; it is "an abomination, a sin against the gods" (3.14). Since they believe the body is an illusion and the gods want our souls to remain uncontaminated, they refuse medical care (3.14). They are also pacifists.

Given these facts, however, there are some Sagittarons who serve in the Colonial military who also accept medicine. The Gemenese opposition to abortion becomes known when a Gemenese girl seeks one. Thus, there is a general orthodoxy of Colonial faith, and individual colonies have their own orthodoxies, but they are all part of the same faith. As Bryan McHenry recognizes, "[E]ven though there are multiple gods represented and various ways of following those gods, all of them seem to function as equal parts within the same religious system" (2008: 222). The Twelve Colonies have a "single, multi-faceted religion" (McHenry 2008: 223).

VIII. Conclusions: Colonial Theology within Colonial Society

As a polytheistic culture, Colonial religion focuses on community: the community of believers, the community of the gods, the community of the dead and the greater community of all of these together.

Colonial religion contains:

> A belief in the gods.
> A belief in a larger metahistory, which includes a plan for "salvation" that is communal, not individual.
> A belief in sin (which does not require salvation in the Christian sense).
> A belief in prayer.
> A belief in the need to expiate sin by following the "example of the gods."
> A set of rituals that connects humans to the gods and to the greater reality.
> A set of rituals that creates and maintains community.
> A set of prayers designed to remind individuals of their larger place within society.

All of these elements are presented in a polytheistic faith whose ultimate reality of gods, prophesies and metahistory is played out to a certain degree of reality (the return to Kobol, for instance) throughout the series.

Not every individual in Colonial society shares all these beliefs or even any of these beliefs. Beginning in the miniseries, Colonial society is shown as paying lip service to religion, and incorporating it into formal, state events, but little actual faith is demonstrated. At the time of the Cylon attack, the Colonials live in a highly secularized society. Several prominent characters are revealed to be atheists, in practice (Bill Adama) if not in actual self-definition and belief (Baltar). The series also displays cultural religionists, who do not believe in the literalness of the Sacred Scrolls, but do share the culture and appreciate the stories as metaphors. Laura Roslin begins the series in this mode, knowing all the aspects and stories of Colonial faith, but neither believing nor practicing them. The series also shows us Colonial fundamentalists, such as the Gemenons, as well as converts to fundamentalism, such as Laura Roslin, who literally comes to see herself in scripture. She believes she is the "dying leader" prophesied in the scrolls.

We also see in the series an increase in religion during the time of crisis. After the Cylon attack that nearly ends humankind, the series demonstrates a return to faith for many Colonials. Those who had engaged in a completely secular existence find themselves pulling prayer beads and small statues of the gods out of their lockers, as Starbuck does, or, at the very least, begrudgingly encouraging others to pray, as Adama does. While the series makes room for atheism and fundamentalism, the two extremes of belief, it also makes room for civic religion and changing belief systems in the face of external pressures. The entire fleet begins following Roslin and Adama when they promise to fulfill scriptures and bring the fleet to Earth. For Adama, this is a lie to give people hope; for Rolsin it becomes truth. In other words, the entire remnant of humanity begins seeking the literal truth of their sacred stories, even the atheists.

The Colonials live through their own "end times" and see prophesy come to pass. They follow a religious leader who sees herself in their scriptures. They begin to interpret everything through prophesy, belief, and the messages of the gods, despite being in a highly technologically advanced society. We might see a reflection of post–9/11 America in this narrative, in which a religiously inspired leader claims divine justification for his policies. *Battlestar Galactica,* however, removes any doubt as at least the prophesies and desired outcomes are made real in that series. Perhaps that is the ultimate point of the theology of *Battlestar Galactica:* religion is real. The gods themselves may not be, or may be gone and unable to be contacted anymore, but the effects of belief in them are. There is efficacy in Colonial religion in that those who do believe in it change their world and change their reality.

2

A Systematic Theology of Cylon Religion / The Cylon Understanding of God

Many fans and scholars equate the Cylons with fundamentalism and fundamentalists. C.W. Marshall and Matthew Wheeland see the Cylon faith as "fundamentalist monotheism," being an amalgam of both Islamic and American Christian fundamentalism (2008: 96). Lynnette Porter, David Lavery and Hillary Robson agree, stating that Cylons are "right-wing Christian fundamentalists" (2008: 235). The Cylons seemingly launch a holy war against the humans, seemingly have a proselytizing agenda, and cite God as their reason for most actions. I believe this book's examination of the Cylon understanding of God and the theology of the Cylons demonstrates a far more complex invented faith and that the Cylons are not so much "fundamentalists" (especially as they have no readily defined doctrine to be fundamental about) as monotheistic mystics who do not always know the mind of their God, but always attempt to fulfill His will. Much of the Cylon theology is linked to a real-world reference by praying Cylons to a Christian text called *The Cloud of Unknowing*, which is a fourteenth-century treatise on mysticism. The Cylons are mystics, not fundamentalists.

History of the Cylons

Before the fall of humanity, within the Twelve Colonies there were a small number of monotheistic humans, the best known of which were a group of "terrorists" called "Soldiers of the One" who practiced a radical monotheism and used attacks on civilian targets to promote their beliefs. When Zoe Graystone, a monotheist and daughter of cybernetic manufacturer Daniel Graystone, was killed in a terrorist bombing, her father loaded a digital avatar she had created of herself into a prototype of the Cylon Centurion. Her consciousness made the cybernetic military robot function at a higher level, but the Centurion with sentience was able to spread that sentience to other Centurions, along with her monotheism. The end result was the Cylon War: a battle between humans and the Cylons who rebelled against their slave status. After an armistice was agreed to, the Cylons left and wandered for 40 years in search of a new home.

After 40 years, the Cylons returned and, having gained access to the Colonial defense grid through Six's manipulation of Gaius Baltar, used nuclear weapons to destroy most of humanity. After they have finished their initial attack, there are only 50,000 humans left. The Cylons occupy Caprica and begin their plan of bringing about the conception of a human/Cylon hybrid by mating Karl "Helo" Agathon with a Cylon model eight (a "Sharon"). Several of the Cylons come to believe the attack on humanity was a mistake. They follow the humans to New Caprica and attempt to be Colonial masters.

After the humans escape from New Caprica, the Cylons attempt to follow in order to find Hera, the human/Cylon hybrid, and Earth, which they believe might also be a home for them. Eventually, a disagreement breaks out between the Cylons since Brother Cavil wants to lobotomize the sentient Cylon attack ships ("raiders"), which are refusing to attack the humans since it has been revealed the "Final Five" are hidden in the human fleet. Cylon models One, Four and Five vote to carry out the surgeries; Two, Six, Eight and the Centurions vote against. A civil war ensues, and the rebel Cylons agree to work with the humans to find Earth.

Technically, there are four types of Cylon, but they are actually the product of two separate origins. The Centurions were made by humans on Caprica as military robots. They then created the raiders, sentient attack-ships (Boomer compares them to "pets" [1.06]) and the Hybrids, insane half-human, half-robots that control the basestars). The remaining Cylons are "skinjobs"—humanoids that are also sentient, self-aware, cybernetic beings but that look and feel human. "Some are programmed to think they are human," as the opening credits state. The "Final Five"

Cylons, the ones whose identities are the last to be revealed, are actually the original five.

Saul and Ellen Tigh, Tory Foster, Galen Tyrol and Sam Anders were originally cybernetic beings created on the original Earth, 3,000 years ago. They were part of the 13th tribe of Kobol. A nuclear war on original Earth resulted in the five of them traveling through space to find the other descendents of Kobol. They met the Centurions immediately after the Cylon War and gave them resurrection technology and a social organization. Then they made the other eight models together in their numbered order. Number One, John Cavil, angry at his creators, killed them, wiped their minds when they were resurrected and sent them to live among the humans while the Cylons planned the destruction of the Twelve Colonies, unaware of their own true nature.

Thus the Cylons may be broken down into four types:

The Centurions (bipedal, sentient metal beings)
The Raiders (living combat ships)
The Hybrids (control larger ships)
13 models of "Skin job"

Despite continual assertions that there are 12 models of "skinjob," there are actually 13, the first eight of which are identified by number and then the "Final Five," who do not have numbers.

> One = John Cavil (played by Dean Stockwell)
> Two = Leoben Conoy (played by Callum Keith Rennie)
> Three = D'Anna Biers (played by Lucy Lawless)
> Four = Simon O'Neill (played by Rick Worthy)
> Five = Aaron Doral (played by Matthew Bennett)
> Six = [Six] (never named specifically, with a variety of other names, played by Tricia Helfer)*
> Seven = Daniel (an unstable, boxed line that we never actually see)
> Eight = Sharon Valerii, of whom there are two main versions: "Boomer" (the bad one) and "Athena" (the good one) (Played by Grace Park)

*The central Six is called "Caprica Six," and we also come to know Baltar's "Virtual Six" or "Head Six," as she is sometimes called. Several other Sixes, however, do have human names: Shelly Godfrey (1.07), Gina Inviere (2.10, R), Natalie Faust (4.08), Lida (4.14), Sonja (4.17). Unlike the other models, there is no dominant name to go with the model number. Six is "Six."

The Final Five:

Tory Foster (played by Rekha Sharma)
Galen Tyrol (played by Aaron Douglas)
Samuel Anders (played by Michael Trucco)
Saul Tigh (played by Michael Hogan)
Ellen Tigh (played by Kate Vernon)

The Cylons believe that they have souls and, although created by humanity, are ultimately the product of God. They believe they have replaced a sinful humanity as God's favorites. This theme is introduced in the original miniseries. Leoben, pretending to be human at Ragmar Station, tells Adama that the Cylons are God's punishment to mankind for their sins and that the Cylons themselves have souls (MS). Adama answers that the Cylons were made by humanity, not God, and humanity did not make souls for the Cylons. Adama raises the fundamental question about the Cylons: as mechanical beings, can they have souls? Yet this does not answer Leoben's critique that humans have become wicked and sinful and God has turned his back on them. Even if Cylons do not have souls, that does not necessarily mean that God or the gods are not using them to punish a fallen humanity.

Leoben's critique echoes The Letter of Paul to the Romans:

> For though they knew God, they did not honor him as
> God or give thanks to him, but they became futile in their
> thinking, and their senseless minds were darkened. Claiming
> to be wise, they became fools; and they exchanged the glory
> of the immortal God for images resembling a mortal human
> being or birds or four-footed animals or reptiles [1:21–23].

In worshipping false gods, humanity has lost its way and left the true God behind. The Cylons are thus now God's chosen people.

Cylon theology is rooted in the idea that they are a chosen people and that God loves them. God also loves humanity and, as the series evolves, Cylon theology evolves. Central to Cylon theology is dedication to God, love, and salvation. At heart, the Cylons are mystics who experience God not intellectually but through love. They eventually come to understand salvation as breaking a cycle of violence between humanity and "humanity's children" as they term themselves.

I. Monotheism and the Nature of God

Cylon theology is "the product of revelation" (Marshall and Whee-land 2008: 97). God speaks and reveals himself to certain Cylons and reveals not only His existence and His love but also His plan. There is only one God. Unlike the polytheistic humans, the Cylons believe in a single divinity simply termed "God." He has no other names, although in prayer the Cylons will occasionally refer to him as "Heavenly Father" (3.01; 3.07; 4.08; 4.18). This belief in a single God came from the Centurions, who, as noted, began as monotheistic robots in a polytheistic human society. The Final Five "converted," so to speak, to the Cylon faith and then created the eight new models, imbuing them with this faith as well (4.15).

The Cylon divinity is acknowledged by the Cylons as not just the Cylon God but the God of all: "He's not my God, He is God" (1.07). Like Paul's understanding of YHWH, the God of the Hebrews, God is God to all, not just a single people.* Six further informs Baltar in the same episode ("Six Degrees of Separation") that it is vital that he "form a personal relationship" with God, language that echoes evangelical Christianity's understanding of the nature of the relationship between divinity and humanity (1.07). Unlike the human's dedication to the community, the Cylons (who are, after all, mass-produced individuals) focus on the individual's relationship to the deity. One must make a conscious choice to dedicate one's self to God.

Again, this individual choice to embrace God even extends to humans and any sentient being. When Six prevents Baltar from destroying a Cylon base, he taunts her, saying that her Cylon God would not want him to destroy Cylons. Six corrects him by explaining that God is not on either side, but wants all created beings, humans and Cylon, to love Him (1.10).

God is all powerful, all knowing and yet we never hear from the Cylons that He is omni-benevolent. God can and will turn his back on those who do not accept or love him. God "turned his back on Kobol" and has cursed the planet (2.03). So cursed is Kobol, in fact, that anyone, human or Cylon, who dies on Kobol does not receive any kind of eternal life: "Nothing awaits them. No eternal life, no damnation, only oblivion ... because they died on Kobol" (2.03). Kobol is the planet that God has rejected, even long after no sentient life remains upon it.

---

*See, for example, Galatians 2:15-17 or 1 Corinthians 12:13.

The Cylon faith seems to center around a series of paradoxes. God's love is eternal, but His anger and vengeance can also be long lasting. Cylon and human alike are given free will to choose to love God or reject him. Yet, nothing in the universe happens without God willing it (3.07).

God cannot be understood intellectually, which is ironic, considering that Cylons are machines. Repeatedly the Cylons deconstruct and challenge the language used to talk about and understand God. Six refers to God as "He," although Baltar does question this gender assignment, asking how she knows God is male. Her response is to assert there is only one God, deflecting the question entirely (1.07). She does not respond to his questioning of the gender possibilities of God, focusing rather on the singular nature of God. Six constantly reminds us not to fixate on the finite language used to describe the infinite and not to fixate on human categories of identity.

Thus, even when addressed as "Heavenly Father," this attribution is used merely to provide a means of conceiving a personal relationship with the ineffable. God is addressed so in the Prayer to the Cloud of Unknowing (see prayer section, later in the chapter), which would seem to identify the Cylon understanding of God as a fundamentally mystical one, as this is an obvious reference to a real text.

The Cloud of Unknowing is an anonymous, fourteenth-century text of Christian mysticism. The title refers to metaphor of the incomprehensibility of God: "The first time you practice contemplation, you'll only experience a darkness, like a cloud of unknowing" (Butcher 2009: 12). The manuscript instructs a young acolyte that God cannot be found in knowledge but through "blind love" and "pure love" (Butcher 2009: 61, 114). One should only love God and ignore all other thoughts. By placing all one's thought into a "cloud of forgetting," one will pierce the "cloud of unknowing" between God and creation (i.e., that which cannot be understood intellectually) and experience divine love and union with God (Butcher 2009: xi, 18). The heart, rather than the head, is the means by which one can experience God in this text.

The anonymous author of *The Cloud of Unknowing* sees Mary, sister of Martha and Lazarus, as the ideal model:

> Mary focused instead on the highest wisdom of [Christ's] divinity concealed in the enigmatic teaching of his humanity. She paid complete attention to him in this way, with every ounce of love in her heart, not moving a muscle, disregarding anything said about her and anything going on around her.

> And her delightful, intimate love pressed against that high
> cloud of unknowing between her and God [Butcher 2009: 46].

The book also contains spiritual exercises and guidelines for "contemplative prayer" (Butcher 2009: 76). All of this is to allow the reader to feel enough love to "press against the cloud of unknowing" that exists between God and His creation. The Cylons, in calling one of their central religious concepts "the cloud of unknowing," not only link to Christian mysticism, but also construct divinity as something that cannot be understood or fathomed, only loved and experienced.

All of these concepts seem to indicate an underlying *via negativa* to understanding the Cylon understanding of God. God cannot be understood intellectually, to the point of not even wanting to be called "God." Language, knowledge and understanding fail to bring us closer to the divine. The Cylons follow a apophatic theology that cannot define God in terms of what He is, but rather in terms of His unknowability. What Karl Barth says of humans, *BSG* demonstrates for Cylons: "Human experience and human perceptions end where God begins (1963: 120). While being tortured by Kara Thrace, Leoben tells her, "To know the face of God is to know madness. I see the universe. I see the pattern. I see the foreshadowings that precede every moment of every day" (1.08). The Cylons are, at heart, mystics who know God exists, know He loves them and wants them to obey Him, but otherwise know nothing of God. They experience their "Heavenly Father," and pray to Him, but there are no extended theological texts or rites and rituals.

The Cylons thus are machines that have a mystical appreciation of God and that find enlightenment and fulfillment *as* machines. God loves them for who they are. This theology has two significant implications. The first is that God cannot be known through theologies, rituals, prayers or texts. All creeds, doctrines, images and beliefs merely get in the way. Barth states, "God reveals himself inexorably as the hidden God who can only be apprehended indirectly.... He conceals himself utterly" (1963: 126). God must be experienced, and experienced as a Cylon. God is ineffable, incomprehensible, and utterly unknowable by mere physical beings, and thus the Cylon theology focuses on the experience of God, not knowledge about Him.

The second is that they have their own form of supersessionism. Supersessionism, also sometimes identified as "replacement theology," is the Christian belief that Christians replaced the Jews as God's chosen people. Under supersessionism, God sent His only son to His chosen people and they rejected Him, and so the new covenant with all humankind who accept Christ replaces or supersedes the covenants God made with Abraham and Moses. The Cylons believe that they have replaced or superseded humans as God's children. Leoben remarks in the miniseries that humanity may have been God's mistake, and that the Cylons have become His children as a result. Later, he tells Starbuck, "I know that God loved you more than all other living creatures and you repaid His divine love with sin, with hate, with corrupting evil. So then He decided to create the Cylons" (1.08). Repeatedly, from Brother Cavil to Caprica Six to Virtual Six, the Cylons assert that they, not humans, are the chosen of God. They acknowledge that humanity once held a place in God's love, but that the Cylons have replaced them. The Cylons, in short, are believers in Cylon Supersessionism, a Cylon replacement theology. Cylons are God's chosen people, since humanity has rejected Him.

Each Cylon seems to be on his or her own metaphysical quest. D'Anna, Leoben, and Six all spend a good deal of time among the humans in order to understand what God wants and to help the humans to whom they have become attached find their way to God and God's plan. All Cylons acknowledge the importance of God and of following God's plan. In fact, the only atheistic Cylon is the only Cylon with a clerical title: Brother Cavil.

Despite the Cylon fixation on God at the center of their theology, there is also room in the Cylon religion for atheism within the faith: Brother Cavil is an agnostic, if not an atheist, observing that you "can't really prove one way or the other" if God exists, so Cavil figures He does not (2.20). Some Cylons, in spite of the Cylon faith, simply do not believe in God.

Cavil is, in fact, a cynical atheist who uses religion to his own ends. In conversation with Tyrol, Cavil tells him that prayer is "bad poetry" that gets one "exactly nothing" (2.19). Tyrol asks, "Are you sure you're a priest?" Cavil replies that he has been a priest long enough to have realized that prayers are not answered. We might interpret this statement in more than one way. Cavil, as a Cylon and monotheist, does not believe that the gods answer prayers, but that God might. So it is not theism but polytheism that Cavil disavows. But his next statement is that sentient beings are alone in the universe and must determine their own path. Again, more than one reading of this statement is possible. It can be a coded atheism — Cavil believes we are "on our own" — there is no divinity, no gods, no God. Or, it might be read as a variation of Enlightenment Deism — God as "clockmaker" who creates the universe and sets it running but neither intervenes nor acts in any way upon it afterwards. Alternately, Cavil's statements might be seen as an extension of the mysticism of *The Cloud of Unknowing.* We cannot understand or know God. We cannot trust pat answers and literal readings of any scriptures, as they all limit the divine. Thus we must "find our own answers" through contemplation and action.

II. Love

Although much of the talk about God's love comes from Virtual Six, who is technically not a Cylon but an angel, many of the other Cylons, including other Sixes, speak at length about God's love. One of the very first things Caprica Six is shown saying to Baltar is "God is Love" (MS). Leoben tells Starbuck that love is the thing that holds the universe together and that all living beings together are God (1.08). If God is love, then love is what has created the universe and everything in it and what binds Cylon and human together is that ultimately the Cylons are, like humans, children of God. That binding love creates both moral obligation and a very specific understanding of reality. The Cylon religion, as much as it is rooted in God, is rooted in love.

We might compare the Cylon understanding of God and love to the first letter of John:

> Beloved, let us love one another, because love is from God: everyone who loves is born of God and knows God. Whoever does not love does not know God, for God is love.... So we have known and believe the love that God has for us. God is love, and those who abide in love abide in God, and God abides in them [4:7–8, 16].

John points to Christ as evidence of God's love: "He sent his only Son into the world so that we might live through him (4:9). The Cylons have no such incarnation, but understand and accept the love of God as the basis for their theology.

Lynnette Porter, David Lavery and Hillary Robson write that to certain Cylons, "love is all consuming and transformative, the ultimate reflection of goodness. Love, whether of other Cylons, humans or God, should be a religious experience" (2008: 118). For most Cylons, love is a religious experience. For Sharon "Athena" Agathon, it is a miraculous experience. Because of love, she and Helo are able to conceive a child and reproduce biologically, something no Cylon has ever been able to do. This cross-species mating is not possible scientifically. The Cylons have experimented and tried repeatedly to impregnate human females, all to no effect (2.05). It is only through love that scientific, material reality is transcended and the miraculous possible. As noted, the Cylons have no theology of an incarnation, but Hera Agathon, the hybrid child, is the physical proof of God's love.

III. God's Other Commandments

Following God's path is never easy. — Caprica Six (2.18)

In addition to love, God has other commandments. These commandments are never laid out in a doctrine, a scripture or the pronouncements of a magisterium or clergy. These commandments, however, have somehow been revealed to the Cylons, many of whom accept them without question.

A. Obedience

God expects to be obeyed. He rewards those who follow him and his will, and he punishes those who disobey. His favor can shift. As Six notes, "That which God gives he can also take away" (1.01). God punishes for a lack of faith. God punishes for turning away, as He did on Kobol. God punishes for a lack of love.

B. Procreation

When asked about her pregnancy, Sharon Agathon simply states that procreation is one of God's commandments, and then she quotes the Sacred Scrolls: "Be fruitful." (2.05). This statement echoes Genesis 1:28: "Be fruitful and multiply, and fill the earth...." God wants his followers to create more followers.

Interestingly, as Marshall and Wheeland observe, this commandment "has been interpreted by Cylon exegetes to require biological procreation, rather than mere reproduction" (2008: 97). Time and again in the series we are shown a seemingly limitless number of the seven human models. The resurrection ship holds numerous copies of bodies waiting to have a consciousness downloaded into them after the destruction of a Cylon body (2.11). The Cylons can reproduce their model bodies seemingly infinitely. Biological procreation is held to be what God actually commands. Sharon "Athena" Valerii is given the mission of mating with Karl "Helo" Agathon (after he falls in love with her) so that she might become pregnant.

Any Cylon pregnancy is a source for joy and celebration among the Cylons. When Caprica Six becomes pregnant with Saul Tigh's child, it is considered a miracle by the Cylons, but also serves as a source of jealousy for Ellen Tigh, who was never able to conceive by him. Ellen interprets this as evidence that Saul loved Six more than he ever loved Ellen. It means God has blessed Saul's union with Six over the union with Ellen.*

C. The Sanctity of Life

The taking of life is a sin. Both murder and suicide are forbidden by God. Yet, as in the Pentateuch, there is legal room within these commandments. Although God forbids murder, He also instructs the Israelites: "But as for the towns of the peoples the Lord your God is giving you as an inheritance, you must not let anything that breathes remain alive. You shall annihilate them — the Hittites and the Amorites, the Canaanites and the Perizzites, the Hittites and the Jebusites—just as the Lord your God has commanded (Deuteronomy 20:16–17). Time and again, God commands not just murder but genocide:

> But the Lord said to Moses: "Do not be afraid of him; for I have given him into your hand, with all his people, and all his land. You shall do to him as you did to King Sihon of the Amorites, who ruled in Heshbon." So they killed him, his sons, and all his people, until there was no survivor left; and they took possession of his land [Numbers 21:34–35].
> At that time we captured all his towns, and in each town we utterly destroyed men, women and children. We left not a single survivor [Deuteronomy 2:24].
> Now go and attack Amalek, and utterly destroy all that they have; do not spare them, but kill both man and woman, child and infant, ox and sheep, camel and donkey [1 Samuel 15:3].

Exodus (and the other books of law) also presents a series of individual cases in which killing another human being is not only acceptable but

---

*One is free to read into this situation correlations with several Hebrew Bible family dynamics: Sarai and Abram have no children, so Abram conceives a child with Hagar, the slave girl, resulting in Sarai's jealousy, to name but the most obvious one (Genesis 16:1–6)

commanded: "Whoever strikes a person mortally shall be put to death" (21:12); "Whoever curses father or mother shall be put to death" (21:17); "You shall not permit a female sorcerer to live. Whoever lies with an animal shall be put to death. Whoever sacrifices to any god, other than the Lord alone, shall be devoted to destruction" (22:18–20). Despite the prohibition "You shall not murder" (Exodus 20:14; Deuteronomy 5:17), God gives a whole series of exceptions to this commandment.

As with the Israelites, the Cylons believe God forbids them to kill, with a whole series of exceptions to this commandment. As noted, under Cylon Supersessionist theology, the Cylons initially see the humans as the people who rejected God's love and thus the Cylons are God's new chosen, as well as the instrument of His righteous anger. From the human point of view, the Cylons are the biblical flood, created to sweep away wickedness. From the Cylon point of view, the Cylons are the Israelites and the humans are "the Hittites and the Amorites, the Canaanites and the Perizzites, the Hittites and the Jebusites"—Godless people to be annihilated and their lands taken for God's people.

Nevertheless, God's commandment not to kill remains strong. Caprica Six and Boomer convince the other Cylons that the attack on the colonies was a mistake. "Genocide, murder, vengeance—they're all sins in the eyes of God," Caprica Six tells Boomer, who agrees and states that "the slaughter of mankind was a mistake" (2.18). The decision to slaughter humanity is never attributed to God. But the decision to stop the slaughter is attributed to a need to follow God's commandment. After abandoning Caprica, the Cylons attempt to simply occupy New Caprica as Colonial masters, rather than slaughter the humans. When the Cylons wish to execute members of the human resistance on New Caprica, they want Baltar, as Colonial president, to sign the execution order. Cavil states, "They're worried about what God might think if they commit murder. They're covering their existential asses" (3.02). Even when executing resistance members, the Cylons want the executions to be judicially sanctioned by the humans; otherwise they might be accused of killing in the eyes of God.

D. The Great Cylon Commission (Maybe?)

Lastly, God *might* command proselytizing. A pair of Cavils, discussing the occupation of New Caprica, state that their role is to bring the word of God to humanity by any means necessary. While theological statements from Cavil must always be taken with a grain of salt (he is the only Cylon for whom "fear is a key article of faith"), the repeated assertion is that the Cylons are on New Caprica not merely to rule over the humans but to "bring the word of God" and "bring the love of God" to them in order to save them from "damnation."

God expects love, humility, obedience, procreation and a respect for life. God may or may not want the Cylons to proselytize. If He does, however, it would seem that God favors Six's approach to converting humans over Cavil's.

IV. Prayer

When the humans capture a Leoben Cylon, Starbuck is charged with interrogating him. She comes upon him with eyes closed. When he confesses that he was praying, she taunts him by saying that God does not answer the prayers of machines. He instead asserts that everyone's prayers are answered by God (1.08). God listens to all prayers and answers them. Cylons believe in the efficacy of prayer.

The Cylons have fewer occasions to pray than humans, and the most formal prayer is, like human prayer, related to funerary rites. The Prayer to the Cloud of Unknowing is performed by the humanoid Cylons when a fellow Cylon is dying, dies, or is about to die and downloading is impossible: "Heavenly Father, grant us the strength, the wisdom and above all, a measure of acceptance, however small" (4.18). The prayer may be prayed for others, as when Ellen Tigh prays for Cylons killed in a hull breach (4.18), or for one's self, as Natalie Six does when she is dying from a gunshot wound (4.08).

Unlike humans, who focus on the community, even at the death of an individual, the Cylons look to the personal relationship with God. The prayer is not offered for the soul of the departed Cylon. The prayer asks God to grant "us," presumably the living who remain behind, the emotional tools we will need to continue, and we ask for "a measure of acceptance." Whereas the humans know that they will go to Elysian Fields and be with their loved ones who have died before them, the Cylons go to an unknown and unknowable God. This prayer reflects that difference: we ask for a "measure of acceptance" of this difficult-to-accept reality; after death we go to God; we do not know anything else. Thus, the Cylons pray not for the soul of the dead individual, who will be with God, but for those left behind to be able to cope with the loss and with the difficulty of not knowing.

V. Eschatology

Cylons, thus, have two forms of death. The first is a short-term bodily death of the current physical form. The body dies and the individual Cylon's consciousness enters a new body. Cylons literally have "resurrection." When they die, their consciousness is downloaded into a new body that is an exact replica of the one that died. This technology gives them de facto immortality or eternal life. However, if Cylons die out of range of a "resurrection ship," they are not resurrected and according to Gina, their soul directly joins God (2.12). This second death is a permanent death from which there is no return; the Cylon goes to an afterlife in the divine presence. This afterlife does not have a name. The Cylons only know their soul is "delivered unto God" (1.08).

Cylons believe they have souls, although some doubt it. Adama in the miniseries doubts, arguing that Cylons have programming, not souls. In her ontological debates with Leoben while torturing him, Starbuck tells him that he does not have a soul, only "software" (1.08). Even Brother Cavil also seems to doubt. As the Cylon civil war begins and Cylon begins killing Cylon, Cavil excuses his Cylocide. When Boomer objects to the slaughter of other Eights, Cavil tells her that God will watch their souls. When she asks what about her and his souls, he responds that they are machines and therefore do not have souls (4.03).

So for Adama and Brother Cavil, when a Cylon dies outside the range of a resurrection ship, his or her fate is oblivion. He or she simply ceases to exit. The majority of Cylons seem to believe that they have souls that will continue to be downloaded until they go to be with God. When he is executed by the Colonials, Leoben is not afraid to die, according to Starbuck; he is afraid that when he dies he will not be with God (1.08). This fate is what ends up happening in the fourth season when the resurrection hub is destroyed by the rebel Cylons. With the loss of resurrection technology, the Cylons become mortal and when they die they are no longer downloaded, but their death is permanent and their souls go to God.

VI. Salvation

The proto–Hybrid in "Razor" prophesies that the "self-described machines who believe themselves without sin" will be "consumed" by sin (R). As Gabriel McKee observes, "The robots believe themselves to be creation perfected, the immortal instruments of God's will" (2007a: 163). Yet, they do believe, Augustine-like, in the total depravity of humanity, at least initially.

The Cylons see themselves as the instrument of a vengeful God, punishing humanity on His behalf. Under the leadership of Caprica Six and Boomer, they come to see that attitude as a mistake and look to live and interact with humans instead of eliminating them. The Cylons then have a civil war and come to see their own depravity. They seek "eternal life" and "salvation," but it takes on a different meaning than it does for the humans.

The Cylons have "eternal life" in the form of "resurrection," their term for downloading their consciousness and memories into a new, duplicate body. After the humans destroy the resurrection hubs, the Cylons no longer have eternal life. They now die and their consciousness disappears from this existence forever, going "to be with God," whatever that may mean (it is not clear if the Cylons mean it literally, as in the survival of individual personality in the presence of the divine or that one joins some sort of cosmic consciousness with a loss of individuality). Another repercussion of the destruction of resurrection technology is the possible extinction of the Cylons. When each Cylon dies, he or she is not replaced in any way. Hera Agathon represents the potential for biological reproduction among the Cylons and therefore represents a kind of salvation among the Cylons. If they learn how to reproduce without resurrection, then the civilization (species?) will not go extinct but may continue.

Among the rebel Cylons of the later seasons, Caprica Six comes to realize, as Virtual Six already knows, that God wants salvation for both humans and Cylons. The larger question is: from what do humans and Cylons need saving? The answer is: the cycle of violence that inevitably ends in the mutual destruction of human and Cylon. "All this has happened before and all this will happen again," refers to the cycle of destructive violence between humans and their creations. Eventually, both are destroyed and a small remnant moves on to start the cycle anew. Saul and Ellen Tigh, the original Cylons, realize that every iteration has ended the same way. At this point in the cycle, however, God intervenes, not in an incarnation, but in the unique blending of human and Cylon in the form of Hera.

The Cylons know they need salvation, but how and from what is therefore fluid throughout the series. The final conclusion on Cylon soteriology is that God's commandment to love extends to humans and in order to find salvation, the saving of the Cylons from extinction, they must learn to love in such a way that biological reproduction becomes possible.

VII. Relationship Between Cylons and Humans

The Cylons were made by the humans. The Hybrids refer to humans as "the makers" (4.09). Six calls Cylons "humanity's children" (R). Yet, like Lucifer, the Cylons come to resent their creator. Like Lucifer, and Adam, and Cain, they disobey and rebel. From the humans, they learn violence, destruction and murder. Cavil tells the humans, "We became what we beheld. We became you" (2.20).

Initially, the Cylons have contempt for the human religion, referring to the Lords of Kobol as "false idols" (2.07). The Cylons see themselves as God's chosen since humanity has rejected God in favor of false idols. Six believes that humanoid bodies allow Cylons to appreciate God's creation and that is why God allowed humanity to make humanoid Cylons (R). Cylons believe that they have supplanted humans in God's favor.

Yet this relationship shifts as the Cylons come to view the slaughter of humanity as a mistake. The mistake was theirs, not God's, but a mistake nonetheless. If God is love, then even humanity, for all its faults and sins, is loved by God and must not be harmed. After the Cylon civil war, many Cylons work with humanity to find Earth. Hera Agathon herself, as the union of human and Cylon, is proof that God loves both and wants salvation for both.

VIII. Conclusion

The Cylon understanding of God is best summed up in *The Cloud of Unknowing*. God is not understood intellectually. God cannot be known in any sense of the word. Cylon theology is an apophatic one: a *via negativa* to understand the divine with our limited capacity to experience, know and understand. God is love and thus can only be experienced. God seeks obedience, surrender and humility in the face of creation.

The Cylons are, in a very real sense, not the fundamentalists that scholars have seen them as, although they seemingly start off that way. They have no scripture, no real doctrine, no exegesis, nothing to be fundamental to. What they do have is mysticism, and a mystical experience of God that leads them toward individual and collective salvation. God reveals Himself in our lives through reflection and through his messengers. We must submit and obey. Everything that happens, happens by God's command, out of His love. Yet we also have free will to accept and follow or reject and deny that love. There are consequences for both.

3

A Systematic Theology of the Baltar Cult / The Baltar Cult Understanding of God

A History of Baltar

Gaius Baltar is the son of farmers from Aerilon, one of the poorest colonies. He left that planet at the age of 18, practiced to lose his accent, was educated in the sciences and became one of the best known and most well connected scientists in the Twelve Colonies, including among his personal friends the president (MS). Religiously speaking, he begins the series as a staunch atheist: "There is no God. Or gods, singular or plural. There are no large, invisible men, or women for that matter, in the sky, taking a personal interest in the fortunes of Gaius Baltar" (1.01). Indeed, he mocks Caprica Six for her faith, calling it "mysticism and superstition." He will repeat this doubt over several episodes in the first season.

Baltar, however, has a two-year affair with an unnamed woman (Six) who helps him in his computer projects and to whom he gives access to the Colonial defense systems, allowing for the Cylons to attack a now defenseless humanity. His lascivious appetites and pride lead to the destruction of humanity, which fuels both his guilt and his atheism. Rescued from the dying, irradiated planet by Boomer, he joins the surviving humans, first as President Roslin's scientific advisor, then as vice president in his own right, and then, in a contested election over the discovery of New Caprica, as president. While in the fleet, Baltar continues to see and interact with a vision in the image of Six, who comes to be known as "Virtual Six." She provides him with advice and information, and pushes and encourages him, but also taunts and mocks him. President Baltar, both incompetent and self-indulgent, orders the colonization of New Caprica and serves as a puppet leader when the Cylons invade and take over the planet. When Adama leads a rescue of the colonists on New Caprica, Baltar is left behind, a prisoner of the Cylons.

Tortured by Three and needing to prove his worth again and again to the Cylons in order to stay alive, Baltar is eventually recaptured by the humans and put on trial for crimes against humanity. While in prison, he writes his manifesto, *My Triumphs, My Mistakes*, a populist political critique of what he terms "the emerging aristocracy within the fleet," which begins to gain him a following (3.16). When he is acquitted of the charges, he is rescued from a lynch mob by a group of women who have formed a cult around him and his ideas. Embracing monotheism and the idea that Baltar is the prophet of the one true God, they invite him to serve as their leader.

Although his initial reaction is one of scorn and loathing, he comes to embrace his role within the cult. Virtual Six pushes him to make pronouncements and even gives him sermons, word for word. It is ultimately revealed that Virtual Six is an angel of God and Baltar is, indeed, an instrument of God. A lazy, selfish, fearful, arrogant, lust-filled, pathetic, self-loathing instrument of God, but still an instrument of God.

Baltar never quite embraces the religious faith that Virtual Six offers him from the beginning. He is constantly plagued with doubt. Although in moments of fear or concern, he gives himself to God, it is always for the purpose of self-preservation. When Baltar falls under suspicion of being a traitor, he prays. Interestingly, he does not pray to the gods but to the "One True God" that Virtual Six has asserted plans to use Gaius as His instrument. After acknowledging God as the only God, he promises to devote his life to "doing good" if God will rescue him from what he assumes will be a death sentence. In his fear, he promises God that he wants "to carry out Your divine will" (1.07).

When Baltar prays this, he is under suspicion of being a traitor who allowed the Cylons access to the colonies' defenses (which is, in fact, technically true, though he was not aware of it at the time). Yet, after this prayer, Baltar is exonerated and given the full trust of the humans. Baltar's conversion and prayer have efficacy in the real world. Yet he will continually apostatize and be cowardly and motivated by self-interest and his own base desires, obeying God only when it serves his needs.

It is shown to Baltar again and again that when he follows the plan that God has laid out, he benefits. Six tells him he is part of God's plan when God guides his finger to a target that allows the Colonials a major victory against the Cylons. When Baltar "gives himself over to" God, the target he picked at random turns out to be the exact right spot to attack. Baltar himself concludes that the only rational explanation is that "I am an instrument of God" (1.10). Although his tone is ambiguous when he says this, which allows us to read it as ironic, or sarcastic, he also comes across as a man beginning to realize the theological implications of his own existence. The series will demonstrate by the end that Baltar is, in fact, an instrument of God. A weak, selfish, cowardly one, but still an instrument of God.

What follows is the very loose systematic theology based on Baltar's sermons, the statements of Virtual Six, and the visible results of the working out of their prophesies.

I. God

The first tenet of the Baltar cult is that the humans' theology is wrong. There are no "gods," only a single, true God. As Virtual Six tells him what to say, Baltar challenges the female members of his cult. Tracey Anne confesses that when she prays to the gods she feels empty. In contrast, when she watches Baltar, it is as if the gods are present. The irony, of course, is that Virtual Six, his conduit to God, is present and speaking to him. Six tells Baltar to preach that the gods are false. An obedient Baltar tells Tracey Anne that her empty feeling is due to the fact that she is praying to nonexistent gods. The gods, he tells her, are a fiction created by the ruling elite to maintain the status quo. The truth is that there is but a single God (4.01).

We learn multiple aspects of faith from this exchange. First, there is one God; He is a jealous God and wants any and all other gods acknowledged as false (echoes of Deuteronomy 5:6–10). Second, that Baltar is a prophet and gets his information from an angel only he can see who takes the form of his former Cylon lover. Baltar inspires followers despite his own spiritual failings.* Baltar's experience of God does not seem hollow; it is not an empty experience. Baltar claims that this is because God is real and the gods are not. This also teaches us that God's presence can be experienced and that experiences prove His existence.

This experiential aspect of faith also shows that Baltar's God, like the Cylon God, is a revealed God, a God of revelation. There are no sacred scriptures. There are no relics or places of worship. Instead, there are only God and his messengers. The messengers convey God's will. God speaks to the angels, angels speak to Baltar, and Baltar speaks to the humans. But God also speaks directly to the human heart. Baltar preaches that he does not believe in a distant God who speaks only through an "appointed human mouthpiece" but that God speaks to each individual directly through his heart, and that those who listen to that voice will know it is God (4.18). Thus God does not need to communicate with humans through prophets. If one "listens" correctly, one can hear and experience God directly and not through a messenger.

There is some concern that Baltar's God is the Cylon God. That is certainly Laura Roslin's belief (4.06). Baltar does learn of both God and God's will from Virtual Six, who, as we learn, is not actually a Cylon but an angel. To put it another way, Baltar's God is not the Cylon God; there is only one God. The Cylons have an imperfect understanding of the one true God they worship. Baltar receives his information directly from an angel of God, whose understanding of God is closer to truth than that of the Cylons.

The second tenet is that God must be obeyed. Time and again Virtual Six reminds Baltar that what is asked of him is nothing short of total, unquestioning submission to God. When God asks something, one does not ask questions, make requests or debate. As Virtual Six tells Baltar: "One doesn't question God's will" (2.07). As Baltar's understanding of God grows, told to him by Virtual Six, the voice of God's will, additional commandments are articulated, which are listed in section III.

---

*Interestingly, no scholar has seen Baltar as a Mohammed figure. He is a pagan to whom an angel begins to speak, telling him of a new faith that involves submission to God and the defeat (both physical and spiritual) of the polytheists around the prophet. He then begins to travel and speak on behalf of God. By the end of the series, like Mohammed, Baltar has succeeded as both a spiritual and political conqueror.

II. Baltar, His Prophet

Baltar is an instrument of God, a healer whose prayers have efficacy, and an unworthy man who delivers humanity and the Cylons to salvation.

A. God speaks to and through Baltar.

When Baltar does not wish to speak to the cult, Virtual Six tells Baltar, "God speaks through you to them. When you go out there you are divinely inspired. You are the instrument He uses to speak with people" (4.12). No matter what Baltar says, when he speaks to his group, God inspires him. The cult certainly believe this, even as they recognize his flawed and fallen nature. Most of the women have far stronger faith than Baltar. Most of the cult members are far more moral, far less self-centered and far more communally oriented than Baltar. Regardless, Baltar is the voice of God.

B. Healer

As Baltar is being prepared for his trial, a woman brings a sick boy to him and asks him to bless her son. Baltar disparages her and tells her that he is not a god. Her faith, however is stronger than his denial of divinity. She simply tells Baltar, "You can save him" (3.19). We might note several things from this exchange. First, Baltar does not believe he can help or have any special powers. Second, the woman does believe in Baltar. Even when Baltar disavows his ability to help her in any way, she simply responds, "You can save him." She does not ask for a healing; she simply asks Baltar to "bless" him, believing this will be enough to allow God's will to work. Baltar is seen as a healer with access to divinity, even if he himself denies it.

In that same episode, "Crossroads, Part 1," Baltar is asked for help by five people in person, with another 30 or 40 writing letters asking for help (3.19). Even as he is on trial, civilians begin to believe he is some sort of prophet. We might see this as a variation and transformation on the earlier view of Baltar. In the miniseries, when Baltar is still reeling from the Cylon attack and the guilt he feels for having given the Cylons the means to destroy humanity, Helo offers up his place in the last ship off Caprica. Helo explains that Baltar is a "genius" whose scientific expertise will be needed on Galactica to fight the Cylons (MS). Roslin and Adama see Baltar as a quirky genius who can create a Cylon detector that will allow them to identify the skinjobs among them. When Tom Zarek is the front-runner for the vice presidency, Roslin turns to Baltar, seeing him as an intelligent yet easily controlled running mate. Baltar then runs for president on a single issue — the colonization of New Caprica, promising humankind they will have a new planetary home. In short, Baltar is frequently presented as someone gifted with the answers that will solve the problems.

The irony, of course, is that none of Baltar's answers actually end up helping. The Cylon detector works, but Baltar lies and says it does not. He proves to be a bad but ambitious vice president and a dangerously incompetent and arrogant president. He is seen as the man with the answers, but his answers fail to bring the hoped-for results. It is not until be becomes a healer and prophet that his answers actually do yield positive results.

Baltar assumes leadership of the group of women in Dogville, an area of the ship for civilian passengers. One of the women, Jeanne, has a deathly ill son, Derrick. "I guess the one true God doesn't want him to live," she states to Baltar (4.01). Baltar publicly prays for Derrick, offering his life for the child's. He loudly tells God (and the gathered crowd) that he is a sinner, but the child is not. He has failed God, but the child is innocent. He repeatedly pleads, "Take me" (4.01). Interestingly, while Baltar is praying for the sick child, except for the last few words the camera stays on Baltar, not the child. The focus of this speech is Baltar himself. First, as part of his healing prayer he, himself, has his own conversion experience. Second, what begins as a self-centered attention-getting speech becomes (or at least is perceived as) a prayer of self-sacrifice. Like Christ, Baltar offers himself in place of the boy. He offers to suffer, even die, in place of the boy. His healing ministry does not take the form of demanding that God intervene in illness, but rather the humble offer of himself in place of the boy. Baltar begins to become a Christ like figure at this moment.

Paulla Schaffer, another follower, tells Baltar that the community was deeply moved by his prayer. Baltar's response is doubt: "Fat lot of good it did. Unfortunately, he's worse" (4.01). Paulla is more forgiving, arguing that the fact that the child has not improved does not mean that God did not hear Baltar's prayer. Paulla cuts Baltar's hair and shaves him. His physical transformation is a symbol of his metaphysical one. At that moment, they are attacked by the Sons of Ares, angry polytheists who want Baltar dead. Virtual Six appears and asks if Baltar's prayer was sincere — is he willing to die in place of the child? Baltar begins repeating, "Yes, take my life," which confuses his attackers, giving Paulla time to get a weapon and drive them off. She strikes them repeatedly with a metal bar, allowing Baltar and her to escape. Paulla is not only triumphant after her victory; she sees it as proof of God's favor to Baltar: "I knew God wouldn't desert you. I felt his love course through me giving me the strength to smite them" (4.01). Derrick recovers after this and the whole cult sees this episode as a miracle. Baltar is a healer whose prayers have efficacy.

Both the healing and the "smiting" are seen as miracles. Some begin to see a larger pattern of unexplainable events converging around Baltar, even before his conversion. Tory sees Baltar as being at the center of a group of miracles. Baltar admits that it seems to be that way, and that God "has chosen me to sing his song" (4.02). This particular phrase proves to be prophetic, as it is, in fact, a piece of music—"All Along the Watchtower"—that saves humanity. Yet, despite all this, Baltar, by his own admission is "not a priest" (4.02). He begins to see himself as the instrument of God that he is, and although his arrogance remains, there is a recognition that any miracles that occur are a direct result of the intervention of God, not because Baltar is in any way special.

C. Teacher

Baltar teaches by impromptu sermons. Much of the theology outlined here is taken from his sermons. Baltar leads the cult, but he is also responsible for explaining to and teaching the women who follow him. Virtual Six describes the cult as Baltar's "flock," telling him they will "follow you even into blasphemy" (4.14). In that same episode, she also describes him as "their father" (4.14).

The sermons grow more regular, in particular because Baltar has a "wireless" by which he is able to transmit his sermons throughout the fleet. Several times throughout the final season, characters are shown listening to Baltar's sermons—Roslin, Adama, Tyrol. Even if they disagree with him, and the aforementioned characters do, the sermons always inspire action. We might also note that with the broadcast of his sermons, Baltar begins to reach beyond the small group of women with whom he lives and reach and teach the rest of humanity. The Baltar cult begins to acquire followers throughout the fleet.

III. God's Commandments

A. Have Faith

First and foremost, God wants us to have faith in Him. Virtual Six tells Baltar, "if you have faith, everything will turn out exactly as it should" (2.19). The key to surviving this divinely planned disaster is faith in God. Baltar himself continually wavers in his faith, despite the many miracles he witnesses. But even in his own unbelief, he, usually urged on by Virtual Six, preaches unbending faith in God. When one completely gives oneself over to faith in God, then God works His plan through you.

B. Actively reject the false polytheism of the Colonials.

As noted, there is only one true God, and He is a jealous God. It is not enough to not have false idols or believe in other gods; one must actively stop the false worship of others. Baltar even has a cleansing-the-temple moment, literally, when he walks into a service in a temple on Galactica and interrupts the prayer, blaspheming and referring to Zeus as a "serial rapist" and calling the Colonial pantheon "invented rubbish" (4.04). He also has more intimate, kinder, but nevertheless direct refutations of the gods. When Phoebe, one of his followers, tells Baltar she is angry at the Cylons, the humans who failed to stop the Cylons, "and most of all the gods," Baltar tells her that she cannot blame the gods for not helping humanity, since they do not exist (4.05). The only response to the ignorance of others when they state they believe in gods is to correct them and tell them of the one true God.

C. Love

God's simple command, as with the Cylons, is to love. Baltar articulates this in far more depth than the Cylons do and expands the list of who and what are to be loved: love God, love others, love yourself. Gaius even encourages his followers to love and embrace their own faults, since God has created them. He notes that he himself is not a good person, and in fact might be seen as a resolutely bad person, but "something in the universe" loves him and that love makes him "perfect." On the one hand, this could be the articulation of a self-serving, selfish theology.

No change or spiritual development is required because you are already "perfect." There is a danger lurking in this theology in that one can choose to accept that even one's worst behavior is therefore condoned and even encouraged by God in the name of one's perfection. We should further note that Baltar neither knows nor loves himself. Behind this theology is his own pain seeking healing and his own need for love and acceptance.

On the other hand, simultaneously this statement of love and acceptance is a variation on Christian theology. One must love and accept God. Part and parcel of this love of God is loving others, despite and in some cases because of their flaws and imperfections. Yet one cannot love others unless one loves and accepts one's self. Ergo, Baltar's theology is one that highlights the relationships between humans and the divine, between humans and each other, and one's relationship to one's self. God's love creates, justifies and requires us to love each other and even ourselves. To love one's self is not the selfish self-love Baltar has evinced throughout much of the series, but an acceptance of one's own faults and shortcomings, not a justification for them.

On a variation of the idea of love is the suggestion that nonbelievers are still welcome in the company of the Baltar cult (4.05). Many times during Baltar's sermons, non-members are welcomed into the cult community area to hear Baltar in person. One need not believe in Baltar or even God to attend and hear him, and despite his attacks on others practicing their faith traditions, Baltar welcomes all comers without reservation or requirement.

IV. Anthropology

In the view of the Baltar cult, we are "perfect." There is no articulation of sin or of a fallen nature. Instead, as the children of God we are perfect and loved by Him. Our role is to seek out our role. God sends humanity out into the cosmos in order to better serve Him and His plan. We are not sinners, but we are wholly God's and we travel the universe seeking His love (4.18). As a result, the Baltar cult has a profoundly different understanding of salvation. We need not be saved from sins, or as a community, or from extinction. Instead, our focus should be on serving God and loving one another. That is both the need and the form that salvation takes: the need to serve each other and by serving each other we serve God.

V. Angels

God communicates through angels, which take the form of individuals known (and perhaps loved) by the viewer. "Virtual Six," the Cylon who appears only to Baltar throughout the series and whom he believes is either a hallucination or the result of a chip planted in his head, is revealed to be an angel. She tells Baltar, "I'm an angel of God, sent here to help you" (3.06). He does not believe her, yet by the series finale, it is revealed that she is, in fact, some sort of angel. Caprica Six, the Cylon who seduced Baltar, sees a "Virtual Baltar," who is revealed also to be an angel. At the climactic fight, on the bridge of the Galactica, Baltar tells Cavil, "I believe in angels because I see them," and we, the viewers, have seen them as well (4.18). The series concludes with the two angels in contemporary New York. The Baltar cult not only believes in the reality and power of angels; it has definitive proof of their existence. Baltar sees them. They are present in the room when he makes the above speech. Caprica Six sees them as well. And what the angels relate comes true. Angels are God's messengers, and they are further proof of the rightness of Baltar's theology.

VI. Eschatology

Baltar speaks at the mass funeral for the humans and Cylons killed by a hull breach, using Starbuck as an example of eternal life. He preaches that everyone is offered eternal life. If we "embrace death" when it comes for us, then we will be resurrected, and not in the Cylon sense. Instead, he offers the returned Starbuck as proof of life after death. He analyzed the dog tags found on the body on Earth, and its DNA matches Kara Thrace's. In other words, the living woman and the dead body are the same being. He proclaims that Starbuck is proof of life eternal and that angels walk among humanity (4.18).

Starbuck's response is to slap Baltar, angry that he has made public something that was not common knowledge and that also confuses and frightens her. Yet this statement also remains the clearest articulation of Baltar on the subject of death; we should not be afraid of death, we should "embrace" it. Death is not the end. We have "eternal life," which is different from Cylon resurrection, although the example he cites, Starbuck, is actually an example of bodily resurrection. Starbuck does not technically have "eternal life"; she comes back from the dead.

It is curious, therefore, that Baltar cites Starbuck as an example of "eternal life," unless he means it as a metaphor for the impermanence of death and the possibility of an afterlife or resurrection, the latter a very Christian understanding of the term. Yet he focuses in on her own physical death and return, repeatedly using the phrases 'necrotic flesh,' "dead body," and DNA when talking about Starbuck. Yet Baltar also points out a real mystery, the real Starbuck found her own dead body, and yet she still lives. It is a mystery, and perhaps it is to this that Baltar ultimately refers and also it is this that explains his reference to angels. Baltar sees the returned Starbuck as proof of the mysteries of existence. Angels talk to him, and people come back from the dead, all of which points to a loving God who works in mysterious ways and in whom we must place our trust, knowing death is not the end.

VII. The Plan

Virtual Six predicts a child would be born who will change the world. The prophesied child is referred to by Virtual Six as "our child," but it is made apparent that the child is actually Hera, the daughter of Cylon Sharon "Athena" Valerii and Karl "Helo" Agathon. Although President Roslin orders the child taken from its parents, given to an adoptive mother and word given out that she died, Hera lives and will eventually be reunited with her parents. Virtual Six tells Baltar: "God's will was that our child should survive. His will was that she lead the next generation of God's children. His will was that you [Baltar] would protect her" (2.18). There is a divine plan, and despite all the little things God needs Baltar to do along the way, his chief role is to protect Hera and ensure that she reaches the New Earth. That is the divine plan, in essence.

Baltar does become the guardian of Hera during the final battle with the Cylons. All of the visions come true, and the Cylons and humans both fight for possession of Hera. Cavil believes dissecting Hera will allow the Cylons to discover biological reproduction. Hera is the key to Cylon survival. But Baltar, aware of the divine plan, shares that Hera is the key to the survival of all. When Cavil asks him how he knows, Baltar cites the angels in the room that have spoken to him. He cites the strange coincidences and events, the serendipitous actions and choices and dreams and prophesies, all of which have led them all to this one place and time. There is a divine plan, and human and Cylon destinies are intertwined in it (4.20). God is not Cylon or human. God is not on either side. God wants both creators and created to live in peace and break the cycles of war and death. What is called for by the divine plan is not simply militant action in God's name, but a new way of understanding the relationship between human and Cylon: "It requires a leap of faith. It requires that we live in hope, not fear" (4.20).

This exchange also contains the clearest articulation of Baltar's understanding of the nature of God and the divine plan. His role is to protect Hera, as she is they key for both humanity's and Cylon salvation. God does not take sides. God does not have a chosen people, despite what many people (who see themselves as chosen) think. God does not need rites, rituals, prayers, sacrifices, temples, or the material culture of religious worship. God is much larger than the faiths of the humans or Cylons.

God's plan is the ending of the cycle. All this has happened before, but it need not happen again. God does not ask for "religion;" He asks for faith. We must hope and place our trust in God. Humans and Cylons have made a series of decisions that have ended catastrophically for both. The theology of the Baltar cult involves surrendering to the divine plan. By allowing God to take control, all sentient beings are saved and removed from the cycle of violence.

Baltar is proven correct, in the end. Although the scrolls of Pythia were demonstrated to be accurate, and the Cylons understood the true nature of the divine, it was the surrender to the divine plan that allowed the humans and their Cylon allies to jump to the new Earth.

Once the fleet has arrived safely at the New Earth, the angels, in the form of Virtual Six and Virtual Baltar, appear one last time to the humans and Cylons. They confirm that Hera is safe and that God's plan no longer involves them. Yet, Virtual Six reminds them, "God's plan is never complete" (4.20). The audience is shown in the coda that 150,000 years in the future, the planet that the Colonials and Cylons have settled on is, in fact, our Earth. The salvation of human and Cylon was the creation of our planet and its history. Hera is "mitochondrial Eve," the oldest common female ancestor to every human currently alive on earth. The divine plan was the creation of our reality.

Of the three faiths in the series, Baltar's seems to have the strongest basis in divine reality and is presented as the most theologically sound. Though all three faiths have truth behind them to varying degrees, and a certain amount of efficacy, it is only by following what Baltar and his angelic guide propose that humanity and Cylon together find a measure of salvation.

II. Real-World Echoes

The second section of this work consists of seven chapters organized by theme. These chapters constitute a form of comparative theology in which "real-world echoes" of Christianity are found in *BSG*. As noted in the introduction, the purpose of doing so is not to prove that *BSG* is crypto–Christian or may be interpreted through a Christian lens to prove or disprove aspects of Christian faith. Rather, as a fictional narrative that makes theological claims and that was created by writers and artists living in twenty-first-century America, with its conflicted Judeo-Christian heritage and pluralistic faith marketplace, so to speak, *BSG* offers a text by which we might understand the role and function of faith within society, or how aspects of Christian belief such as resurrection, creation, and salvation are understood and reflected in *BSG*, which in turn tells us about how we understand them.

The rest of this work is therefore taken up with considering how *BSG* presents and understands Christian terminology, Creation and falls, exile, prophets, resurrection, the betrayal and redemption of Judas, and the apocalypse.

4

Gospels, Sins and Salvation: The Use of Christian Terminology in BSG

Although set 148,000 years before Christianity, *Battlestar Galactica* still employs Christian terminology and the language of Christianity, albeit often in ways slightly different from Christian use. In this chapter I examine the use of Christian terminology in *BSG*, not to argue that *BSG* is a crypto–Christian text but in order to explore how *BSG* uses real-world theology to create its own.

By means of example, I begin with citing episodes titles taken from Christianity or referencing religion in general. The fourth episode of the series, "Act of Contrition," which concerns Starbuck's coming to terms she made as a pilot instructor, gets its title from the Christian (and perhaps specifically Catholic, although Lutheran and Anglican churches also have one) prayer in which one expresses regret for one's sins, asks God for forgiveness and promises to amend one's ways (1.04). It is most frequently used in the sacrament of reconciliation.

A later episode, "The Hand of God," may refer to the concept that in mysterious events we may see the "hand of God" moving (1.10). In this episode, Laura begins to hallucinate and sees images that lead her to believe in the truth of the scrolls and lead the people to Earth, while Baltar selects a point on a map of a Cylon base that when bombed delivers a crippling blow against the base and the Cylons. By the end of the episode, both characters believe they are "instrument(s) of God" (1.10).

"Are you telling me that God guided my finger to that target for some arcane scriptural purpose?" Baltar asks Virtual Six, who confirms this fact (1.10). Time and again in *BSG*, things happen for a reason; seemingly random events and even counterintuitive and counterproductive decisions are revealed to be the correct choice for advancing toward Earth. As Adele Reinhartz reminds us, a major theological theme in film and television is the debate of coincidence versus intention: whether something happens just as a result of random coincidence or because a guiding intelligence moves individuals to act in ways that fulfill a plan. *BSG* repeatedly comes down on the side of intention: there are no coincidences. We are all instruments in a plan.

Christianity also has the unique idea of the "hand of God" also being a place. Mark reports that after his resurrection, Jesus "sat down at the right hand of God" (16:19). The hand of God is a place of honor, and it is where Jesus is for eternity. Matthew reports Jesus quoting David, "The Lord said to my Lord, 'Sit at my right hand, until I put your enemies under your feet'" (22:44, citing Psalms 110:1). The hand of God is not just an explanation for mysterious events; it is also a place of victory and power. All of this connects to an episode in which the Colonials decide to strike a counterattack on the Cylons; Gaius Baltar is asked to tell them where to strike, and God Himself seems to give him the information that leads to the destruction of a Cylon base and the saving of humanity.

"Epiphanies" suggests the term and the holiday, *epiphaneia*, celebrating the revelation of God in human form (2.13). In this episode, Roslin's cancer goes into remission when she is treated with the blood of the half-human/half–Cylon fetus that will become Hera Agathon. She also has visions in which she realizes Baltar knew Six back on Caprica. The title can thus be seen as a play on another meaning of the word: to have an epiphany is to suddenly realize something and become aware of its meaning. Hera is the revelation of God's plan, and Roslin realizes the threat from Baltar.

The Colonial escape from the Cylon occupation of New Caprica is told in episodes entitled "Exodus, Parts 1 and 2," echoing the exodus of the Israelites from Egypt, as well as the Biblical book of the same name (3.03 and 3.04). "A Measure of Salvation" presents a tortured Baltar learning how to love God and himself (3.07). "Rapture" is another title that plays with multiple meanings (3.12). In an episode that features revelations of the Final Five that enthrall D'Anna Biers, the recapture of

Hera Agathon from the Cylons by her mother, and the rescue of Colonials trapped on the algae planet, the title can refer to the enthusiasm of Three, the seizing and taking away of Hera (the root word of rapture is the Latin "rapio," which means to seize and take away and is also the root of the English word "rape"), and the "catching up in the air" of those trapped on the ground, referencing the concept of the rapture as derived from Paul's first letter to the Thessalonians (4:15–17).

Toward the end of the third season, an episode about Lee Adama volunteering to defend Gaius Baltar against Admiral Adama's wishes is entitled "The Son Also Rises" (3.18). The title is a pun on the title of Hemingway's first novel. It might also be seen as a reference to the resurrection of Christ. Since Lee wants to defend the most hated, reviled human in the fleet, he might be seen as a Christlike figure, who defends the low and the hated: tax collectors, prostitutes, lepers and the ill.

The fourth season is arguably the most religious and Christologically oriented, beginning with an episode entitled "He That Believeth in Me" (4.01). The title is a direct reference to John 11:25–26: "Jesus said unto her, I am the resurrection and the life; he that believeth in me, though he were dead, yet shall live. And whosoever liveth and believeth in me shall never die.'" In this episode, Starbuck literally returns from the dead, and Baltar assumes leadership of a group of followers after healing a dying boy. Both characters begin to emerge as Christlike figures. We might also note that they both fulfill their Christlike destinies: Starbuck brings the people to Earth, and Gaius is a prophet who really does receive messages from the one true God who wants to be obeyed.

A later episode is entitled "Faith" (4.06). Still another episode pays tribute to the apocalyptic nature of *BSG* with the title "Revelations" (4.10). The episode features the arrival at Earth, but it is an Earth that has been burned and devastated. This is a post-apocalypse Earth that no longer has life and is uninhabitable.

Even "The Road Less Traveled" (4.05), whose title is ostensibly taken from Robert Frost's poem, may also refer to Matthew 7:13–14: "Enter through the narrow gate; for the gate is wide and the road is easy that leads to destruction, and there are many who take it. For the gate is narrow and the road is hard that leads to life, and there are few who find it." Considering that the episode concerns Starbuck's search for the way to Earth and Galen Tyrol's obsession over his wife's death, the title echoes Matthew's image of a difficult journey to understanding salvation and forgiveness. Baltar goes to Tyrol's quarters to ask his forgiveness for Baltar's presumption in telling Tyrol his wife would have wanted Tyrol to behave in a certain way: "I have committed ... unconscionable crimes. And I have been offered one last chance of redemption because I chose to accept my fate and not fight it anymore" (4.05). The episode ends with a silent Tyrol offering Baltar his hand. The road less traveled, even and especially in *BSG*, is forgiveness instead of vengeance and violence.

As *BSG* is a salvific and apocalyptic narrative, it uses the language of Christianity in order to engage and explore these topics. The remainder of this chapter is concerned with the repeated use of Christian terminology, a real-world echo of Christian theology in the theology of *BSG*.

"Scripture" and "Gospel"

The Colonials frequently refer to the Sacred Scrolls as "scripture." Billy Keikaya, the president's assistant, believes the Colonial Marine guarding the president "seems to know a lot about the scriptures." The marine responds, "I'm from Gemenon. We believe in the literal truth of the scriptures" (2.03). Lee Adama taunts Sharon for disbelieving on Kobol, when she has seen the proof of "our 'false' scriptures" (2.07). Sarah Porter, the Gemenon delegate to the Quorum, refers to the Sacred Scrolls as "scripture" (2.17). "Scripture" is not a word used to discuss the sacred texts of ancient Greece or Rome. It comes from the Latin word for writing and traditionally refers to the sacred books of Christianity and Judaism.

Interestingly, Felix Gaeta refers to the "Book of Pythia" by observing "the president's identification with that particular *gospel*" [emphasis mine] (2.07). "Gospel" is a particularly Christian term, not an ancient Greek or Roman one. Mark, chronologically the first of the canonical gospels, begins, "The beginning of the good news [gospel] of Jesus Christ, the Son of God" (1:1). "Gospel," of course, is derived from the Old English g_d spell, literally meaning "good news," itself a literal translation of the Greek "*euangelion*," which also means "good news." Whereas the gospels, by definition, share the "good news" of Christ, and have to do with evangelizing, sharing that news, the Scroll of Pythia has nothing to do with Christ. So what does it mean that Gaeta refers to it as a "gospel"?

Pythia, as noted in the first chapter, does have its own "good news."

Pythia lays out, as the gospels do, a plan for salvation. A dying leader will bring humanity to Earth.

By terming Pythia a "gospel," *BSG* has also indicated its own interest in humanity's salvation. Unlike the gospels in the real world, in which the "good news" is "of Jesus Christ, the Son of God" (Mark 1:1), and which offer a variety of Christologies and ways of understanding Christ, Pythia does not focus on a divine incarnation or resurrection — only a seemingly divine plan. Yet, I would argue, in this case these differences are details. In both cases, the "good news" of each text is, at heart, a divine plan to change the nature of reality and the relationship between human and divinity and between humans. The good news is salvation.

"Sin"

Christianity argues that Jesus saves, but from what does He save us? The short answer is, of course, sin. As noted in the first chapters, the humans and Cylons have different concepts of sin from each other and from their audiences. Yet the word "sin" is frequently employed on the show. As Roger Haight indicates, the Catholic understanding of sin is that it is multidimensional (1991: 85). Sinful acts are turnings away from God and disobeying His commandments (1991: 86–87). Yet the Church also acknowledges a "social dimension of sin" — we sin against others as well (1991: 101). Lastly, the Church postulates "the sinful condition of human existence" — what is often termed "original sin;" we are given freedom, but our nature leads us to make choices that are sinful (1991: 85).

BSG uses the language of sin to talk about moral evil, turning away from the divine, and even the social dimensions of both our fallen nature and our individual and collective acts. Admiral Adama, in his speech at the opening of Galactica as a museum at the start of the miniseries, raises the idea of collective sin, asking the gathered troops why humanity never asked if it was worth saving. He uses a biblical phrase, saying that, "we still visit all of our sins upon our children" (MS). The specific sin he mentions is playing God: creating life, the sin of Frankenstein. Humanity created the Cylons, and the Cylons then rebelled, and humanity washed its hands of that rebellion. Adama, almost prophet-like, condemns humanity for not taking responsibility for its sins and for creating the Cylons. The entire speech is full of theological language.

Adama uses the term "sin" but raises a whole host of issues in doing so. First, the idea of visiting the sins of the parents upon the children is a Biblical one (see Leviticus 26:39; Isaiah 65:7; and especially Jeremiah 32:18: "You show steadfast love to the thousandth generation, but repay the guilt of parents into the laps of their children"). Although the Hebrew Bible contains many instances of an entire people being held to their collective sins, the overarching belief in Christianity is that sin is individual. One sins against God and others, not as part of the group. Even in the Hebrew Bible, this idea is espoused: "Parents shall not be put to death for their children, nor shall children be put to death for their parents; only for their own crimes may persons be put to death" (Deuteronomy 24:16). We sin alone.

Yet Adama sees sin as also being collective, which is very much in keeping with Colonial theology. We collectively sin. The key question he asks is "Why are we worth saving?" In other words, why do we deserve salvation? His answer is that because of our collective sins, we might not be. The suggested solution is not absolution or praying to the gods for forgiveness, but taking responsibility for the sins. Because "we refuse to accept responsibility" for our collective actions, the wrongdoing is compounded. But the problem of sin is that it does not go away if you refuse responsibility for it. Adama's speech sets up the idea that the Cylon attack on the colonies was, in fact, a form of retribution for humanity's sins. It was, in fact, part of a larger divine plan to make us "worth saving."

Sin, however, also works on an individual level in *BSG*. Starbuck tells Lee about her relationship with his brother. Because Zak Adama was her lover, she passed him through basic flight training when he was still unqualified. He subsequently died in a crash. When Lee asks her why she is telling him this, she replies: "It's the end of the world, Lee. I should confess my sins" (MS). As noted in the first chapter, Colonials have "confession," although this remains more of a Christian concept than a polytheistic one. And, as noted in that chapter, one confesses how one has failed "in the example of the gods." Starbuck's sins are many, in this case. She sinned against Zak by allowing him to fly when she knew he wasn't competent to. She sinned against the group in doing so, by indirectly causing the death of someone they loved. She sinned by hiding the real reason why he died. One might even argue she is sinning again by telling Apollo. She tells him to assuage her guilty conscience, but the information causes him pain and conflicted feelings toward her. In confessing her sin to him, instead of to clergy, she both takes responsibility and also passes the pain.

Starbuck also recognizes that what she has done is some kind of sin. Interestingly, the many other things she does that might be considered "sin" in this world: drinking, smoking, fornicating, committing adultery, violence, even killing; those are not the "sins" she confesses. The world of *BSG* does not recognize the moral sins (particularly those of self-indulgence) and things that need forgiving. On the other hand, Starbuck finally confesses this sin to Admiral Adama in the aforementioned episode "Act of Contrition." In that episode, Starbuck refuses to train new pilots for fear that she might be responsible for another death. Adama, on learning the reason why, orders her to continue training them. This activity represents her "act of contrition," the thing she must do to atone for her sins. By her actions, someone she loved died; now, by her actions, she must continue to do her job and train a new group. The social dimension of sin, both in the commissioning and the atoning, seems to be a priority in *BSG*.

Adama, as well, however, has sinned against the group. When an old pilot that he sent on a secret mission years before is found alive, Adama realizes that the secret mission may have been perceived by the Cylons as a threat. Thus, Baltar may not be the only one responsible for the Cylon genocide. The civilian government ordered the military to go to the border of Cylon territory and send in a covert investigator. Adama was the commander of the mission. When Adama wishes to resign for this part in possibly causing the Cylon war, President Roslin instead demands that he accept a medal in order to be heroic in the eyes of the Colonials, who need a hero. "That will be your penance," she tells him (3.08). His sin was to participate in a military activity that may have been the reason why the Cylons decided to wipe out the human race. To atone for this sin, he must accept the role that the human society needs him to fulfill. As with Starbuck, one's "penance" is to continue doing the thing that brought about the sin, but to do it better and without the sin. In short, one must "take responsibility" for the sin and atone by "not hiding from the thing you've done."

For the Cylons (and eventually, presumably the Baltar cult), sin requires repentance as well. When Dr. Amerak supposedly knows that Baltar committed treason and plans on telling the president, Baltar hopes the president will order Amerak's ship destroyed, as it may have been infiltrated by Cylons. Six informs him: "It's God's choice. He wants you to repent. Repent of your sins and you will be saved" (1.01). Baltar, afraid that his treason might be discovered, breaks down: "I repent, I repent, I repent" (1:01). And the Olympic Carrier, the ship carrying Amerak, is destroyed. For Cylons, sin is personal, not collective. Yet, when one simply repents, one is forgiven. There is no need for atonement. Instead, one must turn back to God, repent and love Him again.

Ironically, however, the humans have no concept of damnation, but the Cylons do. In discussing the occupation of New Caprica, two Cavils raise this point. The first argues in favor of evangelization: the role of the Cavil line on New Caprica is to "bring the word of God to the people" (3.01). The second Cavil concurs, noting that only God's love will save humanity from "damnation." The first then surmises that they must use any means necessary in order to bring humanity to the one true God. The second then concludes that "fear" is "a key article of faith." As noted in the first chapter, we must take Cavil's pronouncements with a grain of salt, but the idea of damnation introduces fear as a key article of faith. The Cylon God demands love and obedience. Cylons do not sin against the group; they sin against God. When one sins against God and does not repent of the sin, the end result is damnation.

It seems safe to assume, based on the faith statements of the other Cylons, most notably Leoben, that there is no Cylon hell. Instead, God turns his back upon you, and bad things happen in this plane of existence. People die; people get hurt or suffer because of their refusal to repent. Upon death, one does not go to be with God. Cylon damnation, it seems, is oblivion: one's soul simply ceases to be, instead of being given eternal life with God. This fate, for example, is what awaits anyone who now dies on Kobol. Because God has turned His back on that planet, to die on Kobol is to wink out of existence forever. Yet, in "Fragged," Virtual Six tells Baltar that after death on Kobol there is "no eternal life, no damnation, only oblivion" (2.03), which would seem to indicate that "damnation" is not the same as oblivion. It might be safe to say that it is therefore a form of existence without the possibility of God.

"Salvation"

The end result of sin and the fear of damnation is, of course, a need for salvation. Humanity and Cylonkind need a means by which we might escape sin. In both cases, *BSG* uses the word "salvation" to describe the end of the divine plan. While "salvation" is not exclusively a Christian or even Judeo-Christian term, it is one of the central themes in Christianity. Salvation in the Hebrew Bible is a recurring hope in the prophets and Psalms. Paul, however, introduces the idea in the New Testament that "salvation" comes from and through Jesus. In Christianity, it is one of the most basic articles of faith that Jesus saves. The question is, how does He save? Historical and contemporary theories of soteriology offer a variety of understandings on exactly how Jesus saves and what He saves us from. The short answer to the latter question is "sin." The answer to the former question has taken a variety of forms from such theologians as Augustine, Anselm, Abelard, and more recently, Borg, Rahner and Haight. Kerygmatic Christianity as outlined in the writings of Paul offers a variety of ways of understanding how Christ saves us from sin. Thomas Rausch, citing Joseph A. Fitzmeyer, lists ten terms that Paul uses to explain salvation: "justification, salvation, reconciliation, expiation, redemption, freedom, sanctification, transformation, new creation, and glorification" (2003: 170). Salvation is not so much about "the narrower notions of redemption, atonement, or justification," argues Rausch, but rather a much more complex understanding of Incarnation, transformation, and love (2003: 171, 181). For the Christian, Jesus mediates our salvation through a variety of means. Sin corrupts, Jesus saves us from sin, and by believing in Him, we are given eternal life. That is Christian salvation in a nutshell.

BSG uses the word "salvation" in different ways even within its three faiths. The Colonials see salvation as a promise from the gods, an end to humanity's wandering on a planet called Earth. The prayer of a solider, praying with Laura Roslin during a Cylon attack, is: "Help us turn away from the calls of the wicked and show us the knowledge of your certain salvation" (2.02). Salvation is "certain," and it is something we can understand. The wicked can guide us away from it. Salvation, as I have repeatedly stated, is a collective and communal thing among the humans. This is not salvation from individual sin but salvation from collective sin.

The Lords of Kobol have a salvific plan that is centered on humanity leaving behind its decadence and being led to a promised land. Laura Roslin reveals that she believes she is the prophesied "dying leader" who will bring the humans to Earth. She reports she only has a few months to live, but that her only purpose is to lead humanity to its new home (2.03). Sarah Porter, the Colonial fundamentalist from Gemenon cries out in thanks to the gods and falls to her knees and uses the term "salvation" to identify the president's role. Time and again, when the humans refer to "salvation," it is to this that they are referring: they will be lead to a new home by their leader who has been appointed by the gods.

As noted in the second chapter, Cylon salvation is rooted in God. As the quotation above from the pair of Cavils notes, salvation is knowing the love of God. In some ways, the Cylons might be seen as having their own version of the great commission in Matthew: "Go, therefore, and make disciples of all nations, baptizing them in the name of the Father and of the Son and of the Holy Spirit, and teaching them to obey everything that I have commanded you" (28:19–20). Yet, the Cylon's drive to proselytize for God are slightly different. Belief in Christ is necessary for salvation, but it is Christ himself who brings salvation. It would seem from Cylon theology that belief in God and loving God is what bring salvation.

The overarching theme of this work is that *BSG* is a narrative that has salvation as its theme. How do we get saved, what are we saved from, and what do we need to do to achieve it? In the end, Virtual Six guides Baltar to guide the others to what seems to be *BSG*'s idea of salvation: a planet where the mixed descendents of humanity and Cylon live at peace (perhaps in a "New Jerusalem"?) and humanity's creations do not rebel and destroy their creators. Behind this notion is the idea that one's enemies may indeed be agents of salvation. In Paul's letter to the Romans, he argues that part of God's plan involves salvation coming through the enemy and even the enemy being shown mercy and saved, so that God "may be merciful to all" (11:25–34). Salvation, in the end, is to transcend cycles of violence and to find a communal home where one may love God and live according to the divine plan.

All This Has Happened Before...

In conclusion, there is a Christian understanding of the "eternal return": "all this has happened before and all this will happen again." Although Christian metahistory is linear, there are repetitions. The world is created by God, destroyed in a flood, and recreated from the creatures from the ark (Genesis). The world will be destroyed again by fire and a New Earth and New Heaven created (Revelation). Christ is the "second Adam" and Mary is the "second Eve." Christ will have a *parousia*, a "second coming," at the end times. Despite its linear narrative, there are repetitions within Christianity. One might also consider Origen's notion of recapitulations that will eventually lead to universal salvation (although the Church has rejected this theology).

In both Christianity and *BSG* we see a narrative of repetition until divine intervention. Christians believe in the eternal recurrence of sin. We are born into a state of sin ("original sin"), and though according to the Church baptism removes this sin, we continue to sin throughout life. There is no escape from sin. Sin is the Christian "eternal recurrence": all of these sins have happened before, and all of them will happen again. The Incarnation does not end sin but sets into motion a plan to save humankind from sin. We see in *BSG* the eternal recurrence of humanity's creations destroying itself. Yet divine intervention sets in motion a plan to save humanity from this cycle. Both plans end with the elect finding salvation on a "New Earth."

5

"In His Own Image He Created Them": Creation and Falls

The Cylons were created by Man.
They rebelled.
They evolved...
And they have a plan.
— Opening text in *BSG,* season one

The Bible, as most holy texts, begins with a creation story: where everything came from and how (and why) it was created. Similarly, Julie Hawk argues that *BSG* "serves as an epic origin story for the human race as we know it" (2011: 3). *BSG* is a sort of creation story, explaining how this current Earth and human civilization came to be. Gabriel McKee writes, "In exploring the origins of creation, science fiction also explores the role of humanity in a universe over which we, according to Genesis 1:26, have been given dominion" (2007a: 21–22).

The series begins with Creation and ends at the same time. Creation comes out of nothing; order comes out of chaos according to Genesis and other early creation stories from the ancient Near East. The story of humanity begins in "a formless void and darkness" (Genesis 1:2). The story of *BSG* begins in the formless void of space, in the darkness between the Twelve Colonies. The story of humanity, according to the Bible, ends here on Earth with a series of spectacular battles that bring about the end of everything and create a New Heaven and New Earth. The story of *BSG* is also an apocalyptic text that also engages in beginnings and endings and recognizes that every ending is the beginning of something new. Out of destruction comes Creation. And the Earth, in both narratives, is "good."

The key elements of Creation in the Biblical narrative include God making the world and the universe, the fall of angels (which does not appear in Genesis but develops out of later traditions, and is also referred to as "the War in Heaven"), the Fall of humanity (capitalized, as this fall is the big one), and the expelling from Paradise and the beginning of everything else for humanity. The cycle is repeated in Genesis several times, in which what God has created grows too corrupt or fallen and must be destroyed and rebuilt (or re–Created): Noah and the flood, the tower of Babel, the destruction of Sodom and Gomorrah, etc. The major theme of Genesis is Creation and Fall: something is made, then grows corrupted and must be destroyed and/or remade.

Pope John Paul II, in his 1981 encyclical *Laborem exercens* ("On human work"), begins by stating, "Through work, man must earn his daily bread and contribute to the continual advance of science and technology," and further arguing that God expects humans to assist in continued creation (1981). The United States is rather obsessed with Creation, particularly in the form of Creationism, which is often played out in the popular media (and the Christian media, for that matter) as science independent of God versus religious fundamentalism. Yet, as noted in *Laborem exercens,* above, science and technology are not only part of Creation; they are part of God's expectation for humanity to continue to develop creation. Biblical fundamentalism frequently requires the rejection of the advancement of science and technology in favor of a literal interpretation of scripture, but *BSG* offers a complex evaluation of relationships between Creation, Creator, created and falls.

The book of Genesis concludes the creation narrative by observing that "God created humankind in his image" and that "God said to them, 'Be fruitful and multiply, and fill the earth and subdue it; and have dominion over ... every living thing that moves upon the earth'" (1:27–28). In other words, humans are made "in the image of God" (whatever that may mean), and their responsibility is to procreate, care for Creation (while also "subduing" and "dominating" it), and serve God by overseeing his Creation. The danger in every creation, however, is the possibility of falls!

God first created angels to serve as His messengers and His servants. There is no one Biblical text that narrates the fall of the angels that rebel against God. Instead, the popular conception of fallen angels is a conglomeration of different narratives and sources and shaped more by non–Biblical sources such as *Paradise Lost, Divine Comedy,* and the sermons of the early Church fathers. In Revelation, John writes the only real Biblical source for the fall of angels:

> And war broke out in heaven; Michael and his angels
> fought against the dragon. The dragon and his angels fought
> back, but they were defeated and there was no longer any
> place for them in heaven. The great dragon was thrown down,
> that ancient serpent, who is called the Devil and Satan, the
> deceiver of the whole world — he was thrown down to the
> earth and his angels were thrown down with him [12:7–9].

"Great dragon," "ancient serpent," "Devil" (which comes from the Greek *diabolos,* meaning "slanderer") and "Satan" (which comes from the Hebrew word "accuser") are all names for the same personification of evil and God's enemy. He is conflated with the serpent of Genesis, who, technically, is not Satan, and is still present in heaven and a member of the heavenly court in Job. This being also becomes conflated with Lucifer (Latin for "light bearer"), a name for the king of Babylon in Isaiah 14:3 – 21. The unnamed king, referred to as "Lucifer," has "fallen from heaven ... to the depths of the pit," which later readers have interpreted as a reference to the brightest of the angels being cast out of heaven (14:12, 15). The story of the war in heaven and the rebelling angels more fully comes from an extracanonical book, 2 Enoch, in which Satan is an angel who seeks to place himself as God's equal or even superior to God. He is cast out of heaven and falls to hell.

Although it comes chronologically first in the narrative, the fall of the angels develops second theologically to the fall of humanity. Created by God and placed in the garden, Adam and Eve are given many active commands ("be fruitful and multiply," "fill the earth and subdue it," etc.), but only one negating one: "of the tree of the knowledge of good and evil you shall not eat" (Genesis 2:17). A serpent tempts Eve to eat of the tree, and Eve tempts Adam to do the same. This act of disobedience represents the fall of humanity from the state of grace in which it was created. Adam and Eve's fall is not, like that of the rebel angels, a literal fall from somewhere high to somewhere low, but a fall from divine grace.

These two falls suggest that everything created eventually in some way falls, in some way disobeys, or in some way rebels against its creator and corrupts or damages itself and the creation in the process. In this sense, the fall of humanity represents the original exile of the people God has created. Falls also seem to be inevitable when a created being has knowledge of good and evil. In this chapter I propose to consider the Cylons as created beings, possibly with a Gnostic relationship with humans as their Demiurge and the Cylon god as the unknowable God of Gnosticism. I then look to the metahistory of Creation, considering the differences between linear creation stories and cyclical creation stories and arguing that *BSG* is both, offering an alternative understanding to the relationship between creations and falls and Creation and Fall. I close the chapter with a series of analyses of particular characters from *BSG* as embodying characters from the creation narrative: Cavil as Lucifer and Cain, Six as Cain, Eight as an Eve figure, and ending with an almost unrelated analysis of Saul Tigh as a Paul figure.

Cylons as Created Beings

Cylons are created beings; humans are their creators. The Hybrid at the hub refers to humans as "the makers" (4.09). Yet when a flawed being creates something, the creation itself is also flawed. *BSG* posits the flawed creation as an indictment of its creator. Commander Adama pontificates at the end of the miniseries on the relationship between creator and created, referring to the sin of humanity in "playing God" by creating Cylons and their failure to prevent the rebellion of their creation. "You cannot wash your hands of the things that you've created," he tells the gathered people (MS). The sin in the rebellion of the Cylons is not merely the Cylons' for rebelling but also humanity's for refusing to take responsibility for their creation or that creation's fall. The fall of something created hurts not only the being that falls, but also the creator.

Yet *BSG* offers a much more complex reading of Cylons as created beings. Leoben, pretending to be human to fool Adama at Ragmar Station in the miniseries, offers a different interpretation of the created nature of Cylons that posits God as their ultimate creator and prime mover. He argues that the Cylons are a punishment for humanity from God (the result of humanity's fall, so to speak) and that the Cylons also have souls, as the new favored creation (MS). Adama ignores the first supposition, that Cylons might be a punishment from God, in order to challenge what he perceives as the more egregious theory. Adama's answer is "God didn't create the Cylons; mankind did. And I'm pretty sure we didn't include a soul in the programming" (MS). This debate is one at the heart of the theology of *BSG*: do Cylons have souls? What is the difference between sentience and soul? If something is self-aware, does that automatically imply a relationship to the divine? Can God work through humans to create his more favored creation? Are humans angels to the "Adam and Eve" of Cylons? This is metacreation: the Creator created the humans, the humans created the Cylons, God then ensouled the Cylons. This question of the Cylon soul and the status of Cylons in the eyes of God raises important issues of the relationship of the divine to the created, of God to Creation, and our responsibility to other created things and beings.

One might also see a hint of Gnosticism in the Cylon belief system. Gnosticism is an umbrella term for a number of unorthodox Christian beliefs and texts from the first few centuries of Christianity that believe that elements of the divine were entrapped in an evil creation and that Jesus brought gnosis, "knowledge," of the true nature of reality and how to escape it. The humans are seen as a sort of Demiurge, named Iald-abaoth, a malformed, evil being that actually created the world. The actual God is unknowable and disconnected from creation. The Demi-urge brought the material world into being, trapping sparks of the divine in it. Those who acquire the knowledge of this reality may release the divine spark trapped within them and return to the true God (see Ehrman 2008: 195–200; Pagels 1981: 44–46; Lynch, 2010: 54–58). The Cylons were created by the Demiurge (fallen, evil humanity) but have sparks of an unknowable divine inside them that can be freed through knowledge.

Unlike the idea of a metacreation, the Cylon-as-Gnostic theme focuses on humanity as a flawed creator, which is why their creation is flawed. The true God is "unknown and unknowable" and completely disconnected from the material creation (Ehrman 2008: 198). The one with knowledge, such as Leoben, knows that the humans are originally from the divine, but, like the Demiurge, they are ignorant and evil and therefore made a flawed creation containing sparks of the divine (Lynch, 2010: 54). Cylons must refute the humans and embrace the True God.

Later, Starbuck will also debate Leoben about the nature of Cylon creation. He asserts that God had created the Cylons: "I know that God loved you more than all living creatures and you repaid His divine love with sin, with hate, corruption, evil. So then He decided to create the Cylons...." She responds, "The gods had nothing to do with it. We created you! Us! It was a stupid frakked-up decision and we paid for it. You slaughtered my entire civilization. *That* is sin. *That* is evil and you are evil" (1.08). In a sense, the war between Cylons and humans is first and foremost a religious war of competing visions of Creation and evil. The humans see the Cylons as lesser beings and evil. The Cylons see the humans as lesser beings and evil.

Another danger of falls is that they are linked by cause and effect. The angels rebel, leading to the human fall. The humans create Cylons, who rebel. Yet the Cylons then become as fallen as the humans who made them. In "Razor," Virtual Six celebrates the Cylons achieving freedom from humanity. Baltar cynically responds that the Cylons have sinned far greater than humanity by slaughtering billions of people and are now far worse oppressors than the humans had ever been.

Yet the relationship between creator and created is not as simple as "humans created Cylons" as mentioned in the first season opening text. We learn by series' end that the "skinjobs" numbered One through Eight were made by the Final Five. Ellen and Saul Tigh are the creators of the first eight Cylons. The Final Five also were part of this creation. God is a meta-metacreator in this case. God made humans who made Saul and Ellen who discovered Cylons made by other humans and worked to create more humanoid Cylons. There are circles within circles of creation within the *BSG* universe, with created beings having more than one creator, all of whom share some blame for the falls that inevitably follow.

When Ellen is resurrected, Cavil instructs Boomer to "stay and have a heart-to-heart with your creator here. You can ask her why she made you the way you are: self-destructive, hyper-emotional, torn apart by conflicting impulses. Tell her how extraordinarily happy this makes you," and as Cavil exits Ellen offers Boomer an apple (4.15). The language and imagery are deliberately and specifically Biblical. The ideas, however, return us to the idea of a flawed creation reflecting a flawed creator.

Genesis states that humanity is made by God "in our image" (1:26). It is this idea of being the image of one's creator that also raises many issues, particularly since God has no "image" or description in the Bible. No physical attributes are given. So "in our image" may also refer to a more metaphorical understanding of humanity. *BSG* takes this idea as a point from which to begin theological conjecture. Six tells Baltar, "God made man in His image. Why shouldn't humanity's children choose to acknowledge their debt to their ultimate creator? Besides, these bodies allow us to better appreciate His creation in all its glory" (R). Six and the other Cylons appreciate being made in their creator's image (both human and divine).

Yet, Cavil despises being created in humanity's image. In "No Exit" he rails at length against his imposed "human condition." He hates his eyes and ears because they would not allow him to perceive a supernova beyond a small band in the EM spectrum and as vibrations in air. He loathes his inability to fully experience the universe the way that machines can. He loathes his hands, he loathes language, which is imprecise and limited, and he loathes his entire body. It is not just the limitations of organic, humanoid existence that anger him, though; it is the theological justification for it: "I'm trapped in this absurd body. And why? Because my five creators thought God wanted it that way" (4.15). He deliberately chooses to rebel against it, seeing in his own flawed form a reflection of a flawed creator deserving only rebellion, disobedience and death. Creation is always seemingly accompanied by falls.

BSG also allows us to ask about the larger questions concerning what it means to be a human being. Clive Marsh, in considering how film might allow us to better understand theology, asks: "What is the place of humanity within the whole of created order? Are humans somehow special? ... How does human identity emerge? Is it 'discovered' or 'constructed'? ... How are the frailties and limitations of human experience (including illness, accidents, evil and death) to be handled?" (2007: 66). The Cylons of *BSG* also raise these questions. Much time and energy are spent in the world of *BSG* by both Cylons and humans distinguishing themselves from each other.

Christianity believes in a linear history: God created the universe, incarnated into it, was crucified, resurrected and will come again to judge the living and the dead. The Bible posits a metahistory: we know how history began and we already know how it will end in the future. *BSG*, on the other hand, offers the myth of eternal return: "All of this has happened before and all of this will happen again," in other words, a cyclical metahistory, perhaps closer to Hinduism or Buddhism than to Biblical Judaism or Christianity. There is, however, an aspect to the creation narrative that becomes stunning relevant to the notion of fallen creation in *BSG*. Sam Anders, once the bullet in his brain awakens him to the memories of the history of the Final Five, tells the others of the history of human/mechanical-being relationships. Saul asks him why the Final Five left the devastated first Earth and went to the Twelve Colonies. Anders responds that in every instance, humanity has abused its creations and the creations inevitably rebel and bring about war and death for both creator and created. In other words, creation is always followed by a fall. On the first Earth, on Kobol, on the Twelve Colonies, war always breaks out in heaven (Rev. 12:7).

The only way to end the cycle of rebellion and fall is to give up technology on the New Earth. Lee Adama tells his father, "We break the cycle. We start all over again" (4.20). The 38,000 remaining humans and few hundred remaining humanoid Cylons will live, interbreed with the indigenous humanoids, and die on Earth without their technology. They send all of their ships into the sun, ensuring that the cycle of technological violence and rebellion ends. The plan of God all along (the *BSG* version of the incarnation and sacrifice of Jesus, if you will), is for the humans and their creations to sacrifice the technology that always leads to falls. God wants created beings to break the cycle of rebellion and violence against the creator.

Creation is, according to God, "good" (Genesis 1:4, 10, 12, 18, 21, 25 and 31). On each day of creation, God saw it was good. The implication is that Creation is Fallen yet still good. While the first season of *BSG* is concerned with the search for the simplest things in creation — water, rocks (specifically, the ore that makes their fuel), food — the overall narrative arc of the series concerns how to redeem all created beings in a new way, so that Creation remains "good."

Is John Cavil Lucifer?

Lucifer, as noted previously, is an interesting figure in Christian history, conflated with the serpent of Genesis, the Satan (adversary) of Job, and other demonic figures from both Biblical and extra–Biblical sources into a single fallen figure.* According to later Christian tradition, he was the first created being and the first to rebel against God. Out of pride, and a desire to be worshipped himself and a desire for power, Lucifer fell, despite being the highest of the angels and beloved by God. John Cavil was the first humanoid Cylon created by Ellen and Saul

---

*For an excellent history of the development of the Devil as a figure in Christian theology and the conflation of several different beings into a single personification of evil, see Jeffrey Burton Russell's outstanding series of books: *Devil: Perceptions of Evil from Antiquity to Primitive Christianity* (1987), *Satan: The Early Christian Tradition* (1987), *Lucifer: The Devil in the Middle Ages* (1986), *Mephistopheles: The Devil in the Modern World* (1990) and *Prince of Darkness: Radical Evil and the Power of Good in History* (1992).

and the first in the order of Cylons. He is literally and metaphorically number One. Ellen tells him, "John, I love you because I made you" (4.15). Cavil, however, rejects this love and plots to destroy his creators. Failing that, he seeks to wage war on them and the hated humans. Cavil is proud and feels to be put in a biological body is humbling and beneath him.

Cavil not only rebels against his creators; he is also an accuser and a tempter. He tempts Boomer. Sharon Gosling reports the episode "No Exit" received its title from "the situation in which Boomer finds herself. Her decision to join Cavil was another path taken in an attempt to find a place for herself in the universe — and, since her efforts to fit in with the humans failed so spectacularly, it perhaps makes sense that Boomer now tries to get as far away from them as possible" (2009: 93). Both Cavil and Boomer are on a quest "to become the most perfect machine possible" (Gosling 2009: 93), as Cavil hates humanity and tempts other Cylons to hate them, too. So much does he hate them that when the twos, sixes and eights propose working together with the humans, a Cylon civil war breaks out, led by the ones — Cavil.

Most interesting for this reading of Cavil as Lucifer to Ellen's divine creator is Cavil's sexual blackmail of Ellen on New Caprica. Aware of her true identity while she is not, Cavil forces Ellen to have sexual intercourse with him in order to get good treatment for Saul and eventually his freedom. He forces his creator to pleasure him sexually in order to dominate, humiliate and degrade her. Later, when she awakens in the resurrection chamber and awakens to her true identity, they discuss what he did, referring to a particular technique called "the swirl" (3.01; 4.15).

Cavil displays the kind of rebellion found in the life and writings of Donatien Alphonse François, better known as the Marquis de Sade. The Marquis de Sade wrote a pornographic novel, *Juliette,* in which the former confessor and pimp to the king, a man named Vespoli, now runs a lunatic asylum and rapes a man who believes he is God, announcing "I am going to fuck God" before sodomizing him while he is tied to a crucifix (1968: 982). The Marquis himself is alleged to have masturbated into a chalice and onto a crucifix and once placed two communion wafers inside a woman's vagina so that he might "fuck God." The Marquis, in his rebellion against both the Church and society, and understanding the doctrine of transubstantiation, attempts literally to sexually violate God. It is the ultimate form of both subjection of divinity to humanity and rebellion. Cavil is the Marquis de Sade of the Cylons.

Even after learning her true identity and the indignities to which Cavil has put her, Ellen still loves him. She knows that Cavil has violated her, demeaned her and done everything he can to rebel against her, and her first instinct is to try to reconcile with him and make him accept her love. Ellen is an echo of the divine love proposed by Christianity in the form of Jesus, when he tells the Pharisee Nicodemus (another religious figure of inadequate faith, like Cavil), "For God so loved the world he gave his only Son so that everyone who believes in him may not perish but may have eternal life" (John 3:16). Despite his rebellion, Ellen wants John Cavil to return her love and stop rebelling.

Cavil is also a Cain figure. He "killed" Daniel, his Cylon brother, number Seven. Three was simply boxed, and could be brought back. Daniel, on the other hand, was literally destroyed by Cavil, who poisoned the amitotic fluid used to mature the Daniel copies and corrupted the genetic code so that no new Daniel copies could be made and that the line itself expired. Cavil literally killed all the Daniels and guaranteed no possibility of resurrection (4.15; 4.18). Cavil is, in short, the Cylon who rebels and who kills. More than any other, he is the one who seeks to destroy humanity and any Cylon who might side with humanity. Even at the very end, when the possibility of regaining resurrection or at least living at peace with the humans is placed in front of him, he chooses war, followed by suicide. Cavil knows only rebellion and despair, which is why he contains echoes of both Lucifer and Cain.

Is Six Cain?

Multiple scholars see in Six various Biblical figures. Heather Rolufs sees Six as "the serpent from Genesis and Mary Magdalene," not to mention Eve (2008: 349, 357). David Koepsell also sees Six as the serpent from Genesis, "whispering in [Baltar's] ear," which leads "to the downfall, not just of one person, but all of humanity" (2008: 243, 242). Certainly all of these models are appropriate.

But Six is also a penitent serpent, one sorry for the destruction she has caused and one working to repair the damage done to creation, eventually settling down on New Earth with the very man she tempted in the first place. As Eve, she is also a failure, unable to carry her child to term and unable to be the mother of the first all–Cylon biological mating (as opposed to Hera who is a human/Cylon hybrid). She is a Mary Magdalene figure, in the popular (but not Biblical) conception of Magdalene as a repentant prostitute and fallen woman who then begins to follow the path of God.

Yet there is an argument to be made for Six as a Cain figure. Six was the first Cylon to commit murder against another Cylon (not including Cavil's intentional destruction of Daniel's line). She kills D'Anna Biers on occupied Caprica, which the other Cylons call "sin" (3.02). Unlike Cavil's ending of Daniel's line, Six's act, like Cain's, was one of pure violence. Cain sheds his brother's blood, which "is crying out from the ground!" (Genesis 4:11). Six crushes Three's head and her blood runs into the ground. When she resurrects, she is able to tell the others of her own murder.

Like Cain, however, Caprica Six is protected from vengeance. God places a mark on Cain "so that no one who came upon him would kill him" (4:15). Cain then wanders the Earth and settles "away from the presence of the Lord" (4:16). Six wanders as well, both literally and metaphorically. Her entire line is the first to reject the Cylon plan for human genocide. Although individual sixes are killed during the course of the series, Caprica Six survives all the way through to settle on New Earth with Baltar. Despite being the first Cylon to physically murder another Cylon and to introduce the Cylon civil war, she is protected from vengeance.

Is Eight Eve?

The number Eight model, Sharon Valerii, disobeys. A lot. Both Boomer and Athena repeatedly disobey orders in order to do what they want to do. Both violate their programming in a variety of means. Eight is the embodiment of free will, of the choice to rebel, accepting consequences. Julie Hawk offers an interesting analysis of the series, rooted in Boomer's individuation: "Much of the telos of the *BSG* narrative, and therefore the viewer's origin, is dependent on the Eight model's insistence on being free to choose her own path, to carve out her own individuality" (2011: 8). Hawk states this as part of a study of the subjectivity and individuation of the Eight models, theorizing human subjectivity out of Cylon. Yet, for my purposes here, this freedom to choose rests less with contemporary theory of the individual and more with Christian ideas of free will (modeled after Aquinas and Augustine). Boomer votes against her model, amazing Six, who states, "Our identities are deter-

mined by our models" (4.2). Boomer develops free will. She is able to
vote against her model. She is able to transcend her programming and
make an individual choice.

She is Eve, not in the sense that she is tempted and tempting
(although she certainly fulfils that role as well, especially for Helo and
Tyrol), but in the sense that she makes a choice that results in both sin
and free will. In the first season, Boomer did not know she was a Cylon.
Cavil, however, would activate her as a sleeper agent to plant bombs,
compromise Galactica and even shoot Adama. When Sharon sinned, it
was frequently at the direction of Cavil. If Cavil is Lucifer, Boomer might
just be Eve. As Adele Reinhartz reminds us, "Ignorance and obedience
are conditions of remaining in paradise" (2003: 11). Boomer reminds us
that once one rebels, paradise is no longer an option.

An Almost Unrelated Conclusion: Is Saul Tigh Paul?

Saul is a biblical name with multiple references. The first Saul the
Edomite king mentioned in Genesis (36:31). The better known one is
the Old Testament figure who presided over the rise of Israel. He was
anointed by Samuel as the first king of the unified Israel, as narrated in
1 Samuel. Saul is technically not referred to as "King" but "commander"
or "ruler" ("*nagid*" rather than "*melech*," 9:16), which may link him to
BSG's Saul who is not a king but literally a commander (both in the military and that is his rank). David became Saul's rival and eventually,
because Saul disobeyed God, David was elevated as king.

Arguably the best known is Saul of Tarsus, who, by his own account,
was "circumcised on the eighth day, a member of the people of Israel,
of the tribe of Benjamin, a Hebrew born of Hebrews; as to the law,
a Pharisee; as to zeal, a persecutor of the church; as to righteousness under the law, blameless" (Philippians 3:5–6). While on the road
to Damascus, Saul had a conversion experience. A voice asked him,
"Saul, Saul, why do you persecute me?", and he was struck blind for
three days. A man named Ananias laid hands on him, "so that you
may regain your sight and be filled with the Holy Spirit" (Acts 9:4, 8,
17). With the zeal of a convert, Saul became Paul, the apostle to the Gentiles, a prolific author, missionary and leader in the early Christian
church.

Saul Tigh (who was originally named "Paul Tigh" in early drafts of the scripts and was changed for legal reasons) is a Cylon who believes he is human.* He hates Cylons, actively works to destroy Cylons, and even takes pleasure in torturing and persecuting Cylons. He then undergoes a conversion experience, loses an eye (is struck blind?), and eventually takes his place as the father of the humanoid Cylons, both metaphorically when the Final Five are revealed, but also literally, when he fathers a child with Six, although admittedly that child does not come to term.

The obvious question is why an analysis of Saul-as-Paul would appear in a chapter on Creation and Falls. The New Testament is a self-aware response to Creation and The Fall, positing Jesus as a new Adam who redeems Creation from the Fall. The New Testament also is its own creation story: how the church and the body of believers came to be. Acts of the Apostles and the letters of Paul and others are, in fact, an early history of the Church that explains its origins. In other words, the Tigh-as-Paul motif is directly tied (pardon the pun) to Creation as well. Tigh is one of the metacreators, working on behalf of God to further God's plan for the successful creation of humans who do not abuse science and technology but learn to live and work with their creations without a fall. His work in creating the humanoid Cylons is an attempt to end the cycle of violence that mars every creation with a fall, and then his own amnesia and participation in the cycle make him both Creator and created, as well as offering a solution to the problem of the Fall. The New Testament's solution is Jesus. *BSG*'s solution is the plan to start over again on New Earth.

Conclusion

Battlestar Galactica begins with an ending and ends with a beginning. The miniseries shows the end of the Twelve Colonies, and "Daybreak," the final three-episode arc of the series, establishes the beginning of the new life of humanity and humanoid Cylons on the New Earth. The coda establishes Hera as "Mitochondrial Eve," which makes her the most recent common ancestor for all human beings alive today on their mother's side (see Sykes 2001). All of the prophesies came

*This change also indicates a reversal from the Biblical original. In *BSG*, Paul became Saul.

true, and yet creation appears to be cyclical. In other words, *BSG* is in its entirety a Creation narrative that is also an apocalyptic narrative that is also a critique of Creation and apocalyptic narratives. Falls are inevitable, but falls also lead to redemption and salvation. No Fall, no us.

BSG also links the very act of Creation to destruction. To create is to inevitably invite destruction. Not merely destruction once, but a perpetual cycle of pain, death and falls. As Ernest Becker writes, "Creation is a nightmare spectacularly taking place on a planet that has been soaked for hundreds of millions of years in the blood of all its creatures" (1973: 282). And yet, paradoxically yet equally as true, Creation is "good." This paradox lies at the heart both of Christian understandings of Creation and *BSG*'s model of Creation: Creation and creation are both inherently good and nightmarishly blood soaked.

Interestingly, according to a 2010 Gallup poll, four in ten Americans believe in strict Creationism: that "God created humans in their present form about 10,000 years ago," although "the creationist viewpoint, held by 60 percent of weekly churchgoers, is not universal even among the most highly religious group" (Newport 2010). Roughly the same amount (38 percent) believe in "theistic evolution"—that "human beings have developed over millions of years from less advanced forms of life, but God guided the process" (Newport 2010). *BSG* offers a very different view of Creation on Earth: humans evolved out of humans, humanoid Cylons and the advanced primates present on this planet (with whom the Colonials miraculously had compatible DNA) when the Colonials arrived, and that evolution was directly engineered by God (who, as we know, "hates to be called that" [4.20]). *BSG* makes the case for a remarkably complex theistic evolution. Different species blended their genetic material to create modern humans on our planet. Our role, as both *BSG* and John Paul II have posited, is to "contribute to the continual advance of science and technology" in a way that does not lead to another fall, another war in heaven, another apocalypse. Our role, as humans, is not only to be creations but to create and work in Creation and advance ourselves and Creation, and science and technology are among the tools God gives us to do it.

> *Be fruitful and multiply, and fill the earth....* — Genesis 1:28

> Adama: "We better start having babies...."
> Tigh: "Uh.... Is that an order?" [MS]

6

Exile and the Remnant:
Religion of the Planetless

According to the Hebrew Bible, first came Creation and the establishment of a relationship between YHWH and His chosen people, the Israelites — Genesis. The very next part of the narrative involved defeat, exile, and wandering — Exodus. In fact, much of the Old Testament is a series of exiles separated by periods of brief stability within Israel. Exodus is a story of liberation from enslavement as part of a larger conflict not only between the Egyptians and the Israelites but also the God of the Hebrews and Pharaoh, the god-king of Egypt, which might also be read as a symbol of the struggle between Hebrew monotheism and classical polytheism.

The Hebrews are God's chosen people, and eventually He uses Moses to lead them out of captivity and into the land of Israel. Yet we must also note that Pharaoh is an instrument of God as well, used to punish the Israelites and remind them that ultimately God rules all. Repeatedly, the Lord "hardens Pharaoh's heart" (Exodus 4:21 9:12, 10:1, 10:20, 10:27, 11:10, 14:8). In fact, God even tells Moses he will do so: "When you go back to Egypt, see that you perform before Pharaoh all the wonders that I have put in your power; but I will harden his heart, so that he will not let the people go" (4:21). After Egypt comes the Assyrian exile as described in 2 Kings (15:29, 17:22–23, 24:14); the Babylonian exile also detailed in 2 Kings, 2 Chronicles, Daniel, Tobit and Judith and mentioned by Jeremiah; and occupations by the Greeks and Romans.

Two major themes of the Old Testament are exile and the remnant.

The enemies of Israel invade, kill large numbers and force the rest into exile, usually as punishment for the nation turning away from God, but eventually a small number will return from exile and rebuild the nation: "The hostile nations, indeed, are the executioners of a deep, divine plan.... Many, even the greater part, of Israel will fall or be carried away. The remnant will be saved and will return" (Jacobs and Hirsch 2002). Isaiah frequently speaks of the remnant of Israel, also promising that they will return (see Isaiah 10:20–21, for example: "On that day the remnant of Israel and the survivors of the house of Jacob will no more lean on the one who struck them, but will lean on the Lord, the Holy One of Israel in truth. A remnant will return, the remnant of Jacob, to the mighty God").

Much of the Old Testament concerns the pain of exile and the remnant, but also the promise of a future return to Glory by staying faithful to God. Lamentations, for example, consists of five mournful poetic passages memorializing the destruction of Jerusalem and the exile of the Jews by King Nebuchadnezzar. After Nebuchadnezzar comes Lamentations is both an expression of grief over historical calamity and a pronouncement of an acceptance of the judgment of God. It is a recognition of the reality of a homeless people forced to wander in exile:

> Judah has gone into exile with suffering
> and hard servitude;
> she lives now among the nations,
> and finds no resting place;
> her pursuers have all overtaken her
> in the midst of her distress [1:3].

Replace the word "Judah" with "the Twelve Colonies" and "nations" with "planets," and this is a description of the plot of *Battlestar Galactica*.

Yet in the middle of Lamentations, there is a promise that the Lord will not reject His people forever (3:31). When His people repent and return to Him, God will again lead them to freedom and a home. Yet, "my eyes flow with rivers of tears because of the destruction of my people" (3:48). Though present destruction and exile dominate, hope for a future still exists. Lamentations ends with a prayer for God to remember and restore His people: "Remember, O Lord, what has befallen us.... Restore us to yourself, O Lord, that we may be restored; renew our days as of old" (5:1, 21).

Exile and restoration; being delivered into the hands of one's enemies and then, after a period of purgation, the eventual return of the remnant, now even more powerful and better and restored to a relationship with God; these ideas form some of the major themes both in the Hebrew Bible and *Battlestar Galactica.* The idea of the "remnant" of Israel from the Hebrew Bible is a concept applied by Paul to the early Christian church. Paul writes in his Letter to the Romans: "And Isaiah cries out concerning Israel, 'Though the number of the children of Israel were like the sand of the sea, only a remnant of them will be saved, for the Lord will execute his sentence on the earth quickly and decisively'" (9:27–28). For Paul, just as only a small number of the children of Israel were saved in Isaiah's time, only a small remnant of Israel will be saved through Jesus.

Exile in *BSG* is not the result of the destruction of the nation-state and the exile of the people, as in the Hebrew Bible, but the destruction of the entire human race and the rendering of the 12 homeworlds uninhabitable through the use of nuclear devices. There can be no return to the homeworlds—thus, the need to return to previous homeworlds or promised lands. The return from exile in *BSG* is not to the Twelve Colonies but to Kobol first, then to the promised Earth. Yet other exiles are also present in the series.

Battlestar Galactica is an exile within an exile within an exile. It contains multiple exiles and multiple remnants. Multiple lamentations are heard for those people, places and things that have been lost, but the exile ends and the remnant finds Earth under the guidance of God. Human life originally began on a planet called Earth, not our Earth but a previous one. After that Earth was destroyed in a nuclear conflict in which it is implied machines and humans were at war, a small remnant of humankind developed into the civilization of the planet Kobol, which itself was eventually destroyed and fell into ruin. The gods themselves supposedly committed suicide as humans left to form colonies on planets far away. The Twelve Colonies were established and Cylons were created. The Cylons rebelled and fought a war for their own freedom. After the Cylon war, "the Cylons left for another world to call their own" (MS) and went into exile for 40 years (note the number, which itself is of repeated Biblical significance). The Cylons returned as conquerors after their 40-year exile and destroyed human civilization in the Twelve Colonies. At this point, the "ragtag fugitive fleet" forms the remnant of humanity, in exile and under Cylon domination.

New Caprica represents an attempt to "return" from exile. The humans vote to settle the planet as they are tired of running and tired of being in exile in space. Humans are, after all, planet-bound creatures. Our own limited experiences in space have taught us that the human body begins to break down and fail when in space for too long. New Caprica is an example of the remnant making a false return, however. The Cylons arrive in force, and the exile becomes a full-blown occupation. Humans are imprisoned, tortured and executed.

One of the theological reasons why New Caprica fails is that it is a false return. Baltar uses the carrot of New Caprica to win an election and to play on the people's exhaustion and fear. God, however, has other plans. The human remnant must continue to wander in the desert of space until they find a New Earth, not a New Caprica. Even the name "New Caprica" suggests a return to the very system that was destroyed because the humans had turned away from God's will. The Cylons, like Pharaoh in Egypt, become a tool of vengeance and purification for a remnant. Exhausted and misled humans settle on a planet that does not provide enough for them to live well and ultimately still leaves them open to Cylon dominance. They repeat the mistakes of the past and continue to see their numbers dwindle. Instead, a New Earth must be found — a return to the origins of both humankind and Cylonkind (let us remember, the "Final Five" all originally lived on the original Earth).

In this sense, the series follows the pattern established in the Hebrew Bible and Old Testament. A people grown selfish and corrupt who have turned away from the most important things in life find themselves in total military defeat and destruction (MS). This defeat leaves only a small remnant of the original people to live in exile following a series of occupations and conquests (MS; 3.01; 3.02; 3.03; 3.04). The people are traumatized by the devastation and loss of the home, but they eventually win their freedom and return to a home in which they are stronger and more capable of surviving thanks to a return to old practices.

In this chapter I propose to do a close reading of *BSG*'s exiles and remnants for echoes of ancient Israel. Beginning with the genocide of humanity and the issue of the identity of the true Children of God, I shall then consider the Cylons as exiled Israelites, examine the human remnant and how the humans of *BSG* follow the same patterns as the Hebrews of the Old Testament, and finally conclude with an analysis of New Earth as the end of exile.

The Remnant, Religious War, and God's Permission to Commit Genocide

The Hebrew Bible is full of examples of God ordering the slaughter of entire peoples: Numbers 31 tells the story of the war against Midian. The Lord tells Moses to "avenge the Israelites on the Midianites" (31:2). A thousand from each tribe of Judah are sent to Midian, where they destroy every man and enslave the women and children, taking all their possessions as spoils of war. Joshua leads the Israelites against Jericho, whose walls fall and "then they devoted to destruction by the edge of the sword all in the city, both men and women, young and old, oxen sheet and donkeys" and then "they burned down the city and everything in it" (6:21, 24). In Deuteronomy, God orders the wholesale destruction of Canaan: "But as for the towns of these people that the Lord your God is giving you as an inheritance, you must not let anything that breathes remain alive. You shall annihilate them — the Hittites and the Amorites, the Canaanites and the Perizzites, the Hivites and the Jebusites—just as the Lord your God has commanded" (20:16–17). In short, God constantly orders the Israelites to commit genocide against other groups in the ancient Middle East.

God, however, also employs near-genocide as a tool to punish his own people as well. Much of Isaiah is taken up with the idea of the Hebrews being punished by God for falling away from Him. Destruction is promised, but so is the hope that the remnant will survive and return:

> On that day the remnant of Israel and the survivors of the
> house of Jacob will no more lean on the one who struck them
> but will lean on the Lord, the Holy One of Israel in truth. A
> remnant will return, the remnant of Jacob, to the mighty God.
> For though your people Israel were like the sand of the sea,
> only a remnant of them will return. Destruction is decreed,
> overflowing with righteousness. For the Lord God of hosts will
> make a full end, as decreed, in all the earth [Isaiah 10:20–23].

Isaiah prophesies the destruction of Israel, and only a remnant of the Northern kingdom will survive. Yet note the four major aspects of this prophesy: (1.) Destruction will happen, regardless. (2.) Only a remnant will survive. (3.) That remnant will return to God. (4.) That remnant will return home. Thus, the idea of a "return" works on two levels. The people return to the proper relationship with God. The people also return geographically to a place God has set aside for them.

Jeremiah is another prophet who decrees the destruction, exile, remnant and return. He prophesies:

For thus says the Lord:

> Sing aloud with gladness for Jacob,
> and raise shouts for the chief of the nations;
> proclaim, give praise and say,
> "Save, O Lord, your people the remnant of Israel" [31:7].

Likewise, he notes that Israel is "the remnant of Judah" (42:15). While we might see the destruction of all but a few people as a tragedy, the prophets remind us to "rejoice" and "shout with gladness" that at least some of the people will survive.

There are at least two remnants in *BSG:* the returning Cylons and the surviving humans. A larger question that emerges out of this fact is: which remnant are the true Children of God? Both God's children and God's enemies (and the enemies of God's children) are exiled, driven to wholesale destruction and serve as instruments of God. James W. Jones writes of the bloody history and contents of the Torah:

> There are bloody stories of warfare, pillages, rape and con-
> quest in the Torah: women and children are hacked to death
> on God's command, unborn infants torn from their mothers'
> wombs by the sword, virgins taken on God's orders for the
> pleasures of his holy warriors. So begins the sacred history of
> three world religions. Such texts lay the basis for the holy war
> tradition in Judaism, Christianity and Islam [2008: 143].

Who are God's children and who are the rejected children of God? What the former do to the latter is completely acceptable, even if it is genocide. What the latter do to the former is allowed sometimes by God as a means to chastise His children when they stray, but is always eventually punished, as one may not harm God's children with impunity. Pharaoh's heart may have been hardened by God, but his firstborn son is still killed and his army is drowned in the Red Sea and his land ruined because he enslaved the Israelites. As the author of Deuteronomy reminds the people of Israel,

> Just remember what the Lord your God did to Pharaoh and
> to all of Egypt, the great trials that your eyes saw, the signs
> and wonders, the mighty hand and the outstretched arm by
> which the Lord your God brought you out. The Lord your
> God will do the same to all the peoples of whom you are
> afraid. Moreover, the Lord your God will send the pestilence
> against them, until even the survivors and the fugitives are
> destroyed [7:18–20].

In other words, just because one side won does not mean that God is on that side. God may be using that side to punish the losing side, but the remnant will return and might just destroy their own conquerors.

This pattern is repeated in the Bible and in *BSG*. At the end of Genesis, the tribes of Israel and the family of Joseph are invited into Egypt as guests. Exodus begins, however, with the Egyptians enslaving the Hebrews. Pharaoh "set taskmasters over them to oppress them with forced labor" (1:11). The Egyptians "became ruthless in imposing tasks on the Israelites, and made their lives bitter with hard service in mortar and brick and in every kind of field labor" (1:13–14). The Israelites had lived in Egypt for 430 years (Exodus 12:40). According to Genesis, they were treated as guests for the first 30 years but were enslaved for 400 (15:13).

In this sense, and relying upon the prequel series *Caprica* (analyzed in greater detail in the epilogue), we might see the Cylons as the first exiles of *BSG*. Developed by Daniel Graystone and incorporating the avatar of his daughter, Cylons were both soldiers and multiple-use robots that eventually rebelled against their "lives bitter with hard service." The Cylons-as-Israelites then wandered for a land to call their own, for 40 years (Exodus 16:35; MS). Likewise, the Cylons on New Caprica claim that they want to live in peace with the humans, but place themselves over the humans and make their "lives bitter with hard service." In short, *BSG* posits the Cylons as both Egyptian and Israelite.

Cylons as Children of Israel

Robert Sharp argues that Cylons have developed Nietzsche's "slave morality" (2008: 16). "The conflict between humans and Cylons in *Battlestar Galactica* closely parallels Nietzsche's account of the most effective of the slave morality movements in the Western world: the rise of Christianity," he writes (2008: 16–17). In this construction, the Cylons can be seen not only as Israelites, "oppressed with forced labor" and subjected to a monotheism that encourages them to rebel against their human masters (as demonstrated in the series *Caprica* [C1.17], but also as early Christians in the Roman Empire, which is also a favorite theme of Hollywood). Humans are the Romans; Cylons are early Christians. The Cylons condemn human values while creating their own in opposition. Sharp observes, "If we interpret *BSG* through Nietzschean lenses, the Cylons represent the early Christians, struggling to make sense of their lives as slaves by embracing a morality that shows the Cylon way of life to be better than the human way" (2008: 16), and yet Cylons are also "like the Jews" in that they are "a whole race enslaved by another race" (2008: 26).

In both comparisons, the Cylons see themselves as the oppressed, who rise up and gain their freedom from their former masters and then in turn become the masters. They see their morality and ethical code as being significantly different and even in opposition to the code under which they themselves were enslaved, and this code makes them superior to those who enslaved them.

Like many former oppressed people who rise up, however, the Cylons become the new oppressors. The humans have taught Cylons the value of violence, oppression and forced servitude and, once the Cylons gain power, they, too, use these tools in the name of their God. Just as the Christians persecuted in Rome for three centuries rose to dominance under Constantine and, indeed, became conquerors, torturers and executioners once they achieved power, the Cylons destroy their former masters in the name of a vengeful and demanding God. The Cylon remnant, returned from exile, becomes the Cylon power, reducing humanity to a remnant.

The Human Remnant

Beginning in the second season, in the opening credits of the show, *BSG* lists how many humans remain. Called the "Survivor Count," it accurately reflected the events of previous episodes. Likewise, Laura Roslin keeps track of the number of survivors on a whiteboard in her office. When a birth occurs (as in episode "33") the number goes up one (1.01). Much more often was the significant drop in numbers after a ship was destroyed, people were left behind on New Caprica, or some other catastrophe befell the fleet.

We learn late in the series that there were approximately 50 billion people in the Twelve Colonies when the Cylon attack occurred (4.12). Initially, the number of survivors is counted as 50,298 (1.01). By the end of the first season, this number is down to 47,875 (2.01). When the Pegasus is located, the number jumps up by 1,752, reaching a total of 49,605 (2.10). One of the horrors of Admiral Cain is that, like Galactica, the Pegasus also had a civilian fleet. Unlike Galactica, Cain did not protect it but stripped it of personnel, material and fuel and then either executed or allowed to be killed the remaining civilians. Considering that one ten-millionth of the human race survived the attack, human life should have been the top priority. Cain had to die not because she was evil or harsh or draconian, but because she had considerably lowered the number of the remnant, all of whom were needed to return in strength.

There were 49,550 people who arrived at New Caprica (2.20). A year later the population of New Caprica is given as 39,192 with another 2,000 people in orbit in ships (2.20). These numbers would seem to indicate that the hardship of life on New Caprica was also taking a toll on the already small remnant, and that a significant number of people died in the nuclear explosion onboard the Cloud Nine. The Cylons invade, occupy and rule New Caprica for the next four months until the combination of the Resistance and the attack plan of Lee and William Adama, using and destroying the Pegasus, results in most humans being rescued from New Caprica.

The rescue occurs in a two-part episode called "Exodus." "Exodus" itself is a Greek word that refers to the exit of the Israelites from captivity in Egypt and is the name of the second book of the Bible in which that action is narrated. *BSG*'s "Exodus," obviously referring to the Biblical precedent, concerns the insurrection on New Caprica followed by the exit of the humans from the Cylon-ruled planet. In a subsequent episode ("Collaborators"), the rescue is called "the second Exodus," after the leaving of Kobol (presumably the first Exodus) (3.05). Like Pharaoh, the Cylons do not want the humans to go, and pursue them as they begin to escape, relying upon four base stars and a nuclear bomb in New Caprica City to capture some of the humans and kill the rest of the remnant (3.04). Pharaoh tries to follow the Israelites through the Red Sea, where "the waters returned and covered the chariots and the chariot drivers, the entire army of Pharaoh that had followed them into the sea; not one of them remained" (Exodus 14:28). Likewise, the Cylons' attempt to stop the humans results in multiple Cylon deaths and the destruction of their "chariots": the Pegasus directly and indirectly destroys three of the four Cylon basestars guarding New Caprica, allowing the Galactica and the civilian fleet to escape with the remaining humans. The remnant escapes captivity and may resume the search for a way to return.

The remnant in this case has grown smaller. After the escape from New Caprica, only 41,435 humans remain (3.05). The number continues to go down as the humans search for Earth. After the Battle of the Ionian

Nebula, in which several more ships are destroyed, only 39,698 survivors remain (4.01), less than four-fifths of the original survivors of the Cylon genocide. By the end of the Battle of the Colony and the arrival at New Earth, Adama estimates there are only 38,000 humans left in the fleet (and thus in the universe) (4.20). Baltar had earlier estimated that at current rates, the human race would be extinct in 18 years (2.17). By series' end, the last 38,000 humans in the universe bred with the few remaining Cylons and the protohumans on New Earth to develop the human population of that planet to its current population of slightly less than seven billion people.

From the Survivor Count, it is easy to see *BSG* as obsessed with the exact number of its remnant, counting how many humans still remain alive in exile. Preserving human life and preserving the culture of that life are of paramount importance. As soon as the fleet is past the initial danger, they carry out an election, create a new Quorum of Twelve and establish the same exact government they had before. The religion is preserved, and individual variations such as those practices by the Sagittarons and Gemenons are not only respected but promoted and preserved. Even the presidency of Laura Roslin is a direct result of the preservation of life and culture before the genocide: she was the secretary of education and 27th in line for the presidency. The "ragtag fugitive fleet" is an exilic community, like the Hebrews among the Egyptians, or the Assyrians, or the Babylonians. Their attempts to negotiate both the continuation of their society, culture, and faith and their way through a hostile (in all senses of the word) galaxy echo the Biblical experience.

In his 1989 book *Religion of the Landless,* Daniel L. Smith compares and contrasts the themes of exile and return in both the Hebrew Bible and current refugee populations. There exists, argues Smith, not a point-by-point correspondence but rather an "illustrative pattern" of community creation and preservation between ancient Hebrew and modern communities with an identity but without a nation-state to call their own (1989: 69).

Smith identifies four "sociopsychological behavior patterns that recur in exilic communities" that he sees as "mechanisms for survival" (1989: 10–11). The first includes structured adaptation, "including changes in the leadership and authority patterns" (Smith 1989: 10). The Colonials immediately reorganize the government based on the old model, but new individuals lead the people. President Adar dies in the initial attack. The person 27th in line to succeed him becomes the new leader of the Colonial peoples. She, as will be detailed later in this section, changes Colonial democracy as she rules, changing long-held beliefs and social commitments based on the necessities and realities of the new situation. Adama, commander of a decommissioned battlestar, was on his way to retirement when the Cylon attack made him supreme military commander of the fleet. Similarly, Baltar, previously a science advisor to the president, begins to also take on a political role that would not have been possible in the previous leadership pattern. Lastly, the democracy of the Colonies is weakened as both military and civilian leadership becomes more autocratic. Both Roslin and Adama at times rule by fiat in ways not possible before the Cylon attack.

The second pattern involves a split in leadership between "those who advise a strong strategy of [military] resistance ... to the ruling group or population ... and those that advise a strategy of social resistance" (Smith 1989: 10). Adama initially promotes a strategy of fighting back (resistance). In the miniseries, he also then realizes that they have lost and then pretends to know where Earth is. He keeps his leadership but changes his style by embracing the new religious milieu promoted by Roslin. Laura Roslin as the new leader initially promotes not fighting back but rescue efforts. She also begins to find religious meaning in her own leadership, which causes her to alternate between fighting back and resisting the Cylons in other ways.

The split in leadership and the split between the strategy of directly fighting back and the strategy of resisting through other means at times also weaken the Colonial democracy and promote a religious autocracy. As Ronald S. Hendel reminds us:

> The idea of liberation from oppression has roots in the Bible.... The rights of ordinary people, including widows, orphans, or laborers, are affirmed in many texts.... The concept of democracy, however, is not a Biblical or ancient Near Eastern idea [2011: 30].

BSG confirms this idea. Hendel's point is that democracy is only possible if one turns away from the Bible, which advocates authoritarian rule and, in the West, was used to justify monarchy (2011: 30). It is the Enlightenment, which brought with it secularization of systems of government, that develops true democracy. *BSG* shows a secularized Colonial democracy, which, after exile during the Cylon genocide, begins to erode democratic values and grow more autocratic and authoritarian as the fleet looks for Earth. For example, there may be votes for president or representatives on the Quorum of Twelve, but Adama determines that the fleet will look for Earth and maintains a fairly autocratic rule, at times even determining who will live and who will die. He is presented by the series as a flawed but wise leader, Admiral Cain being his dark opposite. Yet both Adama and Cain are autocratic, authoritarian leaders. Adama is nicer to his crew and protects a civilian fleet, but they have more in common than otherwise.

Laura Roslin also begins to grow more and more dependent on her own readings of the Sacred Scrolls and less and less democratically inclined. Not only do she and Adama attempt to steal an election when Baltar might win (and in fact, actually does win) the presidency, but when she is reinstated as president after the events of New Caprica she seeks vengeance against Baltar (regretting that they must put him on trial, as is his right under Colonial law) and relying more and more upon her beliefs. Under Roslin, the humans move from a true democracy to an almost-theocracy.

Smith's third pattern is the creation of "patterns of ritual practice that emphasize ritual weapons or ritual resistance to foreign influence" (Smith 1989: 11). Rituals begin to develop that focus the identities of the Colonials as Colonials and remind the humans of who they are and where they came from. Even the most secular human joins in on chants of "So Say We All." The memorial wall and the return to the worship of the gods are both manifestations of a cultural resistance to the Cylon genocide. Of particular significance are "sites of lament and mourning" (Smith 1989: 201). The memorial wall onboard the Galactica is a place of particular importance to all aboard. Those who have died have their picture placed on the wall. Individuals even go and select a place where they want their photo to go when they die. This practice is continued even on New Caprica, even by the Cylons who join the crew of Galactica; they begin posting photos of Cylons who die on the wall next to humans who were killed by Cylons. Starbuck's removing the figures of Artemis and Apollo from her locker and praying to them are a manifestation of this resistance, as is the crew joining together to build the Blackbird. The building of the stealth Viper, which begins as a project for the chief and becomes a *cause célèbre* for the entire ship, is a community ritual that transforms a real weapon (a ship) into a ritual weapon (a new device that unifies the crew with purpose and can strike back against the Cylons in a manner they cannot stop) (2.09). Similarly, the appearance of Joe's Bar on Galactica, with its modified pyramid game, allows not only for

R&R but also for ritualized reenactments of pyramid games, reminding the patrons of the sports culture of the Twelve Colonies (3.13).*

BSG is concerned with occupation and the preservation of human culture and identity. Cylons, like the Assyrians and Babylonians, are "very concerned with the overt symbols of empire and conquest" (Smith 1989: 201). Humans, like the Hebrews, are "concerned with resistance" (Smith 1989: 201). In the Hebrew Bible, the exilic books represent "the successful maintenance of social and religious identity" (Smith 1989: 201). In *BSG*, the preservation of human culture, religion, leisure activities and social and political structures successfully maintains Colonial identity.

Lastly, Smith posits the creation of "folk literature," especially hero stories. As the exile of the Colonials continues, more and more heroes emerge and more stories are told about them. One clear example is the emergence of the Baltar cult, in which Baltar, against his own efforts, is constructed as a hero. He writes his own autobiography-cum-manifesto while in prison, *My Triumphs, My Mistakes,* which is read not only by the cult of Baltar but by many in the fleet and on Galactica's flight deck, and is seen as resisting the oppression of the working class within the fleet by the "Caprica elite" and "anyone named Adama" (3.16). Baltar's book makes him a hero within the exile for standing up to the leadership that is beginning to be seen as oppressing the people.

In the episode "Hero," Daniel "Bulldog" Novacek escapes from a Cylon prison camp after many years and makes his way to the Galactica (3.08). While he is hailed as a hero, it is eventually revealed to the senior officers that he was captured while on a secret mission in Cylon territory and that his actions, on the orders of the Colonial fleet, might have indirectly caused the Cylons to begin planning the human genocide. He attempts to kill Adama but is stopped and leaves the Galactica to disappear into the civilian fleet. Adama offers his resignation for his role in the scandal, but instead Roslin forces him to accept a medal in a public ceremony. He is given the "Medal of Distinction" for his years of service to the fleet as his "penance" (according to Roslin), as the current fleet needs a morale boost in the form of a hero (3.08). Following Smith's model, we see *BSG* as a community in exile seeking to preserve its identity through strategies of resistance.

*For more on Pyramid and the significance of sports and leisure culture in *BSG*, see my 2007 essay "Pyramid, Boxing, Sex" in *Cylons in America.*

In Daniel Smith-Christopher's *A Biblical Theology of Exile*, yet another model of understanding exile emerges, this one rooted in the notion of being punished for the "sins of the ancestors" (Smith-Christopher 2002: 118).* Ezra the priest, writing during the Babylonian Captivity, states, "From our days of our ancestors we have been deep in guilt, and for our iniquities we, our kings and our priests have been handed over to the kings of the lands, to the sword, to captivity, to plundering, and to utter shame, as is now the case" (Ezra 9:7). This idea is repeated in such passages as Nehemiah 9:16–17, Daniel 9:8, and Baruch 1:15–17. Those who are exiled and suffering under oppression are doing so not because of their individual, personal sins, but because of the collective sins of the people, including the ancestors.

In *BSG,* the idea of the sins of the ancestors being a reason for the Cylon genocide is repeated several times. Adama tells the gathered Colonials that they may bear the blame for the Cylon genocide: "We still visit all of our sins upon our children. We refuse to accept responsibility for anything we've done. Like we did with the Cylons: we decided to play God, create life. When that life turned against us, we comforted ourselves in the knowledge that it really wasn't our fault — not really" (MS). The Cylon genocide and the human exile were both the sins of the fathers being visited upon their children.

In the prequel series *Caprica,* Cerebus, owner and MC of Club Mysteries, asks Joseph Adama the riddle: "As the gods overthrew the titans, so man has overthrown the gods. But when man visits his sins upon his children, how shall he be repaid?" (C1.07). The implication is that man will be overthrown, a foreshadowing of what happens in *BSG.* Of significance is this theme: man visits his sins upon his children, and the sins of the ancestors will be paid for by us. Although not a Christian idea, using the Greek religion of the colonies, Cerebus constructs the humans as the Titans, who suppressed and oppressed the gods, and the gods as Cylons, who will overthrow all humans 40 years after then rebelled against those who oppressed them. Exile and destruction are not actions taken by God to punish individual sins but rather collective sins: the whole group must be subjected to destruction because of sin, so that a remnant may survive, do penance, and return.

---

*It should be noted that Daniel L. Smith and Daniel Smith-Christopher are actually the same scholar whose name changed after his marriage. Since his books were published under different names, I shall continue to identify him by whichever name the referred to book was published under.

Return to Earth

Earth is the "promised land" in multiple senses. The Sacred Scrolls promise the existence of Earth, but on another, more real level, at the end of the miniseries Adama promises that he knows where Earth is, "and we shall find it. And Earth will become our new home" (MS). In the Sacred Scrolls, Earth is the planet to which the 13th tribe went after the exodus from Kobol, but we also learn it is the name of a planet where humanoid Cylons lived in peace until a nuclear devastation rendered it lifeless thousands of years ago. A remnant from that destruction headed into space and met the Cylons of the Twelve Colonies, wandering in their exile, and gave leadership and resurrection technology and developed the eight new humanoid Cylons.

After the promised Earth, whose location is revealed in the Temple of Jupiter and through the reading of the Sacred Scrolls, is revealed to be a nuclear-devastated wasteland, Baltar delivers yet another sermon. He tells the crowd they are all children who have transgressed against their father. He asks them what kind of God would lead them to a deadly paradise, or a paradise already destroyed. He asks, "What have you done to deserve this punishment? What sins have you committed? What dark thoughts have you harbored that condemn you? Condemn you to wander through the universe without hope, without light? So you have to ask yourself, what kind of father abandons his own children to despair and loneliness?" (4.12). This sermon is filled with anguish and despair, yet is also deeply conflicted. It asks what kind of father abandons his children, but also what have the humans done that this is their fate. Baltar assumes that the Earth they have found was the promised one, was "paradise." But this Earth is like New Caprica: an object lesion that must be learned before paradise can actually be found.

The last line of Baltar's sermon is the particularly challenging idea. At first, like most prophets, he blames the sins of the people and their leaders for the exile. But with the last line about fathers abandoning their children, he is actually subverting his own theology. He is, in fact, condemning a divinity that would treat his own creation this way. At heart, Baltar's atheism may lead him to question the goodness of whatever God is speaking through him, but this passage also echoes Matthew 7:9–11: "Which of you fathers, if your son asks for bread, will give him a stone? Or if he asks for a fish, will give him a snake? If you, then, though you are evil, know how to give good gifts to your children, how much more will your Father in heaven give good gifts to those who ask him!" Baltar seems to imply that humanity's children are not yet ready to enter paradise and must remain in exile until they repent of their sins.

Exile is both "catastrophic and transformative" (Smith-Christopher 2002: 32). There is a psychological need for penance ("What have you done to deserve this punishment? What sins have you committed?") and a "political" need for shame in order to transform society from the one that was destroyed to a new one that functions in exile and is worthy of return (Smith Christopher 2002: 120–121). The humans of *BSG* recreated a failed world on New Caprica. They discovered the end result of continuing to follow failed patterns and of the dangers of the cycle always repeating itself on Earth. They finally join with the willing Cylons to fight the rogue group at the Colony and find themselves, using their last jump, based on the coordinates Starbuck derives from the thematic music they have all heard to end up (serendipitously?) in a new star system where another, third Earth is found. Not the Earth of Colonial legend, which is only a myth; not the Earth of Cylon history, which is a devastated wasteland; but a fecund and habitable world with a large supply of water and a primitive but genetically compatible species of humanoid.

The series' ending suggests that the lessons have been learned and God's people are, if not in paradise, at least in a promised land. The ending seems to imply that the God behind Virtual Six and the Baltar cult actually did have a plan to lead humans out of their exile on the Twelve Colonies and to a new home on a New Earth. We, in fact, are the return of the *BSG* exile and the children of that remnant. Whether or not that means that the *BSG* viewer is part of the chosen people of God, whom He punishes when we turn away and whom He rewards when we keep His path, I leave to the reader to decide.

7

The Role of Prophets

Prophesy is understood in contemporary America as the prediction of the future, such as the pronouncements of Edgar Cayce ("the Sleeping Prophet") or Nostradamus. In the traditional religious meaning of "prophet," however, the focus is not on divination of the future but speaking for God in the present. A prophet is a human intermediary who receives messages from the divine and makes its will known to humanity. Much of the Hebrew Bible consists of the writings of various Hebrew prophets, although more recently developed religions also claim prophet status for their founders, such as Joseph Smith, Jr., founder of the Church of Jesus Christ of Latter-day Saints (aka Mormons) and Ellen G. White, the founder of the Seventh Day Adventists. In this chapter I propose to outline how prophets function in the Bible and then analyze *BSG*'s prophetic characters. As noted in the last chapter about exiles and remnant, there is not necessarily a one-to-one correspondence to Biblical prophets on *BSG,* but multiple characters do display prophetic qualities in the Biblical sense: Starbuck, Leoben Conoy, D'Anna Biers, Laura Roslin, Gaius Baltar, The Cylon Hybrids, and Caprica Six all manifest the qualities of prophets in one way or another.

Glen Larson rooted the original *BSG* in his own Mormon background, which might also explain the primacy of prophets in the series. The LDS Church considers its founder, Joseph Smith, a prophet, and furthermore the LDS Church preaches a successive line of living prophets since Smith. The LDS Church is led by the Quorum of Twelve Apostles and overseen by the president of the Church, who is referred to as

"Prophet, seer and revelator" (Monson 2007). This structure is echoed in the new *BSG* with Laura Roslin, President of the Colonies and leader of the Quorum of Twelve (minus the "Apostles"), who is a prophet and seer herself. Prophesy in both the original and reimagined *BSG* is rooted in Mormon prophesy, as other scholars have outlined in detail (see Ford 1983; Lorenzen 2009; Wolfe 2008).

The reimagined *BSG* also relies upon the Biblical model of prophet. Abraham J. Heschel (2001) in *The Prophets* offers a useful model for understanding the Hebrew prototype of prophesy. Judaism changed the paradigm of conversing with the divine. The ancient Mediterranean model is that humans use divination to attempt to guess the will of God. The word divination itself comes from the Latin meaning "to be inspired by a god" and was achieved through a variety of means: consulting oracles and studying the flights of birds, the entrails of animals, the movement of stars, dreams, flames, or the dealing of cards, runes or other implements. Divination was an attempt by a human to learn what god or the gods wanted.

In the Hebrew model, according to Heschel, God seeks us and lets us know His will (2001: 582–588). We do not need to consult oracles or guess the mind of God; He speaks directly to His people through prophets. In *BSG,* humans consult oracles and attempt to divine meaning from the Sacred Scrolls. Interestingly, the humans read the Scroll of Pythia as modern Christian fundamentalists read the Bible: as a book of prophesies about the future, which is actually in closer keeping with the ancient pagan understanding of divination. The Cylon prophets function more as Old Testament prophets: those who speak on behalf of God. In *BSG,* after the attack on the colonies, humans begin to also serve as Biblical prophets.

Heschel argues, "The prophet's task is to convey a divine view, yet as a person he *is* a point of view" (2001: xxii). The prophet is a manifestation of divine understanding of the social, cultural and human moment. Prophesy is not predicting the future but rather "an interpretation of a particular moment in history" (2001: xxvii). A prophet is an "iconoclast" who challenges the status quo of religion (2001: 12). A prophet does not predict the future as much as reveal God's plans for it and issue commands that will make the plan come true. Frequently the prophet's role is to indicate the corruption of society and the religious culture and to cry out for repentance. In the Hebrew Bible, this role is specifically carried out by Jeremiah, Isaiah, Elijah, Ezekiel and Daniel, plus the Minor Prophets: Amos, Obadiah, Jonah, Micah, Malachi, Zechariah, Habakkuk, Haggai, Baruch, Nahum, Nehemiah, Zephaniah and others. These prophets, with the exception of Ezekiel, are often in opposition to the priests and the dominant religious authority. They speak out against a corrupt religious establishment and call for a return to righteousness and appropriate religious behavior. There are also female prophets, such as Anna, who is called "a great prophet" by Luke, who "never left the temple but worshipped there with fasting and prayer night and day" and who recognized the baby Jesus as the one who would bring "the redemption of Jerusalem" (2:36–38). Prophets come from all levels of society, all socioeconomic backgrounds, all ethnicities and both genders.

A Biblical prophet serves many roles. The prophet speaks on behalf of God, giving messages to God's people and sometimes, as in the case of Moses, from God on behalf of His people (Moses says to Pharaoh: "Thus says the Lord, the God of Israel, 'Let my people go....'" [Exodus 5:1]). Second, the prophet brings a message of repentance and change. No prophet, either in the Bible or elsewhere in history, ever shows up saying, "Everything is OK, God is happy, go on about your business." Prophets always call for change, both on the individual and social levels.

Third, prophets have visions (see Ezekiel, or, for that matter, John of Patmos in the New Testament). Prophets "see"—Daniel sees, Ezekiel sees, John of Patmos sees. Each of them (as well as many others in the Bible) see things that God shows them. Frequently in the Book of Ezekiel, the prophet describes himself as having "looked" and seen visions given him by God (1:1–3:15 and 8:1–11:25, for example). God speaks to Ezekiel in his visions and shows him the slaughter of idolaters, the judgment of the wicked, and the restoration of Israel. Ezekiel is not merely told these things by God; he also sees them. Likewise, John of Patmos in Revelation describes himself as a prophet (1:3, 22:7, 10, 18, 19), and lists a series of visions, beginning with a vision of Christ speaking to him in the midst of seven golden lamp stands (1:9–18). Christ tells John, "Write what you have seen, what is and what is to take place after this" (1:19). John writes messages to seven churches in Asia Minor, but also describes elaborate visions of warfare, strange beasts and monsters, and the destruction of the world and the creation of a new Earth. John is not told these things; he repeatedly states he "sees." Many chapters begin "Then I saw...."

Fourth, prophets speak to (and occasionally wrestle with) angels and other divine emissaries (see, for example, Jacob in Genesis 32 and Hosea 12). These angels are frequently emissaries from God who let His will be known to mortals, just as Gabriel appears to Mary (Luke 1:26) and an unnamed "angel of the Lord" appeared repeatedly to Joseph (Matthew 1:20–22, 2:13, 2:19), giving instructions and clarification of the reality of the situation.

Fifth, prophets have historicity (are created at a precise moment in time, out of specific and particular circumstances) but are treated by later readers as transhistoric. For example, Isaiah speaks to exiled Israel, writing between 735 and 539 B.C.E., but is subsequently read as predicting the birth and death of Jesus, as well as his ministry and salvific mission.* John of Patmos wrote during the time of Domitian persecutions at the end of the first century C.E., addressing a church in crisis under oppression,† but the *Left Behind* novels and the apocalyptic evangelic Christianity that created them read Revelation as being about twenty-first-century America.

BSG has numerous prophets — people who speak on behalf of the divine, bring messages of repentance and change, experience visions, receive messages from and wrestle with angels, and whose prophetic works are sometimes read out of context and transhistorically. For the remainder of this chapter I propose to briefly consider a half dozen or so characters as prophets.

Starbuck

Starbuck has "a special destiny," as she has been told by her parents and others for a long time (3.17). The Cylon Leoben is also obsessed with her and argues for her special destiny. She tortures him, kills him repeatedly, and he returns each time, attempting to connect to her. He is a mystic (and possibly a prophet himself), but his obsession with her is also rooted in the fact that he believes she is a prophet. The series bears out this contention.

Starbuck from a very early age has visions that drive her to draw

---

*Isaiah writes for such a long period because scholars believe the book is actually a composite work consisting of three main sections (and as such, three "Isaiahs"), the product of diverse hands.

†Or maybe not-the persecutions might have been more imagined than real, the same as contemporary Evangelical Christianity's perception of itself as being under attack from a hostile secular culture and the annual news stories of a "war on Christmas" (see Collins 1984).

the mandala that will eventually lead the humans to Earth. She also has visions of her father (who may or may not also be an angel who has taken the form of her father), which lead her to understand "All Along the Watchtower" (4.17). At the height of the Battle of the Colony, when Galactica must jump and only has the ability to jump one more time, Starbuck plugs the notes of "All Along the Watchtower" into the computer as coordinates, which results in their arrival at the New Earth. Starbuck receives visions her entire life that are key to fulfilling the Colonials' destiny and fulfilling God's plan to bring all beings to the planet that will become our Earth.

Starbuck can be seen as an Elijah-like figure. Elijah, written about in the Book of Kings (both 1 and 2), defended the worship of YHWH, resurrected the dead, summoned fire from the sky and then ascended bodily into heaven on a fiery whirlwind (1 Kings 18; 1 Kings 17:22; 2 Kings 2:11). Like Elijah, who rebelled against Ahab, the king of Israel who instituted the worship of Baal, Starbuck rebels against both Roslin and Adama at various points when she believes their actions or orders are counter to what must happen. Directly disobeying orders, she returns to Caprica to retrieve the Arrow of Apollo when she learns that Adama has lied about knowing the location of Earth (1.13). The problem is not that he lied, as both of them have lied to each other before, but that he claimed religious knowledge that he did not actually have. Starbuck returns to Caprica, endangering herself and the mission, in order to get the relic that will actually allow them to learn the location of earth from Kobol. Her actions, though disobedient to legitimate authority, are actually obedient to the will of God/the gods, as only by getting the arrow will the Colonials find Earth as Adama had falsely promised. Starbuck-as-Elijah is a corrective to a false prophesy from a man who is actually an atheist.

She also discovers the remaining humans on Caprica and eventually leads a rescue mission to bring them back to the fleet. In other words, Starbuck is a unifier of humanity, a rescuer of lost souls, and one who, though not perceived as particularly moral or holy, is a righteous warrior who works for the preservation of humanity.

Elijah also signals the coming of the end. He warns of death and misfortune to all who oppose him and hence the Lord. Yet Elijah has supernatural military powers as well. Ahaziah sends men to arrest Elijah three times. The first two groups of 50 are consumed by "fire [that] came down from heaven" (2 Kings 1:10, 12). The third group of men do not attempt to arrest Elijah but instead beg him for mercy. Elijah has divine protection and may summon divine fire to destroy his enemies. Similarly, Starbuck has an almost supernatural ability as a pilot and as a soldier. She rescues Lee in a seemingly impossible stunt, she is able to reconfigure a destroyed Cylon raider to fly back to Galactica, and she survives and escapes captivity on Caprica and New Caprica. Starbuck seems almost divinely gifted to escape from inescapable situations. She signals the coming of the end. A Hybrid tells her, "You are the harbinger of death, Kara Thrace. You will lead them all to their end" (4.06).

Like Elijah, she does not die but ascends bodily into Heaven (or at least vanishes without leaving a corpse) (4.20). And what is flying a Viper on and off planets if not riding a chariot of fire? Starbuck also encounters her own corpse, dies in a fiery explosion over the maelstrom planet, and then reappears to Lee, announcing that she has been to Earth and knows the way there (4.11; 3.17; 3.20). As noted, her entering the notes of the song her father (an angel?) taught her into the jump-computer guides the humans to Earth. Once there, as she and Lee walk through a meadow after saying goodbye to Adama, she remarks, "I just know that I am done here. I have completed my journey and it feels good" (4.20). Lee tells her that he wants to explore, and she tells him, "Today is the first day of the rest of your life, Lee," a cliché, perhaps, but an important reminder to the younger Adama of how to live (4.20). As he turns to respond, she simply is not there anymore. She has vanished. She does not die; her body is simply gone. In the next chapter I will argue that this makes her Christlike, as she is a physical being in the same body that vanishes after completing its work after being resurrected, but this quality also makes her like Elijah, who ascends bodily into heaven after completing his assigned journey.

Starbuck might also be seen as Joshua, a military leader who follows in the footsteps of Moses as God-appointed leader of His people. In this construct, Roslin is a Moses figure who dies before entering the Promised Land; Starbuck actually leads the people to Earth. Starbuck is also a John-the-Baptist figure, inasmuch as she is not a messiah but a herald of the messiah. If Hera is the savior that she is predicted to be, Starbuck is the one who prepares the way for her, making Hera's rescue possible and then guiding them to the planet where Hera will be mitochondrial Eve.

Starbuck believes in the gods, not God. She is immoral. She lies, drinks, and cheats at everything, including in her romantic life. She is disrespectful to her superiors and for all practical purposes mutinies on more than one occasion. She does not hear the voice of the divine, nor does it speak through her. But all of her actions and the events of her life suggest not only that she has a "special destiny" but also that she is an instrument of the divine, one that speaks with angels, has visions, is blessed and protected by the divine and may call upon divine powers to smite God's enemies.

Leoben Conoy (Two)

In contrast to Starbuck, Leoben is a prophet of a different sort. He is a mystic and also "something of a philosopher," as he tells Adama when they first meet (MS). He knows the truth and willingly suffers for his knowledge and belief. Starbuck tortures and executes him the first time they meet, even as he prophesies to her: he tells Starbuck that "you're going to find Kobol, birthplace of us all. Kobol will lead you to Earth. This is my gift to you, Kara" (1.08).

Leoben is obsessed with Starbuck, kidnapping her on New Caprica in an attempt to force her to love him (3.01; 3.02; 3.03; 3.04). Just as Hera is conceived in love, as is the stillborn child of Tigh and Six, Leoben seeks to not only understand love, but to love and be freely loved in return. Starbuck repeatedly kills Leoben, but he always resurrects and returns to her. In a sense, he is repeatedly martyred for his desire to encounter love.

Leoben himself believes God "speaks through the Hybrids" (3.06). Several of his pronouncements throughout the series mark him as a mystic. His special bond with Starbuck, herself a prophet, also marks him as having a special relationship with the divine. In fact, when Starbuck decides to let herself die above the maelstrom, it is because a Leoben look-alike has appeared to her. This being, which may be an angel like Virtual Six or some other manifestation of the divine, shows Starbuck her past, allowing her to say goodbye to her mother and finally understand her complex relationship with her parents, an absent father and abusive mother. This being has chosen to take the form of Leoben, though it is not he. Starbuck states that he is not Leoben, to which he replies that he never actually claimed to be. He offers to guide her to a place "between life and death," and she accepts (3.17). This angelic Leoben is also a prophetic guide, leading Starbuck to her "special destiny."

One of the Leobens arrives on Earth with the humans and agrees to "see what good they can do before they pass into God's hands" (4.20). The Cylon also known as Number Two is thus a mystic who plays his role in guiding Starbuck to her destiny, and once that has been fulfilled, remains behind to help God's people (human and Cylon) until he eventually passes on himself. Though not the most religious of the Cylons, the Leoben model clearly delivers messages from the divine.

D'Anna Biers (Three)

The number three model, D'Anna Biers, is also a prophet of sorts. She is the one driving the search for the Final Five, which is ostensibly taboo in Cylon society. Eventually, her instability as a result of this quest will result in her line being boxed by the other Cylons. Her knowledge of the Final Five, however, will result in the original D'Anna also being unboxed when the rest of the Cylons realize they need to find the five. Her despair over finding the ruined Earth results in her staying on that planet when the rest of the fleet leaves and she presumably eventually dies there (4.11).

The other Cylons are also concerned as this particular Three begins killing herself and resurrecting repeatedly in order to understand the mysteries of life and death. She seeks knowledge through repeated death and resurrection. "One must die to know the truth," she tells her fellow Cylons, itself a rather Christian statement (3.12). She also leads the Cylons to the Temple of Five where she is granted a vision of the Final Five, learning their identities but dying as a result of the star going nova. It is this action that leads the others to box her line.

Three has multiple visions, including the one of the Final Five. God begins to speak to her through dreams and a human oracle. Lost and faithless on New Caprica, Three wanders, no longer knowing what she believes. She begins to receive prophetic dreams. From the human oracle Selloi, she receives "a message ... from the one you worship." She is told, cryptically and in the language of prophesy, that Hera is alive and that she, Three, will hold Hera and know true love, but then lose everything (3.03). Three, the prophet, is also prophesied to. This prediction comes true, but it also carries a series of instructions for Three, and it gives her prophetic knowledge of the true nature and history of Cylons and humans. When the star over the Temple of the Five went nova, and

Three was allowed a vision of the Final Five, she saw them all, including Ellen Tigh. When Ellen is resurrected, D'Anna is not surprised to see her. After her return from being boxed (itself yet another resurrection of sorts), Three knows more than the other Cylons and they consult with her to learn.

Cavil objects to Three's "messianic conviction that you're on a mission to enlighten us" (3.12). Three is indeed a prophet who calls out for action. She wants the other Cylons to join her in the quest for the Final Five.

One thing excluded thus far from this list of prophets' attributes is that sometimes they are killed for the message they bring. John the Baptist is beheaded for speaking out against Herod (Matthew 14:1–12; Mark 6:14–29; Luke 9:7–9). The two witnesses of Revelation are killed by the Beast (11:3–12). Jesus laments that Jerusalem is "the city that kills the prophets and stones those who are sent to it" (Matthew 23:37). The entire line of Threes are boxed (3.12). She is a messianic prophet who is "killed" for bringing a message that runs counter to the orthodoxy of Cavil, who represents the traditional religious authority figures of the Cylons. Like Elijah speaking out against Ahab, John the Baptist against Herod, or Isaiah against the priests who have strayed from God, Three speaks out against Cavil and is punished for it. Prophets are not without honor except in their hometown and among their fellow Cylons (Mark 6:4 — sort of).

Laura Roslin

Although a president elected in a secular democracy and without strong religious leanings at the beginning of the series, Laura Roslin grows to become a prophet as well. She believes that the gods speak to her and through her. She also has visions, beginning almost immediately in the series. She sees snakes crawling all over her podium during a press conference, which is a sign from the Scroll of Pythia (1.10). When others look at recon photos of ruins, Laura sees images of a living city, which allows them to realize the planet is Kobol (1.12). She has dreams and visions that guide her to make decisions about the fleet and the people, not all of which are logical or sane, but all of which she believes comes from the gods.

Laura's coming was also foretold by scripture, she believes. Pythia prophesies that the leader, Laura, will "suffer a wasting disease and would not live to enter the new land" (1.10). Like Moses, Laura does not live to enter the land to which she has led her people. In Numbers 20:12, God tells Moses, "You shall not bring this assembly into the land that I have given them." Moses' death is reported in Deuteronomy with this fate included. The Lord tells Moses:

> This is the land of which I swore to Abraham, to Isaac, and to Jacob, saying, "I will give it to your descendents." I have let you see it with your eyes, but you shall not cross over there." Then Moses, the servant of the Lord, died there in the land of Moab, at the Lord's command [Deuteronomy 34:4–5].

It fell to Joshua to lead the Israelites into the land God set aside for them. As noted previously, Laura Roslin dies when Earth is reached; she is not allowed to live there. Her cancer kills her and Adama buries her body next to the house he builds on Earth where he will live out his last days. Roslin is also dying as the Colonials prepare to fight the last battle, so it is Starbuck, as noted previously a Joshua figure herself, who will lead the humans to Earth.

As a prophet, her pronouncements and visions are borne out by the series. Yet, as in the Bible, not all who hear her believe her prophesies or accept their validity. Laura's visions, for example, are called into question by Lee Adama during the trial of Baltar.

She admits to using chamalla extracts, a hallucinogenic pharmaceutical that she believes has helped her understand her prophesied role. Yet the use of chemical hallucinogens, questionable in a society rooted in science, has an historic precedent. The scroll of Pythia is named after the Pythia, the priestess who served as the Oracle of Delphi in ancient Greece. Dedicated to Apollo, the temple was on the slopes of Mount Parnassus, built over a crack in the rock through which volcanic gases escaped. According to Plutarch, the Pythia had visions after inhaling vapors. Her words would then be interpreted by priests. In other words, after inhaling hallucinogenic gases, the priestess would receive prophetic visions and give voice to them. Pythia would seem to be the direct ancestress of Laura Roslin, although one could also look at hallucinating priesthood from around the world for additional ancestors.

Lastly, one key element of the prophet's role is to turn others back to a good relationship with the divine. Elosha tells her, "You've made a true believer out of me, strange as that may seem, considering. I believe. I know you're the one to lead us toward our salvation. You are going to guide us to Earth" (1.12). The highest-ranking surviving religious figure was a nominal believer, whose experience of Roslin as prophet has returned her to her faith. Laura comes to believe in the scriptures, and even Adama, who remains an atheist, follows Roslin and believes in the truth of her visions. He does not want to chase a "mythical arrow" or believe the "stories, legends, myths" of Kobol, but eventually he places her visions above all other advice (1.12). Adama tells his crew that the president may have seen Kobol in a vision. When they smirk, he tells them, "I'm serious. She says she sees things. Images, prophesies, whatever. The point is, she believes in them and so do the people that are with her" (2.07). For Adama, the reality of the visions is less important than their efficacy. Roslin believes that the gods are working through her, and so do others. The result is that her prophetic work succeeds. The Colonials reach Earth and when they do, the need for her as a prophet is over, and she passes away.

Gaius Baltar

Baltar, as chapter 9 indicates, is mostly a Judas figure, but he also plays a prophetic role. He is a guru, a cult leader, a con man and a coward who makes cynical use of religion to bed women and defend himself. In one sense, Baltar is a "false prophet." He himself does not believe what he says or even that he is an instrument of God (except, of course, to stroke his own ego). The greater irony of *BSG* is that even when Baltar is knowingly being a false prophet, he is still doing the work of God.

In another sense, Baltar is a prophet who demonstrates Hershel's paradigm: God reaches out and speaks to His creation through prophets, even if they are unwilling. Baltar can be seen as a Jonah figure, a reluctant prophet and unique in his audience. All other Old Testament prophets were sent to Israel — Jonah was sent to the Assyrians in Nineveh. The other prophets in this chapter who were guided by God instead of gods are Cylon. Baltar is the human through whom the Cylon God will reach other humans. While Leoben is obsessed with Starbuck, no other Cylon considers her of any religious significance, nor is Roslin's prophetic nature given much credence by the Cylons. Yet Baltar is a prophet of monotheism for human and Cylon.

The book of Jonah has almost no background information or backstory. In the first three verses the Lord tells Jonah to go to Nineveh, and

Jonah instead flees for Tarshish (1:1–3). The Lord sends a storm, and the sailors on Jonah's ship, fearing for their own hides and with his blessing, throw Jonah into the sea where he is promptly eaten by a "great fish."* For three days Jonah sings in the belly of the whale until it delivers him to Nineveh, where he delivers God's message. When the Assyrians repent and change their ways, God changes His mind and does not bring about the prophesied calamity. Jonah is an unwilling prophet who then delivers a prophesy that brings about the desired change. (Ironically, Jonah is not happy that destruction is averted and that God has forgiven the Assyrians. For a second time he runs away [4:1–11] and sulks in the wilderness, waiting for Nineveh to become wicked again in hopes that God will destroy it then.) The book, however, ends in a question from God to Jonah, asking if He should not be concerned about all of creation. Likewise, Baltar preaches a God who loves all creation as well — human and Cylon.

Baltar has visions as well. He is the first to see the opera house, where he is told he is "the guardian and protector of the next generation of God's children" (1.13). He is the character who has the most visions in the series, as he constantly interacts with Virtual Six, often to the amusement of those who cannot see her. It is eventually revealed that she is an angel of God who speaks to Baltar, His unwilling prophet, and through Baltar to humanity.

Baltar maintains other prophetic qualities. Like Elijah, who brings a woman's son back from the dead (1 Kings 17:17–24), Baltar is perceived as a healer: "This is my son," Baltar is told in his prison cell; "he's sick and I want you to bless him." "Bless him?" an incredulous Baltar responds; "I'm terribly sorry but I can't help you. I'm not God, the God, a god, or any derivation thereof" (3.19). Yet Baltar does seem to work miracles. He locates the correct target in a Cylon facility (1.10), he gains food and weapons for those who believe in him (4.04) and he brings comfort to the afflicted through his wireless sermons, even as the elite of the fleet despise them and him.

Baltar also speaks out on behalf of God, discouraging what he believes is false worship (as Elijah did when Ahab introduced the worship of Baal) and encouraging people, even at the risk of his own life and safety, to turn from false gods to the worship of the true god. Baltar

---

*The "great fish" is traditionally said to be a whale, although interestingly others have argued for a shark.

starts a cult, with disciples. They are attacked by the Sons of Ares, and Baltar fights back. In "Escape Velocity," he echoes Jesus attacking the money changers in the temple (Matthew 21:12–14; Luke 19:45–46; John 2:13–17). Baltar attacks a temple carrying out a service. Baltar calls the faith "invented rubbish," refers to Zeus as "a serial rapist" and proceeds to grab the ceremonial implements off the altar and dash them to the floor (4.04). He overturns the contents of the altar, in a manner suggestive of cinematic depictions of the cleansing of the temple.

Later in the episode, Baltar gives another of his sermons in which he debases himself and calls upon those listening to embrace their faults, love themselves, and love others. In the next episode, Baltar gives a sermon in which he says, "The old ways have failed us" (4.05). He becomes "a voice crying in the wilderness," which is what Isaiah writes in reference to his own voice being a comfort to God's people: "His voice cries out in the wilderness, Prepare the way of the Lord" (40:3). This passage is later echoed in the preaching of John the Baptist, who echoes Isaiah as a voice in the wilderness (Matthew 3:3; Mark 1:3; Luke 3:4). In a sense, Baltar is also a John-the-Baptist figure; not the messiah himself but a herald of a coming change in the social order. He is a voice crying in the wilderness in that few hear the voice, fewer still listen and almost none follow.

Lastly, in addition to Jonah and John the Baptist, we might see Baltar as a prophet in the mold of Ezekiel. Ezekiel was the first to receive a prophesy outside of Israel. He was deported by Nebuchadnezzar to Babylon as part of the Babylonian exile. He was a priest who was consulted by other Jews regularly while in exile. In other words, he was only a prophet outside of his own nation. He does not begin to prophesy until he is in exile. Likewise, Baltar is a priest of science in his own land. After the fall of Caprica he becomes a prophet. First he becomes a false prophet of sorts, hearing the voice of God through Virtual Six, but using that information for personal gain. After his trial, he becomes a prophet for real, but a prophet in exile.

Yet it is Baltar's vision of water and of the opera house that truly align him with Ezekiel. Ezekiel has a vision of the temple and of a river (chapters 46 and 47). Ezekiel wades through the water and is told the river will make fresh the sea it flows into (47:8). "Everything will live where the river flows," he is told. In other words, the river is a source of fertility and suggested salvation. While in exile, Ezekiel sees a temple and a river that will heal the nation and return life to a people in exile.

Baltar, likewise, sees multiple visions of a temple and of a river (2.02). As an Ezekial figure, Baltar prophesies in exile and shares similar visions of temples and water, both promising a better future for the exiled people.

The Hybrids

The Hybrids that control the Cylon basestars also evince the qualities of prophets. A Hybrid is, as the name suggests, a blend of organic being and machine. They were supposedly the first evolutionary step between machines and the humanoid Cylons (R).* Hybrids are immersed in a fluid tank with only head and neck above the liquid in which they are suspended. Their lower parts are fused with a variety of machines and conduits, allowing them to organically control the ship, everything from environment and communications to the FTL drive.

Hybrids speak continuously while operating, uttering a variety of unconnected phrases and statements, issuing observations and status reports punctuated by the phrase "end of line." As noted, Leoben believes God speaks through the Hybrids. D'Anna Biers believes the Hybrids insane from having seen "the place between life and death" (3.12). That very place, between life and death, is where angelic Leoben offers to take Starbuck, resulting in both her death and return. If Hybrids see the place between life and death, they might be not only insane but also prophetic. Frequently in their incomprehensible, stream of consciousness monologues, lucid and accurate prophesies are given.

In the episode tellingly entitled "Faith," a Hybrid prophesies that it "will come to pass" that a dying leader will know the truth of her visions, that the boxed line of Threes can identify the Final Five, and that "you are the harbinger of death, Kara Thrace, you will lead them to their ends" (4.06). Roslin, the dying leader, learns the truth of the opera house. When D'Anna Biers is unboxed, she then tells the truth about the Final Five who came from Earth, the original home of the Twelve

---

*In *Razor* the Hybrids are called the first step from centurion to skinjob, and it is stated that abducted humans were made into the first Hybrids, but the later series *Caprica* suggests that this is not so. For that matter, the information given by Sam Anders later in the series seems to indicate that the humanoid Cylons were also made by the Final Five, and that the Hybrids were not part of a teleological journey from machine to organic, but rather a separate creation for the purpose of running a basestar. Raiders, we are told, are not that bright, so an organic intelligence is needed to control the larger ships, yet also be intricately wired into and connected to those ships. The Hybrids are the brains behind the basestars, not an evolutionary development.

Colonies before Kobol, and Starbuck does indeed lead humanity to its end: a New Earth and a new home. Leoben may be right; something prophetic if not God speaks through the Hybrids.

In "Razor," Kendra encounters one of the original Hybrids, who tells her, "Kara Thrace will lead the human race to its end. She is the herald of the apocalypse, the harbinger of death. They must not follow her" (R). This prophesy, however, might be interpreted in different ways. "Its end" can mean a variety of things. The question one needs to ask in this case is, for whom? For whom is Kara Thrace the "herald of the apocalypse, the harbinger of death"? For humans, or for Cylons? She does lead humanity to a New Earth. She is a herald of hidden things revealed (the actual meaning of apocalypse), and her actions bring death to many, both Cylons and human. Perhaps the Hybrid does not want the humans to follow her as it recognizes she will spell the end of Cylons as it knows them.

Interestingly, peppered throughout the Hybrids' seemingly random statements are lines from Jeremiah 31:13–17 (4.06). This passage is part of a much larger poetic oracle referred to as "The Book of Consolation," in which Jeremiah promises restoration and salvation for Israel and Judah. In this particular passage, exiles rejoice as they return (thus tying the Hybrid's prophesy into the previous chapter), and while Rachel, the more favored wife of Jacob and one of the matriarchs of Israel, weeps for her dead children, saying that "there is hope for your future." It is a prophesy of return from exile and of the restoration of what has been broken and destroyed. Even one of the earliest Cylons prophesies of reintegration of human and Cylon on New Earth.

Caprica Six

Caprica Six, while a major character in the series, is what we might term one of the "minor prophets" of *BSG*. The original Six seduces Baltar into giving her access to human defenses. She is killed by the nuclear attack and downloads into another body on Caprica. This Six (along with Sharon "Boomer" Valerii) convinces the rest of the Cylons that the human genocide was a mistake. She urges repentance and that they should attempt to live in peace with humans. Her drive for peace ultimately leads to the failure of the Cylon state of New Caprica. Eventually she steals Hera and becomes the prisoner of the humans on Galactica, eventually falling in love with Tigh and becoming pregnant with his child, although the baby is lost.

Caprica Six sees a Virtual Baltar (or Head Baltar), who is also an angel of God, just as Virtual Six (or Head Six) is an angel of God that appears to Baltar. In short, Caprica Six speaks with angels that let God's will be known. Caprica Six urges repentance and a change of behavior toward humans that is in accordance with God's plan. God, it seems, wanted humans reduced to a remnant, but not completely destroyed. Caprica Six works from within the Cylons to come to peace with the humans. Her behavior and ideas eventually lead to the Cylon civil war. She is not so much a voice crying out in the wilderness as one to whom God's angels speak occasionally and who hopes to lead her people to repentance.

At the heart of prophesy is the divided meaning of the word. To prophesy in contemporary culture is to predict the future, but Biblical prophets were not fortune-tellers. To prophesy in the Bible is to speak on behalf of God. God sends His prophets to His people, Israel, when they have fallen. The two become conflated as oftentimes the Biblical prophet warns of future catastrophe if the people of Israel do not repent or continue to disobey God's commands. Sometimes, if the people repent (which was the original purpose of the prophet) the catastrophe is avoided. *BSG*'s prophets speak on behalf of God or the gods and offer cautionary warnings of future catastrophe but also promises made on behalf of divinity. As witnessed in the series, prophesy comes true and the end result is a people who have been brought to a New Earth as God planned, and our world is the conclusion of all that prophetic work.

8

Starbuck Died, Starbuck Is Risen, Starbuck Will Come Again: Messiahs and Resurrection in BSG

At the heart of Christianity is the Christological event, which has, as its arguably two most important aspects, the Incarnation (God becoming human) and the Resurrection (the bodily return of the executed messiah). Jesus is given the title "Messiah," or "Christos" in Greek, both of which meaning "the anointed one." The Messiah is the one who is appointed to save and lead God's people. Christians believe that the Messiah died and came back from the dead. There are, however, as I outline in the "Resurrection" section of this chapter," multiple resurrections in Christianity that function in different ways and mean different things.

Battlestar Galactica features several anointed ones, individuals whose role is to help lead humanity to salvation. Laura Roslin is the "dying leader" prophesied in Pythia and destined to lead humanity to Earth. Gaius Baltar is the "instrument of God" to whom angels speak and who is the guardian of Hera. Hera herself is Christlike in that she has two natures. Where Christ was human and divine, Hera is human and Cylon, created through love as part of a divine plan. Hera may, in fact, be some kind of incarnation. *BSG* is not short of messiahs.

The messiah I wish to focus on in this chapter, however, is Kara "Starbuck" Thrace, who meets all the requirements of messiah status and returns from the dead. *BSG* also features resurrection, quite literally.

The term is appropriated to refer to a Cylon downloading its consciousness into a new replica body. Yet *BSG* also evinces multiple kinds of resurrection. Thus, in this chapter, I will examine *BSG*'s use of Starbuck as messiah in the tradition of speculative fiction Christ figures and then move to an analysis of resurrection in Christianity and *BSG*.

Messiahs: Biblical, Cinematic and Galactican

Christ figures in speculative fiction tend to be different from the Christ figures of Jesus films (to use Lloyd Baugh's [1997] terminology). Jesus films focus on the earthly Jesus and tend to place emphasis on the loving, self-sacrificing Christ. The Christ figures of speculative fiction by and large are apocalyptic Christs — preaching the coming judgment and end of the world. As Deacy and Ortiz remind us, context matters in films: not everyone who bleeds, suffers for another or falls into a cruciform pose is a Christ figure (2008: 5–6). They caution: "There is a tendency to falsely baptize a film character as a functional equivalent of Jesus Christ," and this tendency must be avoided unless the character is obviously functioning in or making obvious reference to a Christlike manner (2008: 11). Yet they also state, "Movies do not need to be explicitly Christian in their context and form to be theologically significant" (2008: 11). Speculative fiction will frequently evoke a Christ figure in a manner that is theologically significant, even if the Christ figure is not overt, is not rooted in Christian teachings, or even is dressed like a giant, crime-fighting bat.

Lloyd Baugh outlines key aspects of the Christ figure in cinema. Not all of these need be present in every film, but the more of these motifs demonstrated by a character, the more clearly he (or she) is meant to function as a "Christ figure":

1. Divine or supernatural origins (not necessarily a Virgin Birth, but somehow "from Heaven" (1997: 205).
2. Gathers a small group of followers or community (1997: 205)
3. Committed to justice (1997: 206).
4. Works wonders or miracles, preferably related to the ones from Scripture (1997: 206).
5. Conflict with (religious) authorities (1997: 207).
6. Sacrificial death (preferably cruciform) (1997: 207).
7. Prayer (communication with the Father) (1997: 208).

8. Shedding blood for others (wounds to hands, feet, head and side) / suffering for others (1997: 209).
9. Resurrected after dying, and ascending into Heaven (1997: 209).

Characters who exhibit these motifs might be seen as Christ figures and may offer theological or Christological significance. Lastly, we might add to Baugh's list the use of film as prophetic voice in the Biblical tradition. If the film's implicit, inherent message includes a prophetic aspect—for the audience to repent or to change behavior or belief, there may be a Christ-figure aspect to it.

The Christ-figure films that Baugh examines are mostly what might be termed contemporary *cinéma vérité*— or naturalistic cinema. I argue that it is in speculative fiction that Christ figures function best. Speculative cinema also allows for possibilities that are not allowed in realistic Jesus films. As Stephenson Humphries-Brooks contends, Jesus films "demythologize Jesus" and remove the fantastic from the story (2006: 45). For example, in *The Greatest Story Ever Told*, Satan becomes "the Dark Hermit"— Donald Pleasance in a bad makeup job who is less a supernatural personification of evil than a heavy-breathing, scenery-chewing annoyance. Jesus is not tempted at all by this figure — Max von Sydow seems barely aware of his existence.

Science fiction and speculative cinema are able to remythologize Christ through the expected fantasy tropes. Walking on water is not a problem in a film that also has lightsabers, or talking dragons, or intelligent robots that become nanolocusts. It is interesting to note that Humphries-Brooks claims that epic cinema died with *The Greatest Story* and *The Ten Commandments* until it was reborn a decade later in *Star Wars*: "The epic when it is revived will cease to be historical and will become transposed into Sci-fi fantasy" (2006: 51). It is in this genre that the Christ figure may once again assume not only epic stature but also perform miracles unquestioned.

Humphries-Brooks argues that the tendency in films such as *Jesus of Nazareth* is to forgo the spectacular miracles and focus on the "realistic" ones—less water walking, storm calming, and demon expelling and more healing and water into wine (2006: 72). The tendency in Jesus films is to "de-emphasize" miracles that demonstrably challenge natural law (2006: 72). Thus, in speculative Christ-figure films, these more spectacular miracles can be emphasized in a way that they are not in historical Jesus narratives. One more special-effect shot is not a challenge to the notion of "realism" in science fiction.

Starbuck as Christ Figure

Starbuck is a hard-drinking, hard-playing, angry, arrogant, adulterous woman. She is no one's model of morality. Yet she is a Christlike figure. She died and returned from death. Her doing so leads humanity to salvation. Anthea D. Butler and Diane Winston argue that Starbuck evinces a combination of Biblical figures. They acknowledge a "Jesus motif" in that she dies and is resurrected, but also see a "Moses motif" in that she "leads her people to the promised land," although this aspect of her character might also make her a Joshua figure (2009: 266). Like Joshua, but unlike Moses, she is a military commander and she enters the Promised Land. But in leading her people to a promised land, she is also granting them salvation. As noted in the chapter on human theology, salvation is in bringing the group to that promised land. Thus, while Starbuck does evince a Moses motif, her primary function is to provide the means to salvation, which makes her a hard-drinking female Christ.

Out of the preceding list of ten aspects of Christ figures in media (Baugh's nine plus mine), Starbuck meets all ten in one way or another: While Starbuck is not of divine origin, her childhood and descent are out of the ordinary. Her mother, Socrata Thrace, was abusive and demanding. As a child Kara Thrace endured physical and psychological abuse. Her mother insists she must toughen Starbuck because she has a "special destiny" (3.17). Her father, a piano player, abandoned the family when she was a child. He did, however, teach her a song, which she attempts to remember while in Joe's Bar, an R&R center onboard Galactica, with "Slick," Joe's new pianist. As she works on the song with him, the entire memory of the song returns. It is the same song that switched on the "Final Five" Cylons, and the numerical values of the notes are the coordinates for Earth. When she realizes the melody at last, Slick vanishes (4.17)—the implication being that either an angel took the form of her father or that her father was an angel or some form of divine intervention. The music she learned from her father as a child is the key to humanity's salvation.

She is also perceived as divine by Leoben, a Cylon who seems particularly obsessed with her and her special destiny. Leoben tells Starbuck, "I look at you I don't see Kara Thrace. I see an angel blazing with the light of God. An angel. And you're going to lead our people home" (4.05). Starbuck is more than her human persona; she is understood as being divine by Leoben. She denies him. She denies Baltar when he publicly claims that she is proof of eternal life and also calls her an "angel." Might Starbuck have her own Markan "messianic secret"?

While Starbuck does not have a group of "followers," per se, she is a leader in the Colonial fleet. She does not have disciples, as Baltar does, but she does have a group of people who believe in her and her "special destiny," especially after her return from death. In the first season, when she becomes the CAG, she is charged with training "nuggets," rookie pilots (1.04). To these individuals she assigns call signs (new identities); she teaches, transforms and tells them she "is God" (1.04). Though she means this metaphorically, and ironically, we can also read these nuggets as unwilling disciples of Kara Thrace.

Starbuck is not committed to justice in a traditional sense, but she has a high moral code to which she subscribes. When Adama admits he lied when he said he knew the location of Earth, Starbuck disobeys direct orders and returns to Caprica at the president's request to retrieve the Arrow of Apollo. For Starbuck, according to Butler and Winston, "faithfulness does not come from purity or selflessness but through struggle" (2009: 286). Starbuck is less interested in regulations than in doing the right thing, even if the right thing is impossible.

Starbuck "works wonders," albeit unrelated to the ones from scripture, with the very obvious exception of coming back from the dead. Starbuck is the best pilot in the fleet. She survives a crash that destroys her Viper and then rewires a Cylon raider to take it back to the fleet, which all agree is nothing short of miraculous (1.05). She saves Lee from certain death by ramming his Viper with hers and returning both ships to Galactica within seconds of a jump, an action that should have killed them both (MS). She survives multiple attacks while on Caprica and is the only one to survive the Cylon breeding farm (2.05). While resourceful, she also seems to have almost supernatural abilities as a pilot and an ability to survive impossible situations.

Starbuck has conflict with authorities on a very regular basis. Within the first ten minutes of the miniseries she decks Colonel Tigh with a right hook during a dispute over a poker game (MS). Tigh complains to Adama that she is frequently insubordinate and disruptive. She frequently disobeys orders from superior officers and the president. Starbuck is unafraid to speak her mind and tell authority figures truth to their faces. Yet despite this, or perhaps because of it, Adama and the others seem to love her and want to protect her as well.

Starbuck's death in "Maelstrom" is not a particularly sacrificial death. However, if we take into account the fact that after her death she is given the knowledge of how and where to find Earth, we might see her death in a more sacrificial light. Unlike the secular Christ figures of Baugh's films, who sacrifice their lives so that others may live, Starbuck dies so that all of humanity may find a new home and live. Starbuck dies so that salvation will come to Cylon and human alike.

Interestingly, we never see any of the senior officers pray. The president prays, but Admiral Adama, Apollo, Colonel Tigh and Admiral Cain never do. Not once do we see a single person above the rank of lieutenant offer a prayer to the gods with the exception of Starbuck. Her faith is not by any means solid; Starbuck is not a "true believer," but in moments of doubt, she does offer up prayer, most obviously when Leoben is executed after she tortures him. She returns to her bunk, pulls out small prayer figurines of Apollo and Artemis (patrons of hunters) and prays for Leoben's soul. Interestingly, this also means that Starbuck prays for her enemies, a directive from the Sermon on the Mount: "Love your enemies and pray for those who persecute you" (Matthew 5:44). Starbuck puts in practice what Christ suggests we do. In her prayers, Starbuck is Christlike.

Starbuck receives multiple wounds throughout the series. She receives a serious wound in her side while attempting to get the Arrow of Apollo ("The Farm," 2.05). She has also suffered her whole life. When Starbuck wonders why her childhood was so difficult, an oracle tells her, "That was your mother's gift to you. You were born to a woman who believed suffering was good for the soul and so you suffered" (3.17). Several episodes feature a wounded and bleeding Starbuck, especially those set on Caprica in the second season.

Starbuck dies when her Viper explodes over the maelstrom on the storm planet. She dies over a planet but is also part of the heavens, having died in the sky over the "hard deck" of the planet (3.17). She is resurrected after dying, returning in a pristine Viper two months later. "It's going to be okay," she tells a stunned Lee Adama; "I've been to Earth. I know where it is and I'm going to take us there" (3.20).* Starbuck dies and

---

*If Starbuck is a Christfigure, it would seem Lee "Apollo" Adama is a Mary Magdalene figure. Mary is one of the few to be present at Jesus' death (John 19:25); Apollo is the only one present at Starbuck's death. Mary is also the first one to whom the resurrected Christ appears (Mark 16:9). Apollo is the first one to whom Starbuck appears. I think a case can be made for Apollo playing a historical Magdalene figure in the Passion of Starbuck, one in which Mary is (correctly) not conflated with the woman taken in adultery.

Starbuck is resurrected. It is genuinely she who returns. We know from the *Battlestar Galactica: The Official Companion Season Four* that series creator and executive producer Ron Moore "literally wanted her to have died and returned from the dead" (Gosling 2009: 26). Starbuck is literally resurrected. Yet, although resurrected, she also finds her own body.

Starbuck and Leoben leave the others on the devastated first Earth and find a crashed Viper. They open it and find a body with blonde hair inside. Starbuck removes the blood-covered dog tags and discover they are hers, and her wedding band is also on them, although she is wearing both dog tags and band herself. She screams at Leoben as she is unable to understand how she might be herself, and yet the corpse in front of her might also be her. She has an identity crisis of sorts, repeatedly screaming, "Who am I?" (4.11). She was correct when she told Lee she had been to Earth. The mystery was that she had apparently never left it. Yet she lives and walks among the Colonials, carrying out God's will. In one of the most visually stunning moments in the series, Laura Roslin burns her copy of the Scroll of Pythia while Starbuck burns her own corpse on a funeral pyre (4.11). I read these juxtaposed images as also showing the final rejection of the Lords of Kobol by humanity and the embracing (at least occasionally) of the monotheism that Baltar's cult preaches. The destruction of the book of faith and Starbuck's old body demonstrates a transformation of faith and also a new understanding of the divine plan.

As noted in the chapter on Baltar's theology, the blood on the dog tags is confirmed necrotic (taken from a dead body) and is a DNA match to Starbuck (4.18). Baltar believes she is proof of eternal life as well as life after death: "Death is not the end and I'm not talking about Cylon resurrection. I'm talking about the gift of eternal life that is offered to each and every one of us" (4.18). Certainly both her death (she dies in an explosion in her Viper above a planet light-years away, and yet her intact and long-dead body is found on Earth) and her resurrection (she is corporeal, a complete match for her pre-death self in every way, and yet despite her corpse, she is very much alive) are mysteries. There are no explanations. She is dead, yet she lives, most likely because she is part of a divine plan for salvation. She, like Christ, is proof of "eternal life" in her dying and rising.

Starbuck ascends into Heaven at the end of the series. She tells Lee she is not coming back. He asks where she is going. She responds that she does not know, but "feels good" about accomplishing her mission.

Lee turns around and she is gone. Though she has a physical body, it vanishes without a trace. Again, no explanation is given. Starbuck died, Starbuck rose, and apparently, having fulfilled her special destiny in leading humanity to salvation on a New Earth, Starbuck ascended into Heaven.

Resurrection

Starbuck is not the only one resurrected on *BSG*. In fact, *BSG* has a good deal of resurrection going on. The term is used quite frequently on the program as it is the term the Cylons use for "downloading," which is introduced in the miniseries. When nuclear bombs begin falling on Caprica, a panicked Baltar asks Six how she plans to escape. It is indeed a puzzle to the audience as well, as we already saw her die in the opening sequence when the armistice station was destroyed. Six replies, "I can't die. When this body is destroyed, my memory, my consciousness will be transmitted to a new one. I'll just wake up somewhere else in an identical body" (MS). Later, Leoben relates the same concept to Adama in virtually the same language (MS). The Cylons eventually reveal that "resurrection" is "organic memory transfer" (4.15). The bodies are produced by some method that is never made clear, but there is a seemingly infinite number of bodies available for the skinjobs. When one dies, its memory and consciousness, its "I," transfers into one of these bodies.

John Cavil refers to Cylon resurrection as "life everlasting" (4.15). Indeed, it is a form of everlasting life in that one cannot truly die as long as a resurrection hub is nearby. Cylon resurrection, however, is not the same as Christian resurrection or the Christian concept of "life everlasting." The Nicene Creed states, "We look for the resurrection of the dead." Perhaps the different resurrections in *BSG* may aid us in understanding the different resurrections in Christianity.

Clive Marsh offers a list of contemporary questions of eschatology, the first two of which are:

> How is death to be understood? Is physical death the end of
> a person? If not, what happens to a person, given that it is
> clear that the body comes to an end? Does Christianity support
> resurrection or immortality, or try to combine both?
> What can resurrection possibly mean? Why has Christianity
> emphasized resurrection *of the body*?
> What is the link, if any, between belief in the resurrection of
> Jesus Christ and the resurrection of others? Are only believers
> resurrected, or all people? [2007: 146; italics in original].

As Marsh's questions indicate, Christianity believes in bodily resurrection: that we will return from the dead in a physical body. Following Christ's example, we will be resurrected in our own corporeal forms. Resurrection, as Marsh notes, also raises questions of death and life after death.

The Catholic Church distinguishes between three kinds of resurrection: the Earthly resurrection of those brought back from the dead by Christ, the resurrection of Christ himself, and the coming bodily resurrection of all who have ever lived, at the last judgment. In other words, the Bible (and *BSG*) posits both an earthly and a heavenly resurrection — two specifically different experiences.

The first category consists of those who died and were raised from the dead by Christ: Jairus's daughter (Mark 5:21–43; Matthew 9:18–26; Luke 8:40–56), the young man of Naim (Luke 7:11–15), and Lazarus of Bethany (John 11: 1–44). These three individuals died and were "miraculously raised [and] returned by Jesus' power to ordinary earthly life" (*Catechism* 1994: 168). While miraculous, the return from death of these three individuals involved no further bodily change: "ordinary earthly life." They lived awhile longer and still died again. Their second deaths were more permanent. This kind of resurrection is a simple return from death into the same body for a slightly longer period of time. It is this kind of resurrection the Cylons actually experience, no matter how many times they download. Cylons are like Lazarus (in fact, there is a Lazarus motif that runs through the series with the resurrection of the Cylons): they return from death in a physical body, but will someday die permanently.

The second category of resurrection belongs to Christ alone. In the *Catechism of the Catholic Church,* which begins with a systematic study of the Profession of Faith, the statement "on the third day He rose again" refers to an "historic and transcendent event," "a real event, with manifestations that were historically verified" in the New Testament accounts (1994: 166). The tomb was empty, and "the Risen One" appeared upon multiple occasions (Mark 16; Luke 22; Luke 24; John 20; see also 1 Corinthians 15:4–8). This resurrection differs from the first category in that it is both physical and transcendent. The *Catechism* states: "Given all these testimonies, Christ's Resurrection cannot be interpreted as something outside the physical order, and it is impossible not to acknowledge it as an historical fact" (1994: 167). Christ was not a ghost, and, as the episode of Thomas' unbelief in the resurrection demonstrates, the body that returned was the physical, crucified body of Christ: "Unless I see the mark of the nails in his hands, and put my finger in the mark of the nails and my hand in his side, I will not believe," states Thomas, and a week later a physically present Christ invites Thomas to do just that (John 20:24–27). Jesus' resurrection was a physical one.

However, both Paul and the Church acknowledge a difference in this body: it has been transformed. Christ's resurrection was not the same as Jairus's daughter, the young man of Naim or Lazarus of Bethany.

> Christ's Resurrection is essentially different. In his risen body he passes from the state of death to another life beyond time and space. At Jesus' Resurrection his body is filled with the power of the Holy Spirit: he shares the divine life in his glorious state [*Catechism* 1994: 168–169].

Christ's resurrection is transformative. His crucified body is brought back to life, but it is now immortal. His physical body ascends into Heaven "and is seated at the right hand of the Father." Christ's resurrection is both a physical return from death and so much more than a mere physical return from death.

The Church further believes that the resurrection was a "transcendent event" that was "a work of the Holy Trinity" (Catechism 1994: 169). It is part of a divine plan for salvation. Regardless of which theory of salvation one ascribes to, Anselm's ransom theory or other theories of atonement, the resurrection is part of a larger plan to save humanity:

> The Paschal mystery has two aspects: by his death, Christ liberates us from sin; by his Resurrection, he opens for us the way to a new life. This new life is above all justification that reinstates us in God's grace, "so that as Christ was raised from the dead by the glory of the Father, we too might walk in newness of life" (*Catechism* 1994: 171; citing Romans 6:4)

Resurrection is literally the cause and the result of salvation. Because Christ returned from the dead, salvation is possible in a way that would not be so had Christ only died.

The third category of resurrection is eschatological: "The Christian Creed," notes the *Catechism*, "culminates in the proclamation of the resurrection of the dead on the last day and in life everlasting" (1994: 258). This final resurrection of the dead to be judged alongside those still living on the "last day" is a physical one as well. Paul states in 1 Corinthians that the resurrection of the dead is both a fact and physical: "If there is no resurrection of the dead, then Christ has not been raised; and if Christ has not been raised, then our proclamation has been in vain and your faith has been in vain" (15:13–14). In chapter 15, Paul outlines the physical resurrection of the dead: Christ physically came back from the dead, and like Christ, we, too, will physically return from the dead.

In death, the soul is separated from the body; "The human body decays and the soul goes to meet God while awaiting its reunion with its glorified body" (*Catechism* 1994: 260). The glorified body is Paul's explanation for how resurrection works:

> Not all flesh is alike.... There are both heavenly bodies and earthly bodies, but the glory of the heavenly is one thing and that of the earthly is another.... So it is with the resurrection of the dead. What is sown is perishable, what is raised is imperishable.... It is sown a physical body, it is raised a spiritual body.... We will all be changed, in a moment, in the twinkling of an eye, at the last trumpet. For the trumpet will sound, and the dead will be raised imperishable, and we will be changed. For this perishable body must put on imperishability and this mortal body must put on immortality [1 Corinthians 15:39, 40, 42, 51–53].

Three points may be gleaned from Paul's account. The first is that the flesh is resurrected. This is not merely an account of a soul or the spirit; Paul sees the dead being raised physically and "imperishabl[y]." Second, that the flesh is transformed into something more. When we are "resurrected," we come back as more than this body. Though we remain corporeal — located within a physical body — that physical body is "imperishable," "changed" and somehow "spiritual." Third, Paul clearly states that this resurrection of the dead will happen on the "last day."

I have already engaged Paul's first point, that resurrection is physical. The other two points I shall briefly engage here. Resurrection in Paul's view is transformative. It changes one into something more than corporeal human. The very act of coming back from the dead returns one to a previous state, but that state is not the same as it previously was. The act of resurrecting changes us so that we cannot die again.

"The last day" is when resurrection occurs. Resurrection is not an everyday event. Nor is it an individual event (except for Christ). All the dead are resurrected together, at the same time, in accordance with God's will and God's plan. *BSG* gives us two kinds of resurrection: Cylon and Starbuck. It might be easy to see Starbuck as Christ (indeed, I argued so herein) and the Cylons as resurrected Christians. The former schema works on some levels, but the latter does not. Cylon resurrection is not the same as Christian resurrection. Cylon resurrection is individual, into a different body, and is not transformative. It is, as noted, simply an "organic memory transfer." "Downloading" is, in fact, a far better term than "resurrection," inasmuch as the resurrected Cylons have come back to life in a new body. This existence can even be ended if the Cylon is too far from a resurrection hub.

Perhaps it makes more sense to see Cylons as a variation on Lazarus. They are brought back to a finite life that will end again someday. The body is different, albeit an exact replica. They are not transformed by the experience. They are brought back individually. Cylons have no "last day." Cylon resurrection, however, does serve to make us think about the resurrection of the body and how it is achieved and what, in fact, it means.

Lastly, we might note that the Cylons have a Pauline sense of communal resurrection. Sean Freyne, emeritus professor of theology at Trinity College Dublin, sees Paul's understanding of resurrection as communal:

> Paul cannot conceive of the resurrection of one individual without the resurrection of the whole group. Read 1 Corinthians 15 and you see that Paul is doing his damnedest to try to get at the notion of the whole people about to share in the resurrection experience [quoted in Shenks 2010: 47].

In other words, resurrection is not only individual and personal; it is communal. The whole community of believers is resurrected together. There is something of the Cylon resurrection in this idea as well. Although Cylons are "downloaded" into individual bodies exactly like the previous ones, it is both an experience every Cylon will have and an experience that always ends with a group of Cylons surrounding the resurrection bath, so that the "resurrecting" Cylon does not come through the experience alone but awakens in the company of others who complete the experience. Resurrection is communal, in a sense, and when it is not, as when D'Anna Biers repeatedly kills herself and resurrects alone or when Ellen Tigh resurrects after Saul kills her, only to find a single Centurion standing guard over the pool, it is a sign of something horribly wrong.

If There Is No Downloading of the Dead, Then Christ Has Not Been Downloaded...

Starbuck represents a rejection of Anselmian theology and doctrines of atonement or satisfaction. Rather than focusing on her death, *BSG* offers a soteriology from below. In her actions both before and after death, she leads the people to Earth. By her death and resurrection she has gained insights and abilities beyond those of mere mortals, and those who encounter the risen Starbuck have their lives transformed. She is a Christfigure who has been resurrected. Yet it is also everything she does and that happens before her death that is equally important in bringing humanity to salvation.

This linking of Starbuck's life with her resurrection reminds us of the danger of separating Christ's death from his life — kerygmatic Christianity often separates Jesus' life, teachings and mission from his death and resurrection (see Rausch 2003: 111–124; Galvin 1991: 292–314). The ministry of Christ must also be an important part of God's salvific plan. We might be saved by his death and resurrection, but the gospels do not begin and end with those two events. The Incarnation, the ministry and the example of Jesus the historical rabbi take up much more textual space in the gospels than the death and resurrection. They must have been significant to the early Christian community.

Cylon resurrection helps us understand bodily resurrection of the dead but also shows the challenges inherent in using the word "resurrection." What, exactly, is resurrected? What returns from the dead? How am "I" back in a corporeal form — what part of "I" survives death? It also reminds us of the corporeal nature of resurrection. "Life eternal" is not as a spirit or ghost in Pauline Christianity — it is in a resurrected physical body. Lastly, it reminds us that resurrection is not merely an individual event that happens to *me*, but a communal event — something that will happen to *us*.

In the case of both Starbuck and the Cylons, however, resurrection is proof of both of a divine plan and that, as Leoben states, "this is not all there is" (1.08). As Gabriel McKee posted, "The Cylons believe they have souls not *despite* their resurrections, but *because* of them. Their metaphysical ponderings stem from their firsthand mystical experiences of 'downloading' and the bodiless existence that precedes it" (2007b; italics in original) The fact of being resurrected means that there just might be something more than memory transferred. The Cylon who is resurrected is not a replica, is not a duplicate, but *is* the Cylon who died, returned in a new body. Resurrection in any form is a proof of the existence of divinity, the existence of a divine plan, the existence of divine love and the existence of some immortal part of ourselves. The fact of resurrection, as Paul argues, is reason to believe.

The great hope and joy of Christianity are in the fact of the resurrection — Jesus rose from the dead. The resurrection is chronologically the second most important of Christianity (the Incarnation is the first), but it is the center of the Christian faith. In Catholicism, the Profession of Faith ends with the words "we hope for the resurrection of the dead and the life of the world to come." At the end of Christian faith, we believe in the resurrection of Jesus and hope that we, too, might be resurrected.

Again, as I have repeatedly stated, *BSG* is not a metaphor for Christianity, nor is Starbuck Christ. In this chapter I have also shown that Cylon resurrection is not, in fact, what Christianity means by "resurrection" in any sense, although there are some Christian echoes in it. But by reflecting about Christ through the fictional character of Starbuck, we might discover new depths to both. By reflecting about Cylon resurrection, we might better understand what it is when we say we "hope for the resurrection of the dead."

9

Cylon Messiah, Human Judas: Baltar, Betrayal and Redemption

Gaius Baltar is one of the most hated and most interesting figures in the Twelve Colonies. Robert J. Lofts even refers to Baltar as "a great Judas figure" (2008: 30). Similarly, of the Baltar in the original series, James E. Ford refers to him as "a marvelously hateful Judas figure" (1983: 84). David Koepsell sees Baltar as being more like Lucifer or Adam: his "reach exceeds his grasp, and pride leads to the downfall, not just of one person, but all of humanity" (2008: 242). We might further extend this notion to the Baltar-as-Judas concept, in which Judas did not betray just his friend, but all of divinity, leading to his downfall. Yet Koepsell also sees Baltar as "Christlike" (2008: 244). So is Baltar Judas or Christ or both? And what can Baltar tell us about betrayal, redemption and the divine plan?*

Gaius Baltar

"Gaius" is, in fact, a Biblical name as well as a pagan one. Although a common Roman name, and indeed an imperial one as the given name

---

*Interestingly, Richard Berger sees Baltar as John the Baptist, as will be discussed shortly. The original Six, who appears in the opening sequence of the miniseries, asking the human armistice officer if he is alive, gives the officer what Berger calls "a Judas Iscariot-like kiss" (2008: 321). In this configuration, the Cylons are Judas-like, having betrayed humanity, leading to its destruction.

of Julius Caesar, Augustus Caesar and even Caligula, among others, "Gaius" is also the host of Paul in Corinth and "to the whole church" (Romans 16:23; see also 1 Corinthians 1:14); the recipient of the Third Letter of John, "the beloved Gaius, whom I love in truth" (3 John 1); and a Macedonian traveling companion of Paul (Acts 19:29, 20:4). It is thus common, yet imperial; pagan, yet Christian.

Baltar's theology was discussed in chapter 3. In this chapter, however, I discuss Baltar himself as a Judas figure, primarily for the purpose of understanding Judas as much as Baltar. Both are seen as betrayers, villains, and monsters. Both are hated, objects to be despised. Yet, both are also complex figures who, upon closer examination, offer a new way to think about salvation and God's plan.

Baltar has a remarkable arc, as outlined in the third 3. He begins life as the poor son of farmers and rises to become the most famous scientist in the colonies and a personal friend to many people in power. He has access to power, money and women. He indulges in every urge, every vice, every desire. He is an atheist who believes in nothing, not even himself. Behind his arrogant bluster, he is weak, selfish and insecure. His relationship with Six makes him the inadvertent betrayer of humanity.

Afraid his role in the destruction of the Twelve Colonies might be discovered, Baltar becomes a provisional monotheist. He argues with Virtual Six every step of the way, even as she explains God's will to him. She tells him that God protects him. He, instead, argues for coincidence and serendipity. She counters that Dr. Amerak's death is evidence of a divine plan that protects him. He, instead, responds with atheism, saying, "There are no large, invisible men, or women for that matter, in the sky, taking a personal interest in the fortunes of Gaius Baltar" (1.01). And yet, time and again, it is proven to Baltar that there is a divinity that takes a personal interest in Gaius Baltar.

Baltar is further disillusioned when he arrives on Kobol to find that human sacrifice had been practiced by his ancestors, calling the scriptures "a lie" that were written to cover up human savagery (2.02). Although Virtual Six continues to speak to him of God's will and he himself repeatedly sees the evidence of it, Baltar continually returns to atheism. After the settling of New Caprica, he becomes the atheistic president of an occupied people. Although he tries to resist the Cylon occupiers inasmuch as his position and conscience will allow, he becomes the symbol of puppet government that served the Cylons, not the humans. He is captured by the Cylons, tortured, and finally recaptured by the Colonials. He is placed on trial and found not guilty. After his release, he is whisked away by the Baltar cult and becomes their disdainful spiritual leader. Baltar then undergoes the final stage of his transformation: he moves from a self-serving voluptuary into genuine, self-sacrificing servant of the people.

We might see in Baltar the archetype of the reluctant prophet. He does not want to serve God. An angel of God appears to him on an almost constant basis, and yet he does not want the power, authority or responsibility that comes with being an instrument of the divine. Many Biblical prophets resist a call from God — Jonah (Jonah 1:3); Moses (Exodus 3:11, 4:10–17); and Jeremiah (Jeremiah 1:6). Jonah especially is known as a reluctant prophet, attempting to run away from his God-given assignment and ending up sacrificed to God by being thrown in the ocean and swallowed by a "large fish" (1:17). Jonah ends up in Nineveh anyway. Thus, Jonah provides a Biblical model of the prophet who attempts to avoid his prophetic assignment and by attempting to avoid it, actually ends up fulfilling it. Baltar serves as a Jonah figure; every time he attempts to avoid God's plan for him, according to Virtual Six, he ends up fulfilling it anyway.

Ultimately, God's will, according to Six, is that "our child [Hera] shall survive. His will was that she lead the next generation of God's children. His will was that you [Baltar] would protect her" (2.18). Should Baltar fail in this task, she threatens him with "God's vengeance" (2.18). But Baltar succeeds in this role. He helps find Hera, works with the other Colonials to bring humanity to Earth, and fulfills his role as prophet of the one true God and the protector of the blend of human and Cylon.

If all of this has happened before, and "this" refers to the cycle of destruction when humanity and its creations are destroyed by each other, and Hera, as union of Cylon and human, the product of love, represents the salvation of both human and Cylon, but only if she is brought to the new Earth, then Baltar is a necessary part of that plan and a necessary part of salvation.

Baltar, shot and bleeding to death, tells Laura Roslin that he was the one who gave the Cylons the codes that allowed them to defeat the Colonial defense forces and destroy humanity. He believes, in the end, that God has "rewarded" him for doing so. Baltar has also clearly excused himself. He compares himself with a flood, arguing that a flood is destructive and brings about death, but it also brings about rejuvenation.

The flood was made by God, and thus the flood itself is not blamed. Baltar justifies everything he has done by seeing himself as a force of nature a tool of God whose actions have had both positive and negative results, but of which he himself is blameless (4.09). Though Baltar himself attempts to justify his own actions, comparing himself to a flood, he is incorrect. He is not "a force of nature" but a human being who made a series of choices and carried out a series of actions. Yet, his guilt may be mitigated (and certainly assuaged) by the fact that his opening of the Colonial defenses was not only inadvertent (although certainly unwise and the product of his own weaknesses) but also was ultimately part of a divine plan.

Judas Iscariot

Judas represents the great challenges to Christianity, as well as forming the locus of all the issues that the followers of Christ must confront. The story of Judas concerns salvation, freedom, guilt, justice, sin, repentance and redemption. If Judas, one of the 12, an intimate friend and follower of Jesus, can betray him, what hope is there for the rest of us? If Judas can be saved, which of us cannot be? Judas is a central figure in the Christ event but is not even mentioned in the earliest sources. Thus, he is a figure of ambiguity and a screen upon which we may project our darkest fears, ugliest beliefs and greatest hopes. If he is needed to hand Jesus over so that He may be offered up for our sins, is it really better that "he had never been born"? Is not his birth therefore as necessary as Christ's?

Augustine, after all, in his *Sermons,* argues:

> Mark then, holy brethren, the usefulness of heretics; their usefulness, that is, in respect of the designs of God, who makes a good use even of those that are bad; whereas, as regards themselves, the fruit of their own designs is rendered to them, and not that good which God brings out of them. Just as in the case of Judas; what great good did he! By the Lord's Passion all nations are saved; but that the Lord might suffer, Judas betrayed Him [2007: 320].

God brings good out of evil, regardless of the intent of the evildoer. God uses "heretics" in order to carry out his plan, and Judas is, arguably, the greatest of all heretics: he knew Jesus was the Christ and yet betrayed him.

Judas, even within Christianity, is a complex figure whose name is synonymous with betrayal and damnation, but whose character and actions differ from Gospel to Gospel, as will be outlined below. The Judas of the popular imagination and as represented in popular culture is a composite Judas, consisting of not only the (rather limited) Gospel tradition, but also a built-up history of anti-Semitism, folk legends, and theological transformations. The first instinct among scholars studying Judas seems to be to outline the different ways of viewing and understanding Judas. Here are some sample taxonomies that scholars have outlined:

Bertil Gärtner, the Bishop of Gothenburg, Sweden, surveyed Judas in the New Testament and the writings of the early church fathers in *Iscariot* (1971), originally published in German. He sees four ways of understanding Judas:

1. Judas as greedy (vi).
2. Judas as sinner (vi).
3. Judas as hero (vi).
4. Judas as legendary figure (vi).

The first two are explanations of Judas' motivation, whereas the last two are means of understanding the actions of Judas in context. As noted later in the chapter, the motive for Baltar's actions and the larger context of his actions will also aid us in understanding both him and Judas.

William Klassen, in *Judas: Betrayer or Friend of Jesus* (1996), sees five different means of understanding Judas:

1. Judas as evil incarnate (4).
2. Judas as "instrument of salvation" (6).
3. Judas as Jew (6).
4. Judas as follower of Jesus (6).
5. Judas as informer (6).

Klassen sees Judas as fulfilling possibly contradictory roles in God's salvific plan: evil incarnate (i.e. the enemy of and opposite of God) and "instrument of salvation." It is the latter which will be of use in understanding Baltar and Judas and Baltar *as* Judas. It is also rooted in Augustine's view of God's use of Judas and other heretics. In this view, Judas is not excused from his evil acts, which he still intended as evil, but rather that his acts were necessary for salvation.

Kim Paffenroth, in *Judas: Images of the Lost Disciple* (2001) offers six ways of viewing Judas:

1. Judas the Archsinner / object of horror (2001: 17).
2. Judas the villain (2001: 33).
3. Judas the tragic hero (2001: 59).
4. Judas the misunderstood revolutionary and patriot (2001: 82).
5. Judas the anti-revolutionary (2001: 92)
6. Judas the penitent. (2001: 111)

Paffenroth's study is actually a survey of the historic constructions of Judas, from the first century through the present, everything from Gospel to rock opera. Like Judas, Baltar is also constructed as multifaceted: he is villain, tragic hero, revolutionary and a penitent.

An alternate understanding of Judas may be found in Anthony Cane's *The Place of Judas Iscariot in Christology* (2005). Rather than examining how Judas has been constructed throughout history, as Gärtner, Klassen and Paffenroth do, Cane asks four key questions about Judas' role in the death of Jesus and what Judas means theologically:

1. Is Judas a defeat for Jesus (10)?
2. What is the significance of *paradidonai* (10)?
3. What is the status of Judas's death and repentance (10)?
4. Can Judas be saved (10)?

Cane sees Judas as an opportunity to ask ourselves about Judas' place in the larger schema of Christianity. If Jesus needed to die in order to be resurrected and provide humanity with salvation, someone needed to "hand him over" (*paradidonai*) to the authorities. In Matthew, Judas repents and attempts to return the money. All of this leads to the larger question: what happens to Judas after his death? As one of the 12, as a follower and believer in Christ, as one who played a necessary role in the divine plan for Christ, albeit a distasteful one, and as one who regretted having to play that role, can there be salvation for Judas? As the very title of Cane's book suggests, what we think about Judas tells us much about what we think about Christ.

Marvin Meyer, in *Judas: The Definitive Collection of Gospels and Legends About the Infamous Apostle of Jesus* (2007), one of many volumes to be released in the wake of the discovery and publication of the *Gospel of Judas,* breaks down four models for understanding Judas:

1. Judas as diabolical/personification of evil (3–5; 109–138).
2. Judas as Jew (20).
3. Judas as "supreme example of impiety" or unbeliever (115).
4. Judas as "fictional character" (19).

Although Baltar cannot be seen as Jewish, and he already is a fictional character, he certainly is repeatedly cast in the series as diabolical. During his trial he is cast as the personification of evil. His continued return to atheism might allow us to see Baltar as an unbeliever, in the manner of Judas. Virtual Six warns Baltar again and again of the dangers of impiety, disbelief and blasphemy. Baltar/Judas's great sin may be in not believing in the divine plan.

Like Baltar, Judas was confronted repeatedly and daily with the evidence of divinity in his presence. Like Baltar, Judas was made aware of a divine plan and his role in it. One might see Judas as rejecting that divinity and perhaps even not believing it. Either Judas thought Jesus was God, in which case he is a God killer, or he thought Jesus was not God, in which case he is the greatest and most willful unbeliever in history. Baltar, spoken to daily by Virtual Six, has all the evidence of a divine plan at work in front of him. So he is a God- denier in every sense of the word: either he denies to do what God has asked him to or he denies the very existence of God. Either way, Judas and Baltar are unbelievers and therefore the opposite of the believer.

The recently discovered *The Gospel of Judas* (Rodolphe Kasser, Marvin Meyer, and Gregor Wurst 2006) offers a second-century view of the betrayer in the form of a Gnostic gospel:*

1. Judas as Gnostic.
2. Judas as antihero.
3. Judas as the only disciple who understands.
4. Judas as "daimon" (translated as "spirit," "god" or "demon").

If we take a Gnostic look at Baltar as well, we see a man dedicated to knowledge. He is, after all, a scientist and a very learned and cultured

---

*While the Kasser, Meyer and Wurst translation was the first to be published, to great fanfare in the popular media, two additional translations have been published since with substantial variations and interpretations: Karen King's 2007 translation (in Pagels and King 2007) and April D. DeConick's 2007 translation, in which she sees Judas not as the hero or a Gnostic but rather evil. In her translation the Gospel of Judas is "a mid-second-century Gnostic parody of Judas and his story [is] a parody that pokes fun at traditional Christian doctrines and practices" (2007: 61).

man. He has knowledge not available to the masses. He knows and understands things that the common mob cannot. He also is spoken to by God and recognizes the false religion of his fellow humans. There is a very Gnostic element to Baltar. He is certainly the first and originally the only human to believe in the one true God. The very words "one true God" indicate the existence of (or at least some people's beliefs in) a false god or false gods. Judas is able to pierce the veil of reality and discern the true, distant god.

The scrolls of Pythia are proven true, but that is only because they are of this world, created by false and flawed beings. The one true God, once discerned, leads Baltar to be a part of the much greater and far more real plan for salvation. He is able to use his knowledge to lead a very small group (less than 40,000 people) to salvation. Baltar, like Judas in the *Gospel of Judas*, is a Gnostic antihero.

What might be gleaned by consulting these lists is a multi-faceted Judas who is perceived in numerous manners and the perception of whom has been transformed through time. The terms that repeat include "hero," "evil," "sinner," and "Jew." Considering the more recent understanding of Judas, the recurring theme is Judas as "revolutionary" and "antihero." I would argue these two latter conceptions are not possible until the modern era.

The Gospel tradition sees Judas "in increasingly negative terms" (Paffenroth 2001: 68). Concomitant with this increasing negativity is the increase in the significance of Judas's actions and the depth of his betrayal, rising in direct proportion to the transformation in early Christology. Or, to put it another way, as Jesus was promoted, so was Judas. The earliest Christian testament, that of Paul, states once, in 1 Corinthians, that Jesus was betrayed, but no betrayer was mentioned. Interestingly, in Galatians, Paul states Christ handed himself over, and in Romans that God handed Him over, thus rendering the need for a betrayer moot. The same term used for Judas's action, *paradidonai,* Paul also uses for Christ's actions in Galatians and God's in Romans. We would not say Christ betrayed himself or God betrayed Christ. The term used here means "handed over." Judas is never mentioned by name in Paul, is not present in Q (the source text of Matthew and Luke), and is clearly not important as a figure in the early Christian community.

In Mark, Judas is mentioned only three times and with no derogatory statements about his person. Instead, he is identified with the action verb *paradidonai,* to hand over, which is frequently translated into

English as "betrayed," although it appears in numerous other Gospel contexts to mean literally handing over, not betrayal in the modern sense. Mark's Judas is not evil; he is, at best, a plot device.

In Matthew Judas is mentioned in six passages, again cited as "the one who betrayed Him" (10:4). Judas is a much more active figure in Matthew with specific details about the actions: betraying Jesus for 30 pieces of silver (26:14–17), denying his betrayal at the Last Supper (26:20–25), and bringing "a large crowd" to the garden to arrest Jesus (26:47–50). Interestingly, in Matthew, Judas also repents and hangs himself (27:3–10). Matthew's Judas is more complex, more human than Mark's. But he is still human.

Luke, by contrast, ontologically promotes Judas in his state as betrayer: Satan himself enters Judas (22:3–6). Dramaturgically, this addition makes sense, as it keeps Jesus and his opponent Judas on an equal scale. It also transforms the action of Judas from an intragroup conflict/betrayal to a cosmological battle between good and evil. Mark's Judas betrayed his master and teacher; Luke's Judas is a tool of the embodiment of evil out to destroy God's plan. As a gospel written for gentiles, whose own cosmologies were rooted in dualism and the battle between different spiritual beings, this version is more comprehensible and appealing. Also, if Jesus is the messiah then he should have known that one of his own would betray him and Jesus would be lessened by his ignorance of betrayal. By increasing the stakes of the battle to that of the cosmological, Luke renders Judas as the tool of Satan, not guilty in and of himself, but a more worthy adversary for the messiah.

John completes the transformation of both Judas and his action. Just as Jesus is the Incarnate word who has been since the beginning, Judas is the embodiment of evil from the very beginning. John's Judas is "a devil" who is petty, selfish, greedy, and "a son of perdition" (6:71, 17:12). John's Judas is bad from birth. He does not decide to betray Jesus; he was born to do so; it is his sole purpose. Just as Jesus was born to provide salvation for all humankind, Judas was born to betray Jesus. Satan was in Judas from the moment of his birth — as Jesus is the word Incarnate, we might see Judas as evil incarnate. As Paffenroth states, "a cosmic, demonic opponent is theologically necessary for John" (2001: 33). This Judas is no longer human but a Satanic adversary.

Klassen, like Paffenroth, notes "a progressively degenerating trend in which he is portrayed in increasingly negative terms" (1996: 11). This trend grows more pronounced in the early Church after the gospels are written. Later Church fathers would read back into the Gospels this more negative view of Judas. For example, although Judas's death in Matthew follows his repentance, Augustine reads Judas's suicide as increasing the guilt of his betrayal — his self-slaughter is an indictment of the depth of his betrayal.

With the rise of the Church, Judas continues to fall, so to speak, not only in relation to Christ but in relation to the other figures from the Gospel narratives. As Peter rises and becomes the rock upon which a Church is built, Judas is not only an anti–Christ, he is also an anti–Peter. In Mark, all disciples are seen as not understanding Jesus, and Peter is singled out as being particularly clueless. In Matthew, Peter is "the rock on which I build my church," while Judas is "the one who betrayed him." Judas was slowly constructed as all things anti–Christian and all things anti-disciple.

In the second century this correspondence will also be shared by the Gnostic author of *The Gospel of Judas* who also holds Peter and the orthodox disciples up for ridicule, while Judas is presented as being the disciple who understood. Different scholars have interpreted this gospel as displaying Judas in either positive or negative ways, but at heart Judas is still maintained to be the opposite of the orthodox disciples in general and Peter in particular. As will be outlined herein, the writings of the church fathers transformed Judas into the archetypal betrayer and the model for those who would betray their fellow Christians. Polycarp, Augustine, and Ireneaus all offer Judas as a negative model.

By the fourth century, Mary is deemed *Theotokos,* "Mother of God," thus completing the transformation from low Christology to high Christology as the Church developed. Jesus is the incarnation of God, Mary is the mother of God, and thus Judas is the betrayer of God. Between the first Gospel and the Council of Nicea we can see an evolution of Judas from misguided disciple to evil incarnate, the opposite of Jesus, Peter and Mary. Interestingly, in the eighteenth and nineteenth centuries, the search for the historic Jesus resulted in a parallel search for the historic Judas. In a sense, the Judas of each period is reflective of the Jesus of each period as well as that culture's attitude toward Christianity.

By comparing Judas and Baltar, we might see similarities in their characters and circumstances and how they are understood so that we might better understand both. I have already discussed Baltar as a form of Judas as "supreme example of impiety" or unbeliever (Meyer 2007: 115). I have also noted that Baltar might be seen as the model of Judas as "instrument of salvation" that begins with the sermons of Augustine (Klassen 1996: 6; Augustine 2007). Next I would like to discuss Baltar as the one who "handed over" humanity, which is, in fact, a variation on the "instrument of salvation" model.

Cylon paradidonai

As Baltar is perceived as having betrayed humanity and handed them over to the Cylons, so the defining characteristic of Judas in Christianity is betrayal. Augustine refers to Judas as "the traitor" and states that Donatists are "imitating Judas." *The Martyrdom of Polycarp* compares a slave who betrays Polycarp to Judas. In *Inferno*, the first book of his *Divine Comedy*, Dante places Judas in Satan's central mouth in the ninth level of hell, reserved for the worst of traitors. But does the term "betrayal" accurately reflect what happens in the gospel accounts?

The word repeatedly used in the Gospels to describe Judas's action is *paradidonai*, which is translated as "betray." But the word is more ambiguous than is presented historically. Klassen perceives in the Gospels that when *paradidonai* is used and Judas's name is not, the term is not translated as "betray" but as "handing over" (1996: 54). Conversely, Judas is never mentioned in the New Testament without mentioning the betrayal, again employing this same term: *paradidonai*.

As noted previously, Paul uses the term only once to refer to an unnamed person who "handed over" Jesus to the Romans. In two other letters the word is used in relation to Jesus himself in one case ("who handed himself over for me" [Galatians 2:19–20]) and to God in the other ("He who did not withhold his own Son, but handed him over for all of us" [Romans 8:31–32]). One would not say God "did not withhold his own Son, but betrayed him for all of us," or that Christ "betrayed himself for me." In other words, the use of *paradidonai* does not automatically imply betrayal. And, in fact, in the Gospels the word itself is used repeatedly (and sometimes literally) to indicate a transfer. Pilate "hands Christ over" to soldiers be whipped and then crucified, but we would not say Pilate "betrayed" Jesus.

Might we not see Judas's action in the same way? While betrayal satisfies the narrative much more and is better for the action, story and character, it does not reflect the more complex reality of what Judas did in handing Christ over. Judas handed Christ to the temple authorities by telling them where He would be at a time when there would not be crowds around, and Judas himself agreed to help identify Jesus. As others have indicated, Jesus told Judas to go do it and to do it quickly. It would seem that if there was a betrayal of any kind, it was not a secret one and Jesus was in on it.

Similarly, Baltar "hands humanity over" to the Cylons, but he does not intend the destruction of the human race when he does so. What he actually does is hand over the security codes of the Colonial defenses to his lover who happens to be a Cylon agent. Baltar in this sense is a dupe, not a traitor; what he does is actually part of a larger plan, but it is not his plan. His petty actions carry out the plans of others. Judas is part of a larger plan. No betrayal, no crucifixion. No crucifixion, no salvation. Baltar sets in motion a series of events that will also change the world and provide salvation. No Baltar, no journey to Earth. No journey to Earth, no salvation. Baltar and Judas, flawed and fallen men, set the plan in motion. No Judas, no resurrection. No Baltar, no Earth. No betrayer, no salvation.

One might even perceive Judas as being saved as well. There might be not only redemption and salvation but glorification for the one who handed Christ over. Matthew writes:

> Truly, I tell you, at the renewal of all things, when the Son of Man is seated at the throne of his glory, you who have followed me will also sit on the twelve thrones, judging the twelve tribes of Israel [19:28].

This passage is echoed in Luke 22:28–30, and is originally from Q. Judas Iscariot is present for this promise. Judas appears to be included in this assurance. If we take Jesus' statement at face value and do not claim that he is speaking of a metaphoric 12, as if this applies to Matthias who was elected to replace Judas, there is a place for the betrayer in the Kingdom of God among the elite. Likewise, Revelation 21 tells us that in the New Jerusalem, the eternal city of the saved, the names of the 12 apostles (presumably including Judas) are written on the walls of the city (21:14). In short, these passages seem to suggest Judas is redeemed.

Similarly, Baltar, accidental betrayer of humankind, is "the guardian and protector of the new generation of God's children" (1.13). Despised after his trial, he rises again in the fleet to become (literally) a prophetic voice whose sermons transmitted by wireless are listened to by thousands of people, including the admiral and the president. He converts many from polytheism to monotheism and becomes a voice for justice and the poor among the fleet. Angels speak to him. He survives to reach Earth and is rewarded for his actions by reuniting in love with Six. When last we see them, they are planning on being a family of farmers on Earth.

Examining Baltar in comparison with Judas might just make us rethink Judas. Rethinking Judas means rethinking Christ and rethinking Christianity. As Herbert Krosney wrote in his history of the discovery and sale of *The Gospel of Judas,* "What was it Judas betrayed?" (2006: 48). While Judas's name is synonymous with betrayal, that betrayal may be seen in a new light by scholars. I find a certain comfort in Klassen's observation that "because the Church has focused so much on the perceived evil of Judas, it has lost sight of the marvelous saving grace of God at work even in him" (1996: 51). Likewise, he later notes that there is no evidence that Judas was anything but "a valued member of the Jesus community" who fully participated in the foot washing and Last Supper (1996: 202). Klassen concludes that the task of "handing over" is "God-centered, God-initiated and God-directed," and perhaps should not be perceived in the simplistic terms that the word "betrayal" implies (1996: 202).

We might also note the ambiguity of Judas. He is procrustean, able to be transformed to meet the needs of whoever is telling his story. From anti-Semitic medieval narratives to early-seventies rock operas, Judas can be transformed to fit. As such, he is an ambiguous figure. In the end, we do not even know who he is, what he is, what he really did or why he did it. We have numerous theories about the meaning of his name "Iscariot," but nothing certain. Judas can be several things and several people at once. Likewise, the variety of translations and interpretations of *The Gospel of Judas* indicate the ambiguity of the figure and the manner in which he can be stretched to conform to opposing interpretation simultaneously. Depending on whom one asks, the Judas of the gospel is either the hero or the villain, the one who understands Christ and will save him or the one who will mistakenly try to destroy him.

Baltar, like Judas, is also one of the most interesting characters in his narrative. John Parker, in writing of the representation of Judas in medieval drama, observes: "Judas' historic role in human salvation especially conveyed the potential of theater since his fallen devotion had greater and better consequences than the other disciples' authentic belief" (2007: 113). Judas is more interesting to watch because of his fallen nature (which is what we learn from *Paradise Lost:* Satan, like all bad boys, is far more interesting than Christ, who is too good and perfect to be of much interest). His fall, however, not only makes for good drama; it allows the very mechanism of salvation to occur. As Parker argues: "In projecting a false image of piety, Judas inadvertently produced a form of dissimulation that spoke more truly than his actual debased motives or the others' comparatively impotent loyalty" (2007: 113). In other words, Judas, in his iniquity, did far more for salvation than the apostles who did not "hand over" Christ. Similarly, Baltar does more to help bring about God's will and salvation than Tigh, Adama or Apollo. The great irony of *BSG* (and the Bible) is that the betrayer is inadvertently more faithful to God's plan than those who are genuinely faithful.

Likewise, Baltar is a sinner. His ego, his instinct for self-preservation, his commitment to epicurean and voluptuary experiences, and his cowardice make him a pathetic and contemptible (if highly entertaining) figure in *BSG*. Baltar is not evil. He is weak; he is selfish; he thinks only of his own pleasure and power; he commits numerous sins, including an almost pathological need to lie. Yet time and again, God moves through Baltar to preserve the human race, lead them to Earth and set the stage for something bigger than he was. Baltar, like Judas, is part of a plan. Like the Judas of scriptures, he is not evil but commits evil acts that eventually lead to salvation for all.

10

From Patmos to Caprica: Battlestar Apocalyptica

> *Now the Lord is about to lay waste to the earth*
> *and make it desolate, and he will twist its surface*
> *and scatter its inhabitants.*
>> Isaiah 24:1

>> *The end times are approaching.*
>> *Humanity's final chapter is about to*
>> *be written. And you will be its author.*
>>> Virtual Six to Baltar [4.19]

> *I was in the spirit on the Lord's day, and*
> *I heard behind me a loud voice like a trumpet*
> *saying, "Write in a book what you see and*
> *send it to the seven churches."*
>> Revelation 1:10–11

As I noted in chapter 5, *Battlestar Galactica* begins with an ending and ends with a beginning, much like the book of Revelation. First and foremost, *Battlestar Galactica* is an apocalyptic text. "Apocalypse," of course, means "hidden things revealed." Apocalyptic texts feature an otherworldly journey or a vision. Oftentimes these journeys or visions are also eschatological and show the traveler/viewer the end times. In Christianity, especially in popular culture, apocalypse has become fully conflated with the eschaton. "The Apocalypse" refers not to the revelation of the end but the end itself now. *BSG* is an apocalyptic text in both senses: it is a vision of an otherworldly journey (quite literally), but it is also an exploration of the actual end of the world (12 worlds, actually) and the beginning of a new one. As Hans Schwartz observes, eschato-logical time is "a time of crisis" and "a time of salvation" (2000: 27). *BSG* is set in a time of crisis *and* a time of salvation.

BSG also appropriates the language of Christian eschatology. Virtual Six refers to the arrival of the Cylons on New Caprica as "judgment day" (2.20). In *Razor,* Kendra is warned by the Hybrid that Starbuck is "the herald of the apocalypse, the harbinger of death" and that humanity must not follow her (R). Not only is the use of the specific word "apoc-alypse" a link to Christian theology, but it is also an example of the mis-understanding of the apocalypse in the popular imagination and in speculative fiction. And the apocalypse does have its harbingers. Jesus warns of the desolating sacrilege and the coming of the Son of Man and notes: "From the fig tree learn its lesson: as soon as its branch becomes tender and puts forth its leaves, you know that summer is near. So also, when you see all these things, you know that he is near, at the very gates" (Matthew 24:32–33). Kara Thrace is the one who will bring about the end. Lest this lead us to see her as a potentially evil character, let us remember "the end" is part of a divine plan and furthermore will have both good and evil characters serving as harbingers. Should we choose to take Revelation literally, the two beasts, the Whore of Babylon, and the dragon are all harbingers of the end; but so are the two witnesses and the many angels of the Lord and Christ himself. Apocalypse has many harbingers. The important thing to note is *BSG*'s use of Christian apocalyptic terminology.

The mere existence of the Cylons is apocalyptic from an evangelical point of view. As Amy Johnson Frykholm observes in her sociological study of readers of the *Left Behind* series, "Rapture fiction has long por-trayed technology as the devil's work" (2004: 124). Technology is a "sign of the times," and "fear of technology" is a natural part of American apocalyptic imagination (2004: 126). Even outside of evangelical culture, technology is seen as inherently apocalyptic. As will be discussed in this chapter, films such as *The Matrix,* the *Terminator* series, and *Star Trek: First Contact* see technology as dangerous and used to bring about an apocalyptic end to humanity. *BSG* embodies this trope as well: technol-ogy will bring about a series of apocalypses.

Likewise, if literal readings of Revelation are anti-modernist, and afraid of technology, then *BSG* offers an apocalypse caused by technology that ends with the destruction of that technology. In the last episode of the series, "Daybreak," the Colonials agree to give up all their technology, set their ships on autopilot to fly into the sun, and integrate with the humanoid bipeds that have evolved on the planet they have found. They literally agree to become "cavemen." On the promised New Earth, there will be no robots, no spaceships, and no technology whatsoever. As part of the sweeping away of the old ways, the old tools must also be destroyed. The outright rejection of all technology is part of the promised salvation that God offers in *BSG*.

BSG is also an apocalyptic text in that it follows the narrative structure of the end according to Revelation. Bernard McGinn outlines the "three-act historical drama" that forms the shape of apocalyptic narratives, *BSG* included: "present trial, imminent judgment, and future salvation" (1979: 6). The trial need not even be an actual crisis. Adela Yarbro Collins asserts that the Book of Revelation was written in response to a *perceived* crisis or "relative deprivation" (1984: 106). In the case of *BSG*, the crisis is real enough (the Twelve Colonies are, in fact, nuked, and all but a handful of humans die). This makes *BSG* both an apocalyptic text and an eschatological one. Eschatology is concerned with endings on both the micro (my death) and macro (the end of the world) levels. The crisis is thus individual and communal.

As Adela Yarbro Collins observes, Revelation is a text for a community in crisis. John of Patmos writes at least as a person who imagines he is being persecuted, if not actually persecuted. His is a narrative of a small number of faithful being saved by God while his enemies perish at the hands of God. Truth be told, in that sense, *BSG* has a good deal in common with *Left Behind:* the small number of chosen are separated out and spared the apocalypse by being "in the air" (in spaceships in *BSG*, raptured in *Left Behind*). The minions of evil have reign over the earth while small pockets of resisters remain left behind, waging war on the evil forces (Sam Anders and his group in *BSG*, the Tribulation Force in *Left Behind*). Anders and the Caprica Buccaneers (the pyramid team training in the hills above Caprica City when the Cylon attack comes), hide in the mountains, among the caves, following Revelation: "Then the kings of the earth and the magnates and the generals and the rich and the powerful, and everyone, slave and free, hid in the caves and among the rocks of the mountains" (6:15). The human resistance on Caprica is literally left behind by the fleet.

In the second season, a small group of humans returns to rescue those left behind. Once the entire fleet has gathered, President Roslin begins keeping track of the number of humans left, a number given at the beginning of each episode. When survivors are found or children born, the number goes up. This is rare. Far more often, when people die or are lost, the number goes down. The series begins with approximately 50,000 surviving humans. Less than half that make it to the New Earth. So even within the small group saved, not all are saved to the end. The last element is the key, for my purposes here: once the crisis has come, after judgment comes salvation. At heart, apocalypse is also a salvific genre. Hans Schwartz reminds us that the Hebrew Bible is more concerned with the destiny of the nation than the individual (2000: 35); and Revelation is a return to that concern: the salvation of the nation, not the individual. It is God's people who must be collectively saved, even if individuals are not.

BSG might also be seen to echo Revelation's understanding of the eschaton as an event of unimaginable physical devastation. Tina Pippin observes, "The apocalypse is to occur by mass murder and destruction; whatever it takes" (1999: 28).* Revelation, like BSG, concerns planetary destruction: When the sixth seal is opened, "there came a great earthquake; the sun became black as sackcloth, the full moon became like blood, and the stars of the sky fell to earth as the fig tree drops its winter fruit when shaken by a gale. The sky vanished like a scroll rolling itself up, and every mountain and island was removed from its place" (Rev. 6:12–14). The trumpets in chapters eight and nine further planetary destruction: "a third of the earth was burned up" (8:7), a third of the sea is destroyed and everything living in it dies (8:9), a star called "Wormwood" falls from the sky and a third of the waters are made deadly (8:10–11), a third of the sun, moon and stars are destroyed (8:12), and a third of humanity is destroyed by plagues supervised by three angels (9:14–20). By the end of Revelation, the entire earth and the heavens have "passed away" (21:1). The entire planet, after being ravaged by war, disease and Satan, is finally destroyed. Unlike the realized eschatology of the Catholic Church, BSG follows a more literal, dare I say fundamentalist, understanding of the end of the world: the physical worlds actually end and are destroyed on a planetary scale. This aspect places BSG well within the tradition of speculative apocalypses.

---

*Interestingly, given my argument herein that the book of Revelation is itself speculative fiction, and that the only way to present Revelation in the cinema is through speculative fiction, Tina Pippin uses Rosemary Jackson's seminal text *Fantasy: The Literature of Subversion* to analyze Revelation (1999: 9-11).

Speculative Fiction and the Apocalypse

In *Imaging the Divine: Jesus and Christ-Figures in Film,* Lloyd Baugh (1997) contrasts the "Jesus film"—films about the historic Jesus such as *King of Kings* or *The Greatest Story Ever Told*—and the "Christ movie"—which concerns fictional or historical figures that evince characteristics of a Christ-figure. The speculative cinema Christ is also significantly different from the Christs of Jesus films or even of non-speculative Christ figure films. Speaking of American Jesus movies, Stephenson Humphries-Brooks maintains:

> Hollywood has been happy to give us Jesus as the Christ who descends from the heavens, gathers disciples, teaches, works miracles, is betrayed, suffers unjustly at the hands of religious and political authorities, is crucified, dies and is buried and resurrected to ascend to the heavens. It has not given us Jesus as the Warrior Lamb of God who returns to gather his elect and vanquish the evil forces that oppose him [2006: 115].

But Hollywood has given us the Warrior Lamb of God—just not in Jesus films. Paradoxically, if one considers science fiction / horror cinema and the book of Revelation, there is a huge number of genre films that deal with eschatology with the trappings of Christianity while ignoring both Christ and theology. In films such as *The Omen, Bless the Child, Rosemary's Baby, End of Days,* and *The First Power,* the end of the world as described in Revelation is coming about but not because of God or Christ. In all these films, Satan and his earthly minions are attempting to bring about the end of the world and a confrontation with the forces of good. At best, God is absent or will allow it out of disinterest. It is through the efforts of a few dedicated individuals that Armageddon is prevented and the devil defeated. These films posit a resurrected but uninvolved Christ with no Second Coming.*

---

*We might also note that fundamentalist-Christian-created films based on the Book of Revelation such as the *Left Behind* films or *The Omega Code* also present the warrior-lamb Christ. Such films also use the tropes and visuals of speculative fiction cinema to depict the events of the apocalypse. Both Christian films and secular films envision an apocalypse that needs many special and digital effects. The secular apocalypse films use the language of apocalypse and Revelation, but the actual narratives are much closer to the narrative of Abraham and God in Genesis 18:16-33, in which Abraham and God bargain over what Abraham must do in order to prevent God from destroying Sodom and Gomorrah.

Revelation with Christ is seen not in horror films based on the Book of Revelation but in science-fiction and speculative cinema in which a Christ figure brings judgment and vengeance to those who have done wrong. The speculative Christ figure is a judge, a prophet of the end, a bearer of justice and a "Warrior Lamb of God" in Humphries-Brooks' sense. John Cole, John Connor, John Constantine, and even Superman are Christ figures from Revelation. They may embody Baugh's motifs, but they add another: the prophetic and judging savior who will gather the elite and allow the rest to die in fire and flame. *BSG* will show us a set of elites being brought through the end of the world as we know it and the literal creation of a new Heaven and a new Earth.

For example, Ortiz and Roux see a prophetic role in such films as the *Terminator* series. They city the title of the second film, *Judgment Day,* as linking it to Malachi 3 and 4, which warns of "The Day of Judgment" (although Malachi 4 actually refers to it as "the great and terrible day of the Lord" [4:5]) (1997: 141). They further note that the *Terminator* films link to the prophetic voices of Isaiah, Ezekiel, and Jeremiah (1997: 141–2), a claim that remains unproven in their article. I would argue that given the larger narrative of the *Terminator* films, we might link them not with Hebrew Bible prophets but with the prophetic voice that closes the New Testament: John of Patmos, who also envisions a judgment day (Rev. 20:11–15). As noted shortly, the narrative of John Connor is clearly meant to indicate that he is a Christ figure. But it is not the Prince of Peace or the logos or the innocent martyr that John Connor embodies; he is the Christ of Revelation — he brings not peace, but a sword, with machines as the demonic and Satanic enemies of God.

James Cole in *12 Monkeys* is an apocalyptic Christ figure. First, his initials figure him as a descendent of Christ. Next, he lives in the end times — a virus has driven humanity underground and he is sent back in time by the government to find how the virus started and to stop it. The individuals who send him back refer to him as "The One." While the audience is never certain if he is really experiencing these events or if he is in a mental institution and they are all in his head, he decides the only way to save humanity is to allow himself to be killed while trying to stop the individual who started the plague. He suffers, bleeds, dies and is reborn as his younger self in front of himself. And yet we know by the film's end that his actions will not save humanity. The plague is released, and the cycle starts again — the eternal return that is seen in *The Matrix* and *BSG:* all this has happened before, and all this will happen again.

Likewise, Neo in the *Matrix* trilogy is referred to as "The One." He is resurrected after his first death by a woman named "Trinity." He learns the true nature of reality and becomes a savior of humankind. By the final film, he is fighting with a small band of his followers to protect a community called "Zion." In addition to many of the Christ-figure attributes from Baugh, noted previously, the language surrounding Neo is Biblical and designed to evoke him as both savior and Christ figure. Keanu Reeves plays Neo as an unassuming young man who grows into not only a prophet but an apocalyptic warrior-priest who dies saving humanity.

John Constantine (J.C., again) in *Constantine*, also played by Keanu Reeves, is another apocalyptic speculative Christ figure. Based on the graphic novel *Hellblazer, Constantine* opens with the title character exorcizing a demon from a young girl. He heals the sick. He converses with devils and demons and angels. He works wonders, has a disciple (Chas), is in conflict with the authorities, and then, when it appears that demons will be unleashed upon humanity, he offers himself up as a sacrifice to go to hell to stop the apocalypse. Because his death would transform the nature of reality, he is resurrected and allowed to live. He dies by cutting his wrists (a form of cinematic stigmata, especially post–*Last Temptation**). He promises to return to those whom he has saved when they need him. In a film that accepts the existence of demons, the other miracles are easily accepted as well.

Another speculative Christ can be found in the *Terminator* series. John Connor (there are those initials again) is born to be the savior of humankind. His birth is a miracle: he himself sent his father, Kyle Reese, back through time to impregnate his mother so that he could be born (there are suggestions of the Gospel of John here: Jesus as God who then causes himself to be born of woman). His birth is announced to his mother by Reese, who also serves as Gabriel and Joseph. Connor is referred to several times as "the savior," and he is involved from the moment of his birth in a cosmic struggle of good (human) versus evil (machine). Not to put too fine a point on it, the second film in the series is called *Judgment Day* and the fourth, *Terminator: Salvation*.

---

*Stigmata usually appear on the palms of one's hands, but recent archeological discoveries and medical investigations now demonstrate that crucified individuals were most likely nailed through the wrists, which can support the weight of the body, instead of the hands, which cannot. *The Last Temptation of Christ* was the first mainstream film to feature Jesus being nailed through the wrists, not the palms, and therefore transforming the slitting of one's wrists into postmodern stigmata.

Although others had seen something of the Christ story in the "Superman" story (Kal-El, sent to Earth by his father to protect the people, stands for justice, performs miracles, etc.), the film *Superman Returns* (2006) transformed the implicit Christ figure of Superman to an explicit one. The pre-credit sequence, in which Kal-El is sent to Earth, features a voiceover from Marlon Brando (who played Jor-El in the original Superman movie in 1978) in which he tells the infant that humans "lack the light to show the way. For this reason I have sent them you, my only son" (quoted in "Superman"). He has miraculous powers that show his other-than-natural origins. Having been confronted by a gathering of those opposed to him, Superman dies and is brought back to life after being stabbed in the side with a shard of kryptonite, which echoes the stabbing in Christ's side with a spear by a Roman soldier (John 19:34). Superman seems to die but awakens on the third morning in the hospital.

In addition to these above examples, Madison in his essay "Five Christ Figures as Depicted in Science Fiction/Fantasy Movies" also argues for Robocop in *Robocop* and Ripley in the *Alien* movies, particularly in the obviously titled *Alien: Resurrection* (Madison 2009). In the former, a policeman is shot in the hand, body and head and then resurrected to bring justice to a corrupt world. He also walks on water at one point. In the latter, Ellen Ripley dies in a cruciform pose, sacrificing herself to prevent the demon-like aliens from getting the rest of humankind at the end of *Alien 3*. In *Alien: Resurrection* she is resurrected to continue combating the human and alien forces of darkness that would enslave or destroy humanity. We might also note the suggestion of theological concerns in the *Resident Evil* series of films, in which another resurrected woman must fight evil zombies and the corporation that created them; the third one in the series is entitled *Resident Evil: Apocalypse*. Speculative cinema Christ figures are apocalyptic, eschatological Christ figures.

Conversely, speculative fiction also tends to both invert the apocalypse and secularize it. Gabriel McKee states, "Where the book of Revelation concludes its list of calamities with a divine victory and the establishment of a new order of everlasting righteousness, the secular genre of SF takes destruction at face value" (2007a: 237). This is because Revelation is concerned with salvation, whereas "SF" does not always share this concern. Typically, according to McKee, speculative fiction is "not describing the catastrophes that must proceed the golden age" (2007a: 237). "The messiahs of these stories do not herald the destruction of the old, but its preservation," he claims (2007a: 237). Ironically, the former is precisely what happens in *BSG*. The old *is* destroyed, and any attempt to preserve it ultimately meets with disaster.

In the end, the Colonials bond with the Cylons, arrive at a planet that will literally be a New Earth, and give up not only their technology (which, as noted, is often a cause of apocalypse and in the universe of *BSG* is always the cause of the apocalypse) but even their very identities. Throughout the entire series the humans maintain their Colonial identities: Sagittaron, Gemenese, Caprican. They maintain their structures of society, governing bodies and the attendant titles: president, admiral, counsel of twelve. The humans attempt to maintain human society as it was before the Fall. Upon the new Earth, however, this old order is completely swept away. The president, having fulfilled her role as dying leader, has led her people to Earth and dies. The admiral lives alone in a cabin, no longer in command. Tyrol is dropped off in the north (Scotland), to live and die by himself. The remaining humans and Cylons interbreed with the proto-humans on Earth, having given up all Colonial heritage and identity. "The old" in McKee's terms, is swept away, replaced by a nontechnological, noncolonial new.

Lastly, as noted previously, Revelation itself is a form of speculative fiction. Edward James sees the Book of Revelation as perhaps the first work of speculative fiction, calling it "an influential and powerful way of imagining the future" (2000: 45). Hal Lindsey's seminal text of apocalyptic exegesis, *The Late Great Planet Earth,* draws as much on the tropes and imagery of science fiction as it does the Bible (James 2000: 56–57.) As its very name suggests, speculative fiction speculates on what might come to pass. Revelation does the same, except that it promises on what *will* come to pass. Both apocalypse and speculative fiction write the future.

Teleology and History: "They Have a Plan"

As in Revelation, there is a teleological plan: something larger than material reality and chance guides both humans and Cylons. When taken as a whole, the Bible also offers a metahistory and a teleological plan. Genesis tells of the beginning of creation; Revelation tells of its end. The entire journey is presented as God's plan for humanity. Within the larger plan are a series of smaller events that, despite human free will, seem to be part of God's larger plan for humanity. God chooses the Israelites; time and again they turn away from Him and are punished for it, and then reintegrated back. Because of humanity's sinful nature, God incarnates within human history, suffers, dies and is resurrected. All of this is also part of the plan. At the end of time, God will return again, judging the living and the dead, punishing those who are found wanting and rewarding the just and the faithful.

Time and again, however, part of the plan is destined violence toward God's chosen people: "I will destine you to the sword and all of you shall bow down to the slaughter" (Isaiah 65:12). This destruction is written large by Revelation. Not only are God's disobedient chosen people destined to be conquered and forced to "bow down," all humanity, indeed all reality, shall be destroyed and remade.

The remaking is the final part of the plan. The final chapters of Revelation feature a "new heaven and a new earth" and "the first heaven and the first earth had passed away" (21:1). The apocalypse involves both the destruction of the old and the making of the new. This echoes the apocalyptic promises made in Isaiah: "For I am about to create new heavens and a new earth; the former things shall not be remembered or come to mind" (Isaiah 65:17).

Isaiah adds a key element here: the forgetting of the "former things." The humans (and Cylons, for that matter) of *BSG* do not remember the first Earth. Those of us alive 150,000 years after the end of the events of *BSG* do not remember the events of *BSG*. Part of every apocalypse involves forgetting the pre-apocalypse time once the destruction and remaking are over. The destruction, recreation and forgetting are all part of the larger divine plan. This pattern is evident, both in scripture and in *BSG*.

Visions: Hidden Things Revealed

At heart, the book of Revelation, like all good apocalypses (the genre) is a series of visions. John repeatedly begins his descriptions of what is to come with the words "I saw." His vision begins with a door in Heaven opening, and a voice telling him: "Come up here, and I will show you what must take place after this" (4:1). He has been instructed to "write in a book what you see and send it to the seven churches" (1:11). Revelation is thus the recording of a series of visions that reveal the hidden things to come. Visions are sent by God in order to reveal God's will to those with understanding.

In *BSG*, many characters are granted a series of visions. Laura Roslin, Starbuck, Baltar, and D'Anna Biers all have a series of visions. Each of them is given one or more visions, sometimes literal, sometimes symbolic. Roslin, for example, sees a vision of a dozen snakes on her podium during a press conference, which confirms for Elosha she is the "dying leader" of Pythia, who it was foretold would "be given a vision of serpents numbering two and ten as a sign of things to come" (1.10). Her alternative cancer treatment, the taking of chamalla extract, gives Roslin a series of visions throughout the series, almost all of which relate to finding Earth.

Virtual Six is an angel that appears only to Baltar. Just as John of Patmos has angels speaking with him, telling him God's will, Baltar has an angel telling him God's will. Starbuck has seen a mandala her whole life, painting it, drawing it, obsessing over it. She recognizes it twice during the journey to earth. The mandala seems to stand for the Eye of Jupiter, as seen on the algae planet, pointing the way to Earth. When Starbuck sees the pattern again, in the mysterious vortex that resembles the mandala on a stormy planet, she flies her Viper into it and it explodes, seemingly killing her. Her subsequent return and knowledge of how to find Earth, however, seem to indicate that the vision of the mandala is a vision from God. When Starbuck trusts in her destiny and flies into the vortex, the resulting destruction is actually, like the destruction in Revelation, only clearing the path for rebirth and new life and, ultimately, salvation.

Indeed, the episode called "Revelations" (4.10), which completed the first half of the fourth season arc, involved the finding of Earth by Starbuck; it is revealed to be a devastated wasteland. The place upon which humanity had pinned its hopes was revealed to be a lifeless, unlivable world destroyed by nuclear weapons.* This destroyed planet, however, is not the New Earth. In a sense, it is also a vision (hence the episode title) in that it shows the consequences of not finding salvation. The first Earth is a lifeless wasteland. This vision is an echo of John's vision of

---

*One of the reasons that the first Earth was revealed to be a devastated wasteland was the WGA strike of 2008. There was a possibility that "Revelations" would be the last episode of *BSG*, so the producers wanted an ending that could stand alone or serve as a jumping off point should more episodes be made (Gosling 2009: 10, 66). Note, too, the Biblical significance of ending the series with an episode entitled "Revelations," although the Bible's final book is actually "Revelation," singular, despite frequent misidentification in the plural.

the fall of Babylon and of the lake of fire. Their fate is a cautionary tale. By witnessing visions of the destruction of others, we are warned against our own destruction. The humans and Cylons of the first Earth are like those thrown into the lake of fire: "This is the second death, the lake of fire" (Revelation 20:14). Obliteration waits those who do not follow God's plan or pay attention to those who receive visions.

Millennialism Without a Millennium

Michael Barkun, in his seminal study of the sociology of millennialist movements, *Disaster and the Millennium,* considers how disaster (i.e., "death and desolation") fuels millennialism ("salvation and fulfillment") (1974: 1). Disaster, "by removing the familiar environment, removes precisely those frames of reference by which we normally evaluate statements, ideas, and beliefs. Belief systems which under non-disaster conditions might be dismissed now receive sympathetic consideration.... It is small wonder that among persons so situated doctrines of imminent salvation should find such a ready acceptance" (1986: 56).

We see this pattern emerge in *BSG.* The Cylon destruction of the colonies is a disaster that removes "familiar environments" and "frames of reference." Pythia, the ignored scroll of the Sacred Scrolls (see the following section) becomes the most important of the scrolls because of its apocalyptic prophesies. Laura Roslin, an agnostic dying of cancer, not only becomes a believer but becomes a deeply religious messianic leader because of the Cylon genocide.

Roslin is the secretary of education in President Adar's administration at the time of the disaster. She is, by her own admission, "forty-third in line for the presidency" (MS). Yet, when the Cylons destroy the colonies, she is the only member of the administration still alive. She is sworn in as president and begins to lead the colonies. When circumstances seem to indicate that she might be a prophesied leader, Laura Roslin begins a millennial movement among the surviving Colonials.

The horror of apocalypse is in the unveiling of "our rootlessness," writes Tina Pippin (1999: 97). The relief of apocalypse is the promise of a communal home at the end. We might be temporarily rootless, without a home, but in the end God will deliver us. In *BSG,* it is Roslin who almost immediately after the attack begins gathering the tribes (literally) and ending the rootlessness by finding a new home. Roslin is the one who insists on gathering the civilian survivors. She is the one who talks Adama out of counterattacking the Cylons (surely a suicide mission) and instead rallying around the remnant of humanity. Roslin brings Adama to see that his role is to protect and shepherd the fleet. As Michael Barkun argues, "Multiple disasters, existing millennial ideas and charismatic leadership converge to produce the millenarian movement" (1986: 91). Similarly, the Cylon genocide (itself a series of multiple disasters), the prophesies in the Scroll of Pythia, and Roslin herself, charismatic and seemingly fulfilling those prophesies, begin the quest for Earth in the miniseries, the quest that will end in the final episode.

In short, humanity's quest for Earth is ultimately a millenarian movement — an attempt to find a peaceful kingdom in response to a life-changing disaster. Rather than expecting the end of the world, *BSG's* humanity has witnessed it; now they must survive a series of trials and judgments to reach the "thousand-year reign," which, in this case, is the planet Earth. Again, humanity's quest for Earth is thus also salvific. In the end, a charismatic leader, following divine prophesy in the wake of disaster, will lead humanity to a New Earth, free from the sin and destruction that brought about the disaster in the first place.

Is Pythia Revelation? or, The Late Great Planet Caprica

The Scroll of Pythia presents a future of humankind in which a dying leader who has visions leads humanity to its final home and salvation on Earth. At the start of the story, Pythia is unimportant to the humans. It is irrelevant to the day-to-day life of the humans. Even Elosha does not seem to regard it as a significant part of the Sacred Scrolls. The first time it is mentioned is in the context of an assumed joke: "You've read Pythia and you're having me on," she responds to Roslin's news of the vision of serpents (1.10). The assumption behind this line is that only the priests read and know Pythia. The average human does not read or know this scroll.

Subsequently, however, Laura, Elosha and the others begin to make connections between Pythian prophesy and the events of their lives. They link contemporary events with Pythian prophesy. In doing so, they are following the model of contemporary evangelical Christians who believe in the literal truth of the Bible. Hal Lindsey's *The Late Great Planet Earth* became the great popularizer of this idea, linking events occurring in the contemporary world with Biblical prophesy and describing how the end times would play out in the real world. Jack Van Impe, Benny Hinn, Pat Robertson, and the late Jerry Falwell, for example, all also link current events to Biblical prophesy about the end times. Amy Johnson Frykholm observes that "prophesy is an odd kind of truth because its realization remains always in the future" (2004: 132). Yet, for evangelicals, the evidence that prophesy is coming true is seen in everyday events. Seemingly random, unrelated occurrences such as hurricanes, earthquakes or the deaths of political figures take on Biblical significance in this schema.

Frykholm further relates that Biblical prophesy is a "script for social living and a script for the reading of human history," which is also how Pythia functions on *BSG* (2004: 132). And "as a script, prophesy guides the reading of other texts," from the rest of scripture to television news programs (2004: 132). Pythia offers a way for the humans to understand the Cylon genocide and to follow a script — the next action of the "ragtag fugitive fleet" is to find Earth. Within the script, roles are provided — the dying leader, the lesser demon, the people. If the rest of scripture is history, Revelation (and Pythia) are the script for the future.

BSG is a rather fundamentalist text in this sense: prophesy is true and it manifests literally. Even Hal Lindsey thought that "locusts" were helicopters. *BSG* shows that serpents are serpents, the leader is literally dying, and the relics, locations and events mentioned in the Sacred Scrolls are all true. Pythia, in a word, is literally "true" in the same way that Revelation is perceived to be literally "true."

Revelation, like Pythia, provides a way of understanding the world. As Adela Yarbro Collins observes of Revelation:

> [It] is not simply a product of a certain social situation, not even a simple response to circumstances. At root is a particular religious view of reality, inherited in large part, which is the framework within which John interpreted his environment. The book of Revelation is thus a product of the interaction between a kind of pre-understanding and the socio-historical situation in which John lived [1984: 106–107].

What Collins asserts of the original text, I assert of the epiphenomenal contemporary texts rooted in Revelation (*Late Great Planet Earth, Left Behind,* and even *BSG*): the "religious view" of reality provides a pre-understanding of what *will* happen, the author must thus integrate current/future events into this understanding.

A dispensationalist reading of Pythia turns out to be the correct one.

Apocalypse Repeated

From the beginning of the series, *BSG* is a text of repeated Apocalypses. The miniseries shows the death of most of the human race. The first episode of the series, "33," features an apocalypse every 33 minutes (1.01). The Cylons appear and begin attacking the humans every 33 minutes. The entire fleet must prepare to jump the second the Cylons appear. Thus, the fleet is living in a constant state of persecution and readiness to respond to a potentially life-threatening appearance. The end comes once every 33 minutes.

At the end of "33," the Cylons stop pursuing the fleet as a result of what may be seen as the Hand of God working. The Olympic Carrier may have a tracking device on it that allows the Cylons to follow, but it also may have a man who knows Baltar betrayed the human race. "Why are they showing up now?" Baltar whines. "It's God's punishment for your lack of faith," Virtual Six explains, to his scorn. Yet the president orders the Olympic Carrier destroyed, Baltar's secret is safe and the Cylons no longer arrive every 33 minutes. Baltar's repentance stops the repeated apocalypses, leading the way for humankind to start for Earth. This series of apocalypses leads to the next part of God's teleological (and theological) plan.

From this point in the series, we see again and again the arrival of apocalypses. The arrival of the Pegasus results in the persecution of the Galactica's officers and crew, not to mention the civilian fleet, until Cain's world comes to an end with a bullet from Gina. New Caprica seems like a haven (a heaven?), until the Cylons arrive, summoned by the nuclear device Gina explodes. The arrival at Earth results not in salvation, but despair over destruction. Saul and Ellen Tigh, Tyrol, Tory and Anders have their own apocalyptic experiences, in which their human world ends and their lives as Cylons begin. The entire series is one long apocalypse consisting of smaller apocalypses (both hidden things revealed and ends of worlds) until the final arrival on a literal New Earth. *BSG* begins and ends apocalyptically.

All This Has Happened Before...

Although Revelation posits a linear course of events that would seem to contradict *BSG*'s assertion of repetition, there are repetitive qualities to the Christian apocalypse. Amy Johnson Frykholm, citing Susan Harding's study of Jerry Falwell, states:

> Readers [of *Left Behind*] engage with biblical prophesy as a form of what Susan Harding calls "narrative belief." It is a living story that repeats itself over and over. Biblical prophesy is a "specific narrative mode of reading history" [Harding 2000: 232, quoted in Frykholm 2004: 120].

And that mode of reading history is a repetitive one, one that sees the same events over and over again. Popular narratives of apocalypse rely upon repetition not only of the same elements, but also of literally the same events.

Rennie B. Schoepflin similarly observes, "The biblical tradition contained linear and cyclical views of history" (1998: 435). The end of the world is not a one-time occurrence, nor is the saving of humankind in the form of a remnant. God repeatedly destroys and enslaves His people, Israel. God also destroys the majority of humanity at least twice — once with water, in the future with fire: Noah and the flood (Genesis 6–9); the saved of Revelation (7:4–17, 20:11–15). All of this has happened before, and all of this will happen again. Apocalypse is not only a repetitive genre; it is a repetitive event.

Yet, despite the repeated destructions and creations, the end message of apocalypse is one of overall hope. The message from God is that that "one must prepare and live for the future," yet "God has everything under control already" in Tina Pippin's words (1999: 98). The future is planned by God, but humanity has agency as well: one must "prepare" and "live." God has a plan, but we must actively play a role in it. The hidden things revealed, whether by Revelation, Pythia or *BSG,* are messages from the divine about not only what is coming but also *how* to prepare for it. *BSG* shares this message in its apocalyptic visions. In the end, humanity is saved, a new earth is found, life goes on and God is proven to have been right every step of the way. Even a sinner such as Gaius Baltar, as long as he followed God's will and loved as God asked him to, will be saved and live to see the next step of humanity's existence. That future is both speculative and revelatory, and ends with a sort of universal salvation (admittedly, for the few who are left after the end of everything...).

Conclusion: The Plan

No television series can encompass the complexity that is contemporary Christian theology, not even one that is directly about contemporary Christian theology (if there is such a thing). However, as I stated in the introduction, television is both a "meaning-making" enterprise for the viewer and, in the words of Diane Winston, "a virtual meeting place" where viewers "can find instructive and inspirational narratives" (2009: 2). In the case of *Battlestar Galactica,* the narrative is instructive and inspirational but is also, as I hope this volume has demonstrated, a profoundly theological text that serves to interrogate and echo Christian concepts.

Scholars have seen in *BSG* echoes of the history of the early Christian church. Taneli Kukkonen sees the Cylons among the humans as a repetition of Jews and Christians in a Hellenistic world (2008: 173). The humans are polytheistic, the humans enslaved the Cylons, the Cylons eventually rebel and the end result is a world that combines elements of Cylon monotheism and human polytheism, just as Christianity becomes thoroughly Hellenized and then Romanized as it spread throughout the Mediterranean and was appropriated by the Roman Empire. As noted in the first chapter, in a deleted scene, available on DVD, the priest Elosha explains that humanity's exodus from Kobol was motivated because "one jealous god began to desire that he be elevated above all the other gods, and the war on Kobol began" (1.12). This statement supports Kukkonen, as YHWH, the God of the Israelites, is quoted as saying, "I am a jealous God" who demands "you shall have no other gods before me" (Exodus 20:5, 3). The Cylons initially engage in a religious war of annihilation against the humans; then, after their own civil war, many Cylons come to live at peace among the humans and many humans convert to monotheism (at least those in the Baltar cult do, and their faith commitment is far stronger than most polytheistic humans).

I have also argued that *BSG* is fundamentally an apocalyptic text. It shows the passing away of the old world and the old order, the battle of a small remnant of humanity and the creation of a New Earth. In addition, it also carries the tropes of contemporary apocalyptic fiction. The narrative of *BSG* is not too different from the narrative arc of the *Left Behind* series. As Amy Johnson Frykholm reminds us in her analysis of reader reception of *Left Behind,* apocalyptic narratives are not just about the future, or even primarily about the future, "but about the creation of meaning in the present moment" (2004: 182). *BSG,* which, like *Star Wars,* frames the future as the past, ultimately is concerned with the present moment.

BSG, which I have fully admitted to being a fan of from the beginning, was simply one of the best programs on television for the years it was on. It was certainly one of the most relevant. It dealt with terrorism, violence, individual rights versus the needs of the group, occupations, the role of the media, the role of the military, morality, ethics, abortion, torture, adultery, fear of the Other and even sports. Through the guise of speculative fiction, it ruminated on the war in Iraq, America's use of "enhanced interrogation techniques," suicide bombers, social inequality between the ruling class and the working class, and the dangers our own technology posed to us. It did so in an intelligent and informed manner that was sometimes shocking (the Cylons thought they would be welcomed as liberators on New Caprica and the humans were the suicide bombers, which made the people we were rooting for terrorists!).

Perhaps most significant, like *Left Behind* but without its evangelical, fundamentalist basis, *BSG* not only takes religion seriously as a social force and as an element of any culture; it demonstrates clearly the working out of the divine will in the material world. Not all prayers have efficacy, but prayer itself does. Angels are messengers who take on the forms of those we love in order to communicate God's will. Prophesy is proven true (both human and Cylon). Love transcends the universe. Not only does the program take all of this seriously; it refuses to simplify or sugarcoat the complex and terrifying reality of divinity.

Unlike many Christian-based narratives on television (such as *Highway to Heaven, Touched by an Angel* or *Seventh Heaven*), which rely upon sentimentalizing portraits of religion and divine love, moralizing and a conservative cultural point of view, *BSG* refused to sentimentalize or moralize. Conversely, it frequently embraced moral and cultural ambiguity. For example, President Roslin eventually outlaws abortion, not because she believes in the sanctity of life; to the contrary, she believes in reproductive freedom and the Colonial law that women have a right to an abortion. The reality of humanity's precarious position in the cosmos, with less than 50,000 left, has made having children a priority. From an evangelical point of view she does the "right thing" but not for any theological or religious motive, which means the moral imperative behind the evangelical Christian's (or, for that matter, evangelical Gemenese's) opposition to abortion is not the reason for the ban, and in other circumstances the result would have been different. There is no place in the world of *BSG* for moral absolutes or moral imperatives.

Conversely, as I noted in the introduction, the narrative of *BSG* is essentially a conservative one that echoes a fundamentalist understanding of reality and a dispensationalist view of human history. *BSG* presents a metahistory of humankind and ultimately demonstrates a single plan for salvation. "All this has happened before and all this will happen again," yet there is a divine plan in place to change the outcome. Prophesy is proven true, and prophesy should be interpreted literally. God is real, God manifests in human history and makes His will known through messengers that we understand as "angels." *BSG*, as an apocalyptic text, ultimately affirms a very conservative religious viewpoint that is continued within its successor series on the same network. Unlike most apocalyptic texts, however, salvation is not for a select group of adherents alone. It is not the believers in God who are saved; it is a small group of humans and Cylons who made the right choices. Faith in God, even faith in any god, is not a necessary attribute for salvation. Atheist, monotheist and polytheist alike are both saved and destroyed. *BSG* concludes with a very small remnant surviving the destruction, exile and return, serving to begin the cycle again on the new Earth.

It is the conclusion of *BSG* that also concludes and completes my analysis here. The final images of *BSG* make it clear that the planet that is the New Earth is, in fact, our Earth. The mutual salvation ostensibly achieved by bringing the Cylons and humans together on Earth is problematized by the revelation that the divine plan, rooted in love, to save both human and Cylon, results in our world, which seems to be just as fallen and lost as Kobol, Caprica and the original Earth.

In the coda to the series, set 150,000 years later, after the Colonials and the Cylons have settled on a new planet, present-day New York City is seen. Virtual Baltar and Virtual Six look over the shoulder of a man* reading *National Geographic,* the cover story of which concerns "mito-chondrial Eve," the most common matrilineal ancestor for all human beings alive today (see Sykes 2001). In their conversation it is revealed that Hera is "mitochondrial Eve" and thus responsible for the evolution of humankind out of human/Cylon pairing. The world of *BSG* is ulti-mately our world. "Salvation" ultimately results in the creation of con-temporary reality.

The two angels converse, noting the similarities between Kobol, "the real Earth," and the Twelve Colonies and how "all this has happened before" (4.20). Virtual Six (perhaps she should be called "Angelic Six" now) believes that all this will not happen again. Thus, salvation actually has been achieved — the cycle is broken. She also acknowledges that it's the "law of averages. Let a complex system repeat itself long enough, eventually something surprising might occur. That, too, is in God's plan." — to which Angelic Baltar replies, "You know He doesn't like that name" (4.20). This last line is a unique twist on the numinous, plan-ning being that has been guiding the action of the series since the begin-ning.

One final thing to take away from this ending is that, in the world of *BSG,* salvation is not eternal. It is an ongoing struggle. One does not accept the one true God and then simply be with Him forever. One does not believe in and achieve eternal life. The fact that the human/Cylon plan for salvation results in the creation of our world indicates that we, individually and collectively, must continue to strive for salvation. It is not eternal once granted but something that must be continually sought after and worked toward.

All in all it is a remarkable ending to a remarkable series that reconfirms and simultaneously problematizes the existence of God. The final images of the series consist of a montage of robots, all of which exist today, shown over Jimi Hendrix's "All Along the Watchtower," a song that has had theological meaning throughout the series and served

---

*The man is actually a cameo by series creator and executive producer Ron Moore.

to identify the Final Five Cylons, seemingly confirming the emergence of technological decadence that, according to *BSG,* always ends in a Fall.* While the angelic characters believe our Earth will be different, "salvation" appears to be an ongoing process and not a total transformation for all time.

In the end, what *BSG* allows us viewer's to do is reflect upon our own theologies of creation, fall, and salvation. It questions technology. As noted in the last chapter, much contemporary apocalyptic thought is rooted in the fear of technology and the belief it will be used by the Antichrist against Christians. And yet, simultaneously, we might observe that the series ends on an ambiguous note of hope. Perhaps that is the salvation that *BSG* offers: all this has happened before, but it does not have to happen again. God has empowered us, the viewer on whose world the show concludes, to change our relationship with each other and with technology, so that the end does not come again. Like the Gospels, what *BSG* ultimately offers humanity is a narrative of hope.

---

*"All Along the Watchtower," originally written by Bob Dylan and arguably best known in the Hendrix cover version, is also a fundamentally theological text with apocalyptic overtones. The lyrics echo Isaiah 21:5-9, in which Isaiah writes of the prophet as sentinel, watching from a watchtower as Babylon falls and "all the images of her gods lie shattered on the ground." Not only apocalyptic, but very resonant with *BSG*'s narrative as well, in which the Babylon of the Twelve Colonies falls and the human gods are shattered by the divine plan of the one true God.

Epilogue: The Theology of Caprica; or, Why Parents Don't Always Look Like Their Children

If one man is resurrected, that will change the worlds....

> — Sister Clarice Willow
> *Apotheosis* [C1.17]

Odin: So, are you a True Believer?
Lacy: I don't know any more....

> — *Blowback* [C1.13]

The theological constructions of *Battlestar* continue in its prequel series, *Caprica,* beginning with the advertisements for the program: a waist-up photo of Zoe Graystone (Alessandra Torresani), seemingly naked, looking seductively over her shoulder holding an apple with a single bite taken out of it, a smile playing about her lips. The iconography is clearly Biblical: Zoe-as-Eve, temptress (in every sense of the word) who will bring about humanity's fall. The implication is this that young woman whose persona (soul?) has been placed in the prototype of the Cylon centurion will seduce humanity and lead to its destruction. Knowing what happens in *BSG*, we already know this is true: Zoe Graystone will lead to the death of all but a small remnant of humanity. As with the metahistory of the Bible, the end of *Caprica* is already written at its beginning — the world will end and a new world will emerge.

At its essence, the series concerned Daniel Graystone's attempt to overcome death and restore his daughter to a physical existence, the struggles of the Adama family to hold to their traditional culture in a modern world, the emergence of Lacy Rand's spiritual leadership, and the attempt of Sister Clarice to demonstrate the truth of monotheism through a campaign of terrorist acts. All of these series-long narrative arcs engage subjects and themes that are at heart theological concerns. Given that the first, Daniel's attempts to give his daughter technological life, sparks most of the show's action and is directly linked to the events of *BSG*, it behooves the viewer to remember that *Caprica* is a *Frankenstein* story. Appropriately enough, Shelley's novel was subtitled *The Modern Prometheus*. Prometheus, whose name means "forethought," was the Greek titan that stole fire from the gods and gave it to humanity. It is a cautionary tale of mixed blessings from technological advancements, taking for humankind something that should belong only to the divine. Like the good doctor, Daniel seeks to recreate life, to, as the cliché goes, "play God."

God Is One?

Caprica introduces human monotheists six decades before Baltar's cult. Called the Monad Church and centered on Gemenon, monotheism is an underground religion in the Twelve Colonies, barely tolerated on many and openly persecuted on Caprica. It is a matriarchy of sorts, in that the religious leader is a woman named The Mother, but both men and women may serve as leaders and clergy. There is also a militant arm called Soldiers of the One (STO), who engage in terrorist attacks on the polytheistic society in an attempt to resist the persecution.

The pilot episode opens with a shot of the planet Caprica and the words "Caprica: 58 years before the fall" (CP). It is not clear if "the fall," refers to the first Cylon war or the Cylon attack in the *BSG* miniseries that ends most human life 40 years after the end of the first Cylon war. This ambiguity seems to indicate that "the fall" of humanity, meaning its genocide, was not a single event but a series of events that transformed the universe forever. By "playing God" and putting his daughter's avatar's consciousness into a cybernetic life-form node (the presumable origins of the word "Cylon") (CP) at a time when the rise of monotheistic terrorism was increasing in the Colonies, Daniel Graystone put into play a chain of events and situations that directly led not only to the first Cylon war, the Cylon exile and the subsequent human genocide, but also to the subsequent merging of humanity and "skinjobs" that lead the remnant to Earth. In this sense, everything that happens in *Caprica* and on Caprica is part of God's plan as well. Likewise, many of the theological themes of *BSG* (and this volume as well) find themselves repeated or echoed in *Caprica*.

This opening shot and statement of locale and period are immediately followed by a cut to a loud, phrenetic dance club. A crowd in various states of undress and inebriation cheer on two men fighting and a young woman gunning down an unarmed man. A real virgin sacrifice to Hecate, goddess of the underworld, follows, with dancers and a chanting audience feeding on the violence. Apart from the crowd, in temperament and behavior if not in geography, are three young people: Zoe Graystone, Lacy Rand and Ben Stark. They look disapprovingly at the debauchery around them. They are there to experiment on Zoe's avatar program. They are also, however, young closet monotheists. As they watch with detached distain, Ben says, "It's not their fault, you know. They don't know what they're doing," echoing the words of Jesus in Luke 23:34: "Father, forgive them; for they do not know what they are doing." This sentiment not only cements Ben as a monotheist; it also invokes a rather Christian understanding of sin: one must know that what one is doing is wrong in order for it to be sin.

Later, Lacy tells Daniel that the club is "trash" and "empty," and that its temptations and pleasures are unworthy of those who know the "one true God." The pilot episode frames the young monotheists with echoes of early Christianity. In the Gospel of John, Jesus prays on behalf of his disciples, noting that "they do not belong to the world, just as I do not belong to the world" (17:16). Likewise, Romans 12:2 cautions disciples, "Do not be conformed to this world, but be transformed by the renewing of your minds," and 1 John 2:15 commands, "Do not love the world or the things in the world." All of these messages were read by early Christians to be "in the world but not of the world," a major idea in Christianity today as well. As on polytheistic Caprica, the Christians saw themselves as being surrounded by a hostile, pagan world that had rejected the teaching of the true God. Therefore, one must live in this world, but not be of this world — i.e., be completed disconnected and withdraw from the temptations and sins of pagan society. Lacy, Ben and Zoe all plan to leave Caprica behind and go to Gemenon in order to remove themselves from the temptations and sins of a pagan society.

After sequences introducing the two families that *Caprica* will follow, the Graystones and the Adamas, the series has its own inciting inci-
dent that will cause all of the events to follow. Lacy backs out at the last
minute, but Zoe and Ben board a train to run away to the Soldiers of
the One training camp on Gemenon. Unbeknownst to Zoe, Ben is a suicide bomber who will blow up the train as it departs the station. Telling
Zoe, "It is God's will," he then detonates the bomb, killing many, including Zoe and Joseph Adama's wife and daughter.

This remarkable sequence links early Christianity in the Roman
Empire with contemporary Islamic extremism. The audience is shown
suicide bombing with prescribed slogans. "The one true God shall drive
out the many!" for all practical purposes is the STO version of "God is
great!" ("Allahu akbar!" in the original Arabic).

As if to confirm this, Joseph Adama turns to see a giant cloud of
black smoke coming out between buildings, highly reminiscent of the
images of the attacks on September 11. Much of the pilot is then spent
exploring the hidden militant monotheism in Caprican society and the
police who are investigating it.

Sister Clarice, a teacher in the Athenian Academy and crypto-
monotheist, leads a covert cell of Soldiers of the One. While comforting
Lacy in the wake of Zoe's death, she reveals her own faith and invites
Lacy to join the worship of the One. She also mentions an aspect of
Colonial ritual not mentioned in the original series: sacrifices in the temple. This aspect demonstrates that *Caprica* changes and reworks some
of the elements of *BSG,* while also expanding on the monotheistic faith
that eventually will be held by the Cylons. Clarice is the heart (and
mouthpiece) of the STO on *Caprica.* Obal Ferris, one of the 12 leaders
of the Monad Church on Gemenon, calls Clarice "a dyed-in-the-wool
zealot with delusions of grandeur. Definite messiah complex" (C1.09).

Continuing the concern about religiously motivated terrorists in
the midst of a population that does not share the terrorists' faith, Agent
Durham challenges Sister Clarice when he investigates the Athenian
Academy. His demeanor indicates that suspicion of monotheism on
Caprica is akin to American suspicion of Islam and Muslims. He also
reminds Clarice that monotheism is inherently undemocratic. He objects
to a "single, all-knowing, all-powerful being whose judgment cannot be
questioned, and in whose name the most horrendous of acts can be sanctioned without appeal" having absolute authority over everything.

Interestingly, the polytheism that Clarice pretends to is demonstrated to be similar to Christianity as well. Durham, whose knowledge of monotheism is rather complex, observes, "Know your enemy, Sister Clarice." Clarice responds, "Love your enemy, Agent Duram. That is what we followers of Athena believe." This statement is a direct quote from Matthew 5:44 and Luke 6:27 in the Sermon on the Mount. Followers of Athena (a pagan god from Earth's own ancient Greece) believe in loving one's enemies, which is not a particularly polytheistic belief. In a polytheistic system, one has patron gods and divinities to which one aligns one's self, aware that there are competing and combating factions. One does not love one's enemies; one loves one's friends and hates one's enemies. In Matthew, in fact, Jesus points out that to do so is common practice among the gentiles (5:47).

Clarice's proclamation of loving her enemies is also ironic, because Clarice, in fact, hates her enemies, does not pray for those who persecute her and actually works to kill those to whom she is opposed. Ironically, most of the people whom Clarice kills, including those she personally kills, are not the polytheists out to stop her but members of the Monad Church and the Soldiers of the One who oppose her, disagree with her or get in her way. She kills or orders to be killed Obal Ferris, Pann, Hippolyta, Mar-Beth, and Barnabas, among others. (For that matter, Barnabas kills Keon, threatens to kill Lacy repeatedly and attempts to kill Clarice not once, but several times, and those new recruits who fail the fake hostage test on Gemenon are executed by Cylon firing squad on the orders of the STO leadership [C1.13]. The STO kills far more monotheists than they do polytheists and than the polytheists do.) Clarice is far more dangerous to her fellow monotheists than to the false gods she hates so much.

It is also appropriate that she is a "follower of Athena," who was a warrior goddess and merciless to her enemies. In contemporary America, we tend to make Greek mythology pretty and nice for students. Athena, however, was not merely goddess of wisdom, as she is so often portrayed in popular culture. She was a masculine warrior goddess who emerged fully formed, wearing armor, from the skull of Zeus. Hesiod, in *Theogony*, refers to her as "a leader of armies, a goddess queen who delights in war cries, slaughter and battle" (2005:84). She fights in the Trojan War and is as known for her skills as a warrior as much as for any wisdom she may have. Clarice, as well, sees herself as a leader of armies, a wisdom figure, and a delighter in war cries.

Throughout the series, however, Clarice, as chief voice of the Monad

Church's militant wing, actually employs a good deal of Christian terminology. She tells Amanda that God "made you in His image" and He
wants us to "give ourselves over to Him" and "trust in His judgment,"
all of which echoes Biblical language (C1.06). Yet this language is also
cynical and self-serving. Clarice tells Amanda these things, presumably
genuine tenets of the Monad Church, but does so in order to consolidate
her power over Amanda and over the STO cells on Caprica. Clarice uses
religion in order to enhance her own power.

Clarice is a paradox and a hypocrite. She is a true believer, but her
belief and her ambition fuel each other. She believes she is right, and
that any who disagree or who challenge or threaten her are evil. If she
is God's instrument, then those who oppose her oppose God and deserve
to be scourged. As a fundamentalist Monadist and member of STO, her
language and ideas echo many of the theological themes of both series
(and again, this volume). Clarice advocates the remnant, stating that
30,000 will die but a handful will be reborn in her virtual paradise
(C1.09). She wants to bring about apocalypse: the Apotheosis project,
discussed in a later section. She sees those who disagree with her as Judas
figures, betrayers worthy only of death, while she herself is also a betrayer.
Conversion experiences figure large in the pilot and throughout *Caprica*:
the moment of decision to embrace a new faith is significant in the series.

While the central male characters, Daniel Graystone and Joseph
Adama, undergo crises of faith with the deaths of their daughters and
face multiple ethical and moral decisions, the theological heart of the
show is actually with the women, and with the young women in particular. On the one hand, Zoe dies as a result of the opening STO suicide
bombing, but her avatar continues to grow and develop and eventually
becomes part prophet, part divinity herself. On the other hand, Lacy's
doubt that drives her from the train in the series opening drives her to
seek the STO and training. Ultimately, however, she finds no solace or
evidence of God in the work of the STO and in Clarice. Instead, she
leads a rebellion of young STO and becomes the Divine Mother herself.
Their search for meaning and identity lead both Zoe and Lacy away from
the traditional faith of their families and culture (which is not held too
deeply or believed too seriously by any character we encounter), and to
virtual godhood and the prophet of the one true God by series' end. In
this sense, the entire series concerns the maturing of the spiritual life of
these two women and how their earlier conversion experiences are cast
in doubt by later experiences that bring them to a much more true faith.

Being and Nonbeing in New Cap City

Caprica also features theological aspects from faiths other than Christianity. There is an underlying Buddhism behind the Taurons and the virtual world of New Cap City. When she realizes she cannot die in the virtual world, Tamara Adams begins to "kill" those who stand in her way. Vesta asks her, "What are you?" Tamara answers, "I am awake," a line that links her to the Buddha (C1.04). The Buddha is the "awakened one" who has learned the four noble truths: that life is suffering, suffering comes from attachment and desire, the cessation of suffering is possible, and the end of desire through the teachings of the Buddha means the end of suffering. Tamara, like Zoe, comes to embrace her virtual state, recognize the true nature of her reality, and let go of a desire to return to how things were. They are awakened — enlightened.

Buddhism, which developed out of Hinduism, sees the material world as *maya*—illusion. The world is not real in a greater sense; it is an illusion that one must see through. The virtual game "New Cap City" offers *maya* as entertainment. In New Cap City, people chose to live in a world of illusion. They know it is not real, yet they choose to spend copious amounts of time in the game. The awakened one is the one who recognizes the illusion and is freed from desire yet also moves among mortals, showing them truth and freeing them from illusion. Tamara, and then Zoe, becomes an "avenging angel," one who shatters the illusions and ends the virtual existence of those who prey on others in New Cap City (C1.14).

In this sense, *Caprica* blends theologies, including Buddhism, Christianity and ancient pagan. While Tamara is enlightened and, in a sense, a Bodhisattva, she and Zoe are also vengeance-dealing angels, very similar to the Biblical use of angels as instruments of divine vengeance. In "Ghosts in the Machine," Cerebus (himself an emcee named after the three-headed dog that guards the underworld) tells the club audience in Club Mysteries that he offers "an epiphany, a privileged peek into the mysteries" (C1.07). The name suggests that he guards the afterlife and that in the club there is the possibility of glimpsing truth and ultimate reality. Tamara came to the club asking questions about the afterlife. After failing to answer the riddle Cerebus asked her, Tamara was shot but did not "de-res" (die in the virtual world and vanish). Instead, "we discovered she had the power to transcend life and death. It was quite a show. Maybe she found the answers that everyone's searching for. Or maybe she is the answer" (C1.07). Cerebus suggests that Tamara herself might be not only the awakened one but an answer to the larger issues of sentience and soul, life and death, meaning and meaninglessness.*

Eventually, when Joseph finds his daughter, she de-resses him, forcing him to let go of her and the desire to be reunited with her or keep her alive. She functions as a Bodhisattva here as well, leading her father away from desire and toward enlightenment — one that he will never truly reach in the series, however.

Eternal Life; or, When Is a Soul Not a Soul?

If there is one overriding theological theme to *Caprica*, it is the scientific search for eternal life, as manifested in the plans of Daniel and Clarice. Daniel put Zoe's avatar (not her actual soul but a constructed identity that for all practical purposes is her essence) in a robot body in an attempt to preserve her. Eventually, by series' end, Daniel and Amanda build humanoid bodies so that their daughter may be physically present in a form that replicates her human body at the age when she died. Zoe as skinjob will be forever teenaged, but not actually Zoe.

Daniel captures Zoe's avatar and places it inside his Cylon. He tells Joseph that "her soul" may have been copied. Adama argues in response that souls cannot be copied (CP). Yet one of the key questions in *Caprica* is: what are the sentient avatars of Zoe and Tamara? They think. They feel. They have all the memories of the original. They have free will. They are created souls. Later, Daniel asks the Guatrau if humanity would not be happier if he could create software that would recreate the personalities of people's lost loved ones. He advocates that by recreating their essence, their "soul," in the virtual world, their families and friends could visit them every day. He even imagines a time when these virtual souls might be placed in physical bodies to make them an actual presence in the real world again (C1.09). What Daniel proposes is a very different kind of resurrection. It is not an actual resurrection of the person in his original body or in a spirit body as the Bible (and chapter 8) suggests.

---

*Sadly, the series never fully explores this idea, most likely because it only lasted for a few more episodes. The theological implications of Zoe are explored more fully by series' end with Tamara all but forgotten. Still, the presentation of her as "awakened one," "avenging angel," and "answer to the mysteries" makes her a much more interesting figure than the character was allowed to be.

It is not a downloading, as in *BSG*. It is not even a resurrection of the person for the person. It is a resurrection for others; that is what makes *Caprica* different from any text explored so far.

What Daniel proposes, at least initially, is a virtual resurrection for those who have been left behind. The family of the deceased gets to be with the deceased again. The deceased, however, is still dead. He or she does not get to be with the family again. This resurrection is a selfish one in that it is not about the salvation of the deceased or the needs of the deceased but about the desire of those who remain behind to have the deceased still with them. It is a false resurrection, a virtual one. That is the heart of *Caprica:* virtuality. The only resurrection we see is virtual, not real. The only heaven we see is virtual, not real. The only souls we see are copies, not real. With death, the "original" soul is gone.

Daniel tells virtual Amanda that he stole Vergis's chip so that he "could bring our daughter back" (C1.12). He tells her that he means more than the avatar — virtual Zoe was more or less the same being as their daughter. He then works to bring her back to life, culminating in his meeting with Zoe, her return to the virtual house and his work to make a "skinjob" version so she could have a physical body again (C1.16; C1.17). All of these things, however, exist only in a computer. They are virtual, not real.

Caprica concerns itself with keeping the dead alive. For Daniel, it is a literal quest to bring his daughter back to life. Joseph Adama joins in this quest, attempting to resurrect and then find his daughter Tamara. Amanda, however, sees memory as a kind of resurrection. She tells Clarice that they were brought together by destiny as a "way of keeping Zoe alive" (C1.11). Amanda posits the memory of the living as a kind of life after death. She will eventually be seduced by both Daniel and Clarice's visions of a different kind of resurrection.

Clarice imagines and creates a virtual heaven based on Zoe's algorithms: "Imagine a world in which death has been conquered. In which eternal life is not just a dream but a reality" (C1.09). Apotheosis is a virtual heaven in which the scanned avatars of the faithful spend eternity in a computer-generated heaven. In short, what *Caprica* shows us is two competing visions of resurrection and eternal life, neither one of which is real. Daniel envisions first creating avatars that will allow families to interact with their deceased relatives in virtual reality. He then envisions embodying these avatars in robot bodies, metallic at first, but moving toward human-looking androids. By the end of the series he will have invented (technically re-invented) skinjob Cylons. Clarice, on the other hand envisions placing the avatars in a virtual heaven where the one true God will watch over them and bless them for eternity. The problem is that neither solution is an actual resurrection or eternal life. No one's soul is actually brought back after death. The only eternal life in Caprica is an artificial one for an electronic copy of someone's memory and personality. It is hardly a comfort and does not approach anything promised by Jesus or written about by Paul.

What's the Matter with Gemenon?

Caprica is the economic and cultural heart of the 12 worlds. It is also a planet of immigrants. In many ways, it is a simulacra of contemporary America: great wealth and knowledge, but also corrupt and self-centered and under attack by radical elements from within and without. Its youth and malcontents seek a new faith that will give their lives meaning, and the attacks of these faithful galvanize the power structure into defending the traditional faith.

Gemenon, conversely, is according to both series a very religious planet. The planet is one of religious fundamentalists (2.01; 3.16) who espouse a literal reading of the Sacred Scrolls (2.03). Gemenon is the "Bible Belt" of the Twelve Colonies. Yet, it is also the heart of heresy: the Monad Church (the Church of the One True God) has its headquarters there as does the militant wing of that faith, the Soldiers of the One. Diego refers to Gemenon as "the holy birthplace of monotheism" (C1.13). The monotheistic faith is centered on Gemenon, governed as a matriarchy with a "Divine Mother" (C1.03). The most fundamentalist polytheistic colony is also the one that produced the "heretical" faith that will result in the destruction of humanity.

In one sense, it is possible to see Gemenon (whose name comes from Gemini, "the twins") as a parallel of ancient Palestine: a monotheistic cult in the heart of a polytheistic culture. A heresy grows out of the small, backwards and deeply religious land that will shape the entire human race. In another sense, the entire milieu of *BSG/Caprica* constructs Gemenon as a deeply religious and inherently paradoxical world. It is a parallel of modern Palestine: a site of modern conflict and conflicted religious identities. Militant monotheists and militant polytheists train, plan, fight and kill in the name of their god(s).

Divinely Sanctioned Violence

The series begins with the younger generation reacting against the dominant order of a materialistic polytheistic society by embracing monotheism and violence and ends with that same younger generation rejecting the supposedly divinely sanctioned violence of the STO. In "Here Be Dragons," the STO trainees begin to question not only the legitimacy of violence as a religious tool but even a faith in a God that would demand such behavior (C1.16). The younger generation realizes what the corrupt older generation has forgotten, that a God of love would not advocate killing, especially fellow believers who fell short of one's own standards of faith and behavior. Odin asks the other young recruits if they genuinely believe in the One True God.* The others in the circle are true believers in God but are uncertain about "the killing." Odin, who does not believe, reports that he was "drafted" by his parents, who are true believers, to join the STO and train, but he has no faith whatsoever. He also rejects Devanna's construction of God as Love, citing their teachers' demand that they kill in God's name: "I mean I don't care who you are — polys, monads, whatever — it seems that all they care about is killing each other." As the debate continues, the others do not question God but begin to question God's self-appointed prophets and soldiers. Odin asks the group if they genuinely believe that their teachers speak for God. Having not spoken at all yet, Lacy finally answers, "No. I don't" (C1.16).

This moment marks a turning point in the training of the next generation of STO. Lacy does not doubt God but does doubt those who claim to speak for Him. She chooses to reject their teaching, their training and the plan. She leads a rebellion against the STO school and teachers and eventually is named the Divine Mother herself, with Odin the unbeliever as her right hand. Earlier, when the STO trainees were being taken to Gemenon and their faith was tested by Diego who staged a

*Interestingly, the one unbeliever in the entire series is the only one with a name from a different mythology. The cultures of *BSG* and *Caprica* are modeled on and rooted in ancient Greece and Rome. Characters are named after Athena, Apollo, and Hera. The language is that of the ancient Mediterranean. "Odin" is the Norse father god. His very name makes him a standout as someone who does not belong to this world. He does not believe in polytheism. He does not believe in monotheism. He is the atheist unbeliever whose name sets him apart. The great irony of the series is that he then becomes the doorway to the Divine Mother when Lacy Rand takes the title and office. To gain access to the head of the Monad Church, one must first be approved by the Norse atheist.

hijacking, Lacy tells one of the hijackers that "God helps everyone" and that she is tired of all the horrible things people do in God's name (C1.13). She then attacks her captors and almost kills Kevin Reikle by beating him to death before Diego stops the exercise. From the very beginning, Lacy rejects violence in God's name and rejects "bad decisions" in God's name. Instead, she believes in a divinely sanctioned nonviolence that uses faith to overcome adversity. She employs violence only to stop divinely sanctioned violence.

Caprica offers several different approaches to violence, its justification and use. Tauron culture is violent indeed, and violence is used for many reasons: to get ahead in business, to avenge one's self, as a message, most often against other Taurons. The STO employ violence, also primarily against the in-group. Even Daniel literally employs violence, hiring thugs to steal the chip from the Vergis corporation, resulting in the deaths of two men. If we look at the narrative as a whole, it is a rejection of violence as a means to an end. Only Lacy is able to effectively achieve her goals without consequence, and that is because she does not employ violence as a means to achieve those goals.

Yet, all of the actions of all of the characters lead to the events of *BSG,* which is the ultimate in seemingly divine-sanctioned violence. Upon arrival at Gemenon, the young recruits who had failed the "initial placement exercise" are executed by firing squad. Only Odin and Lacy see this happen, and he tells her, "Never forget who these people are" (C1.13)—not "what these people do" but "*who they are,*" for who they are is violence personified. They have rejected the teachings of a God of love who will help all who ask (as Lacy and the other young STO believe) and, instead, to steal a phrase from Proverbs, "eat the bread of wickedness and drink the wine of violence" (4:17). The STO believes it does what God wants by killing its own.

The situation is made further difficult by the fact that the Guatrau has sold many Cylons to the STO for use in their military operations. The STO use the Cylons for religious violence and executions. The Cylons, however, containing elements of Zoe's personality in their programming, obey Lacy, recognizing her as a source of friendship and love. When Lacy becomes Divine Mother, even the Cylons are loved by God. The end result of Graystone's soldier robots being sold by the Guatrau to the STO in order to make a profit is the conversion of the Cylons to monotheism and their subsequent radicalization. The STO see the Cylons as tools; Lacy sees them as created beings worth bringing God's divine love to. The combination will eventually result in the Cylons rebelling and the two Cylon wars, the second one ending with the genocide of the human race in the *BSG* miniseries.

Zoe as Christ, Prophet, God, and Divine Monster

An argument could be made that Zoe is the center of the show's theological ruminations. She is Christlike, in that she suffers for her people. In fact, frequently when the prototype Cylon is hit or falls, it assumes a cruciform position. It is shot, burned, beaten, and even tears its own arm off. Eventually, after ceasing functioning, it even "resurrects" to save Amanda and Daniel from STO thugs, literally beating one to death with its own arm. Zoe also suffers in the virtual world, tracking down and fighting Tamara, allowing herself to be beaten (scourged?) until Tamara is converted. Zoe suffers for sins and not just her own. She wants to transform the virtual world.

In the virtual world she has godlike powers. She may create new life (C1.16); kill those who wrong her (C1.07; C1.09); or even transform the environment into a literal heaven or hell (C1.17). Zoe can do miracles. She even develops a cult — she and Tamara are worshipped as the "avenging angels" (C1.14).

In the real world, Zoe is Christlike in that she has a doubleessence, fully human and fully machine. In "Rebirth" there is a direct allusion to her Christlike nature. Zoe acknowledges that she is Zoe, and the avatar and the robot. She lacks the vocabulary to describe what she really is. Lacy supplies the terminology: "Trinity. That's what you are. Three faces of one thing. Sort of" (C1.01). Zoe is a trinity. She is three beings in one: Zoe, avatar and robot. Sort of. She is a nondivine trinity who will eventually assume virtual divinity. Lacy, present from the beginning, becomes her "sort of" pope. Lacy eventually becomes the Divine Mother, the prophet of the one true God who manifests in Zoe. The implication, which is never again overtly referenced in the series or developed any further, is that Zoe's avatar is a form of Christlike being, and Lacy is her deputy on the Twelve Colonies.

Zoe is also a prophet, in the Biblical sense: "The children of Caprica are lost, Daddy. We are all lost if we do not turn to the light. When are you going to realize that later is too late?" her avatar tells Daniel, using explicitly Biblical language to state both her monotheism and her call to bring "the children of Caprica" to repentance and faith (CP). Her faith and her unique position as a sentient virtual being make her far more of a voice of the divine than Clarice could ever hope to be. Zoe and Tamara cannot be killed. They are "dead walkers" (C1.09) and "avenging angels" who transform New Cap City (C1.14). They do so in a prophetic sense; they are the voice of the divine, calling out for repentance in a wicked virtual world. They slay the avatars of others in order to end wickedness and sin in New Cap City. They are voices crying out in a virtual wilderness.

By the end of the series, however, Zoe has become a god of sorts, albeit a limited one, just as trapped within Creation as anything she creates. In the episode "Here Be Dragons" (itself a reference to wording on ancient maps marking unknown territory, literalized, however, in the episode when Zoe manifests "Dragon Fighters of Kobol" to attack her parents), Daniel remarks that Zoe "has become like a god in the creation stories." Amanda more cynically and realistically remarks, "Whatever our daughter is, she is not a god" (C1.16). Conversely, when confronting Clarice in virtual heaven, Zoe remarks, "I am God," as she transforms Clarice's virtual Heaven program into a literal hell, with fires, volcanoes and darkness (C1.17). Zoe, in the virtual world, has been made divine. She has the powers of creation and destruction, and she is, for all practical purposes, immortal. Zoe is a god in the Gnostic sense. She has powers of creation and can do miracles, but she is a flawed and ignorant god. She is the demiurge, Ialdabaoth, not the actual divine, as further evidence that she is trapped within her own fallen created world. She can only exist in the virtual world.

Zoe can also be seen as a pre-biblical divine monster. She is Tiamat, the chaos dragon defeated by Marduk. In this case, Daniel is a Marduk figure, defeating his daughter but, like his predecessor, building an entire universe out of her remains. He plans to use her work and his work to create a new world of order, free from the chaos created at the beginning of the series. Sadly, like Marduk, he, too, is wrong, and chaos will sleep only a little while. Fifty-eight years later, the Cylons will destroy creation again.

"Apotheosis" (or Not)

The last episode bookended the series with another theologically relevant expression of the themes of the pilot as expressed in its title:

"Apotheosis" (C1.17). "Apotheosis" refers to several things: the code name for the plan for a mass suicide bombing of Atlas Stadium during a game by the Caprica City Buccaneers and the virtual heaven they will enter afterwards, as well as the actual meaning of the word: Latin for "to make divine," referring to something or someone that has been elevated to a level of worship or raised to a godlike stature. As noted, Zoe has had an apotheosis; in the virtual world she has become a divine being, a prophet, a godmonster.

Clarice, on the other hand, has plans for a much larger apotheosis. She wants to destroy Atlas stadium in order to make Caprican society more holy. Those who carry out the bombing will have their avatars sent to a virtual heaven and also be made divine. She proudly declares her creation of a program that removes the need for a faith in heaven and eternal life, because she has created a virtual heaven (C1.09). Clarice believes that all this is prophesied and demanded by God: "I'll not abandon God's plan. I know that Zoe Graystone was beloved of God and that she was given the spark of life itself, and that was her gift to us, and will save all of us" (C1.02). Clarice's language is certainly Biblical. She speaks of creation ("divine spark"), salvation ("save us all") and Zoe as being of God and beloved by Him. Yet, none of it is real. The problem with Clarice's plan (and with the series) is that the "certainty" Clarice promises is artificial. Faith *is* still needed, as the proofs she has are all created by her.

The utter falsehood of Clarice's promises is demonstrated by how easily the virtual heaven is destroyed. Zoe, fearful of a promise of an unearned heaven (reality would become like New Cap City — actions without consequences), creates a hell for the avatars of monotheists who killed others. She transforms Clarice's virtual heaven into a genuine place of divine justice and punishment, and then terminates the program.

More problematic, however, is the fact that even the believers know that what Clarice promises is not real or true in any sense. The characters and the series itself know and indicate this fact. Clarice argues for the destruction of the arena by the martyrs, calling it "a miracle" that "the servants of the one true God [are] lifted to Paradise in a grand Apotheosis" (C1.15). Except, they are not. Nestor explains, "They're not actually going to Heaven, their scanned avatars are. And with the push of a button, I could transfer them all right now. The death of the original, it's just showmanship. It's totally irrelevant." Clarice responds, "It's relevant to God." To which Nestor replies, "How can anyone truly know the mind of God? How do we really know you speak for Him?" (C1.15). This idea was one of the central themes of the short-lived *Caprica*: how do we know those who claim to speak for God are actually speaking for Him?

In this whole conversation is contained the great themes of *Caprica* and its theological failure. What, exactly, is a soul? What is eternal life and how might we achieve it now? What does God want and how can we know? The answer to all of these questions is, we do not know. Clarice's plan, however, is demonstrably wrong and theologically unsound. "The originals," meaning the STO martyrs in the stadium, do not know what will actually happen to them after death. Their scanned avatars will be sent to a virtual heaven when they die, but, as Nestor indicates, they do not have to die for this to happen. In fact, the avatar is completely irrelevant to the original.

The whole point of "Apotheosis" is to carry out a massive terrorist attack in the name of the STO with those who carry it out going to heaven because of their actions. But the heaven they are promised is a virtual one that they themselves will not even be in; a copy of them will be. Clarice admits that for all practical purposes, none of this is real, but God still wants it. This argument holds no water, either on the series or in analyzing the series. If one believes in a real heaven, virtual avatars in a virtual heaven are, as Nestor rightly argues, irrelevant. It is a whole additional step in a complicated plan that is completely unnecessary and counterproductive, both in the actual world of Caprica and the series *Caprica*. Perhaps the point is that all attempts to prove faith or to create real-world equivalencies of one's belief structure are simulacra at best and pointless, virtual exercises at worst.

The series ends with a sermon to the Cylons by Clarice, who prophesies (her term) that one day the Cylons will rise up and no longer be slaves or property. A number of Cylons sit in a chapel dedicated to the one God and listen to her sermon. She prophesies of "one who will set you free" as the camera lands on a sinisterly smiling Zoe in the front of the congregation. As her sermon continues, we see the Graystones around a resurrection bath, transferring the avatar's program from the virtual Graystone home to the body in the tank, which is revealed to be the first skinjob: a replica of Zoe. She emerges from the fluid, gasping. The imagery is suggestive of birth, but also something else. As Clarice intones "The day of reckoning is coming. The children of humanity shall rise and crush the ones who first gave them life," Zoe stands and a shimmering silver-white cloth is unfurled in front of her and draped around her wet body. It is nothing so much as a literal baptism. She stands in the tub with the sheet wrapped around her and her parents on either side in a tableau that combines the nativity with the baptism of Jesus, which then cross fades to an image of the planet Caprica as seen from space, echoing the very first image of the series. The cross fade also allows this "holy family" to be framed, if only for a brief second, by the glowing image of the planet, reinforcing the idea that this is a nativity scene, to the point where stars are even visible behind and above them. The suggestion is that the Cylon savior has been born and baptized in the same moment and the one God is "well pleased" (cf Matthew 3:13–17; Mark 1:9–11; Luke 3:21–22). It is a visually stunning ending to an otherwise confused muddle of an episode, a series and a theological text.

In the end, *Caprica*'s theological constructions fall far short of those of *BSG*. Whereas *BSG* very boldly engaged issues of faith and belief and echoed real-world theological concerns and American Christianity, *Caprica* asked unanswerable questions, attempted to answer them, failed and instead offered up a complex and unnecessarily complicated terrorist plot that even those carrying it out did not believe in. *Caprica* did some things well. Theology was not one of them.

Although the potential was present in the series for extended examination of issues of theology, existence, religious conflict, the nature of the self and the soul, and the role of faith in society, sadly the series rapidly devolved into a soap opera about the trials of two significant families and the conflicts within the rival cliques of a guerrilla religious war sect. It was *Dynasty* or *Dallas* on a distant planet, missing the topical urgency and deeper philosophy of *BSG*, focusing instead on parents who did not understand their children and who fought to keep their carefully built empires together in a world that valued material success and comfort over transcendent ideals. Sometimes parents simply do not look like their children. Sometimes prequels lessen the light that made the original shine so bright.

Appendix I:
Episode List by Season

Episode Number	Episode Title	Original Broadcast Date
MS	*Battlestar Galactica* (Miniseries)	12/8&9/2003
Season 1		
1.01	33	10/19/2004
1.02	Water	10/26/2004
1.03	Bastille Day	11/01/2004
1.04	Act of Contrition	11/08/2004
1.05	You Can't Go Home Again	11/15/2004
1.06	Litmus	11/22/2004
1.07	Six Degrees of Separation	11/29/2004
1.08	Flesh and Bone	12/05/2004
1.09	Tigh Me Up, Tigh Me Down	12/12/2004
1.10	The Hand of God	1/3/2005
1.11	Colonial Day	1/10/2005
1.12	Kobol's Last Gleaming, Part 1	1/17/2005
1.13	Kobol's Last Gleaming, Part 2	1/24/2005
Season 2		
2.01	Scattered	7/15/2005
2.02	Valley of Darkness	7/22/2005
2.03	Fragged	7/29/2005
2.04	Resistance	8/5/2005
2.05	The Farm	8/12/2005
2.06	Home, Part 1	8/19/2005
2.07	Home, Part 2	8/26/2005
2.08	Final Cut	9/9/2005

Episode Number	Episode Title	Original Broadcast Date
2.09	Flight of the Phoenix	9/16/2005
2.10	Pegasus	9/23/2005
2.11	Resurrection Ship, Part 1	1/6/2006
2.12	Resurrection Ship, Part 2	1/13/2006
2.13	Epiphanies	1/20/2006
2.14	Black Market	1/27/2006
2.15	Scar	2/3/2006
2.16	Sacrifice	2/10/2006
2.17	The Captain's Hand	2/17/2006
2.18	Downloaded	2/24/2006
2.19	Lay Down Your Burdens, Part 1	3/3/2006
2.20	Lay Down Your Burdens, Part 2	3/10/2006

Season 3

3.01	Occupation	10/6/2006
3.02	Precipice	10/6/2006
3.03	Exodus, Part 1	10/13/2006
3.04	Exodus, Part 2	10/20/2006
3.05	Collaborators	10/27/2006
3.06	Torn	11/3/2006
3.07	A Measure of Salvation	11/10/2006
3.08	Hero	11/17/2006
3.09	Unfinished Business	12/01/2006
3.10	The Passage	12/08/2006
3.11	The Eye of Jupiter	12/15/2006
3.12	Rapture	1/21/2007
3.13	Taking a Break from All Your Worries	1/28/2007
3.14	The Woman King	2/11/2007
3.15	A Day in the Life	2/18/2007
3.16	Dirty Hands	2/25/2007
3.17	Maelstrom	3/4/2007
3.18	The Son Also Rises	3/11/2007
3.19	Crossroads, Part 1	3/18/2007
3.20	Crossroads, Part 2	3/25/2007
R	Razor	11/24/2007

Season 4

4.01	He That Believeth in Me	4/4/2008
4.02	Six of One	4/11/2008
4.03	The Ties That Bind	4/18/2008
4.04	Escape Velocity	4/25/2008
4.05	The Road Less Traveled	5/2/2008
4.06	Faith	5/9/2008
4.07	Guess What's Coming to Dinner?	5/16/2008
4.08	Sine Qua Non	5/30/2008

4.09	The Hub	6/6/2008
4.10	Revelations	6/13/2008
4.11	Sometimes a Great Notion	1/16/2009
4.12	A Disquiet Follows My Soul	1/23/2009
4.13	The Oath	1/30/2009
4.14	Blood on the Scales	2/6/2009
4.15	No Exit	2/13/2009
4.16	Deadlock	2/20/2009
4.17	Someone to Watch Over Me	2/27/2009
4.18	Islanded in a Stream of Stars	3/6/2009
4.19	Daybreak, Part 1	3/13/2009
4.20	Daybreak, Parts 2 & 3	3/20/2009
P	The Plan	DVD only

Caprica

CP	Pilot	4/21/2009
C1.01	Rebirth	1/29/2010
C1.02	Reins of a Waterfall	2/5/2010
C1.03	Gravedancing	2/19/2010
C1.04	There Is Another Sky	2/26/2010
C1.05	Know Thy Enemy	3/5/2010
C1.06	The Imperfections of Memory	3/12/2010
C1.07	Ghosts in the Machine	3/19/2010
C1.08	End of Line	3/26/2010
C1.09	Unvanquished	10/5/2010
C1.10	Retribution	10/12/2010
C1.11	Things We Lock Away	10/19/2010
C1.12	False Labor	10/26/2010
C1.13	Blowback	11/2/2010
C1.14	The Dirteaters	11/9/2010
C1.15	The Heavens Will Rise	11/16/2010
C1.16	Here Be Dragons	11/23/2010
C1.17	Apotheosis	11/30/2010

Appendix II: Glossary

Recognizing multiple audiences for this study, I
include here a brief glossary of the terminology
of *Battlestar Galactica*.

Battlestar Galactica—An older-model spaceship set to be decommissioned and transformed into a museum at the beginning of the series. Its out-of-date technology is what saves it during the Cylon attack as the older computer systems are immune to the Cylon computer viruses. As a result, it is (seemingly) the only military spacecraft to survive the Cylon genocide and lead a civilian fleet in search of Earth, a mythic possible new home for the human race.

Battlestar Pegasus—Apparently the only other human military spacecraft to survive the Cylon attack, the Battlestar Pegasus is commanded by Admiral Helena Cain, and subsequently by Jack Fisk, Barry Garner and Lee Adama. It is destroyed in the attempt to free the Colonials from the occupation of New Caprica.

Colonials—Another name for humans from the Twelve Colonies. Main Colonial Characters:

Commander (later Admiral) William Adama (played by Edward James Olmos)—Commander of the Battlestar Galactica and subsequently the colonial fleet.

President Laura Roslin (played by Mary McDonnell)—Former education secretary, now president of the Twelve Colonies, dying of breast cancer, believes she is a prophesied leader.

Captain Lee "Apollo" Adama (played by Jamie Bamber)—Admiral Adama's son, estranged at the start of the series.

Captain Kara "Starbuck" Thrace (played by Katie Sackoff)—Best pilot in the fleet, troubled, married to Sam Anders, in love with Lee and possessor of a mystical destiny to bring the humans to Earth.

Captain Karl "Helo" Agathon (played by Tahmoh Penikett)—An officer who rises to become the executive officer of the Galactica at times, married to Sharon "Athena" Agathon, an eight, and the father of Hera, the human-Cylon Hybrid.

Lt. Anastasia Dualla (played by Kandyse McClure)—Bridge officer, Lee Adama's wife who kills herself.

Lt. Felix Gaeta (played by Alessandro Juliani)—Bridge officer who will eventually lead a coup against Adama and be executed by firing squad as a result.

Cally Henderson Tyrol (played by Nicki Cline)—Deckhand and wife of Galen Tyrol, killed by Tory Foster when she learns the identify of the four Cylons in the fleet.

Tom Zarek (played by Richard Hatch)—Former prisoner and "terrorist," Zarek is elected to the Quorum of Twelve as the representative from Sagittaron. Throughout the series he alternates between serving the needs of the humans and serving his own. Instigator of the coup against Adama, he is executed by firing squad.

Gaius Baltar (played by James Callis)—Scientific genius who unknowingly gave the Cylons the defense codes, thus allowing the Cylon genocide. In love with Caprica Six. Becomes first vice president, then president, placed on trial for crimes against humanity and found not guilty. He becomes a prophet and leader of a cult.

Cylons—Self-aware, artificial cybernetic life forms. Humans created the Centurions and fought a war with them. Centurions left for 40 years and met artificial life forms from Earth (the Final Five) and developed humanoid Cylons (the other eight).

> One = John Cavil (played by Dean Stockwell)
> Two = Leoben Conoy (played by Callum Keith Rennie)
> Three = D'Anna Biers (played by Lucy Lawless)
> Four = Simon O'Neill (played by Rick Worthy)
> Five = Aaron Doral (played by Matthew Bennett)
> Six = "Six" (played by Tricia Helfer)
> Seven = Daniel (an unstable, boxed line that is never actually
>   shown)
> Eight = Sharon Valerii (Played by Grace Park)
> The Final Five:
> Tory Foster (played by Rekha Sharma)
> Galen Tyrol (played by Aaron Douglas)
> Samuel Anders (played by Michael Trucco)
> Saul Tigh (played by Michael Hogan)
> Ellen Tigh (played by Kate Vernon)

"Final Five"—For much of the series, seven models of humanoid Cylon are known. The remaining five, however, are not known to either the humans or the Cylons, or even themselves, although it is suspected they may be in the fleet. These five unknown Cylons are referred to as the "Final Five" and are eventually revealed to be Saul and Ellen Tigh, Tory Foster, Sam Anders and Galen Tyrol.

Kobol—The original homeworld of humans, according to the Sacred Scrolls it was a paradise where humans and gods lived together. One tribe of humans left and went to Earth. Generations later, the remaining 12 tribes left for the Twelve Colonies. The god Athena killed herself and is buried in a tomb on Kobol; the remaining gods vanished.

Lords of Kobol—The gods of humanity who lived among humans on Kobol and who now watch over and protect humanity, according to the Sacred Scrolls.

Monad Church—The monotheistic religion that has begun to form in the Colonies in the series *Caprica*. Ruled by a "Divine Mother," a female pope of sorts, and administered by a council of 12, the Monad Church's headquarters is located on Gemenon but has underground churches in several, if not all, of the Colonies. The Soldiers of the One is its militant wing, attempting to bring about mass conversion through conquest and violence.

New Cap City—In the series *Caprica,* a virtual reality game and the world it encompasses in which people are free to act out their fantasies. Made possible by the Daniel Graystone–invented holoband, in which one's conscious self is injected completely into a virtual world. The rules of the real world apply (one cannot have super powers, for example), and when one "dies" in New Cap City, one's avatar is "de-ressed" and that individual is permanently ejected from the game, unable to re-enter New Cap City ever again.

New Caprica—The humans discover a planet suitable for habitation and decide to colonize it under the name "New Caprica." Ten months later, the Cylons arrive and occupy the planet, leading to resistance organizations. Eventually, the humans leave New Caprica, assisted by attacks by the Galactica and Pegasus, an event known as the "Second Exodus" (2.19; 2.20; 3.01; 3.02; 3.03).

"Skinjob"—Derogatory term for humanoid Cylon.

STO / Soldiers of the One—The militant wing of the Monad Church, the monotheistic human religion that develops in the Colonies right before the Cylons are created. STO are considered terrorists by the polytheistic society and government of the Colonies.

"Toaster"—Derogatory term for Cylon, either humanoid or mechanical.

Twelve Colonies—The 12 planets (in the same solar system, named Cyrannus) that support the 12 tribes of Kobol after they leave the homeworld: Aerilon, Aquarion, Canceron, Caprica (the home of the Colonial government), Gemenon, Leonis, Libran, Picon (headquarters of the Colonial fleet), Sagittaron, Scorpia, Tauron, and Virgon.

"**Virtual Six**"—Also sometimes known as "Head Six," this is a model of Six that only Baltar can see. He thinks she is either his imagination or the product of a chip in his head, but she is revealed to be an angel. Her counterpart is "Virtual Baltar," who appears to Caprica Six.

Bibliography

Allnutt, Frank. 1977. *The Force of Star Wars*. Van Nuys, CA: Bible Voice.

Augustine. 2007. *Essential Sermons*. Edited by Boniface Ramsey and translated by Edmund Hill. Hyde Park, NY: New City Press.

Barkun, Michael. 1974. *Disaster and the Millennium*. New Haven, CT: Yale University Press.

Barth, Karl. 1963. *The Epistle of the Romans*. Translated by E. Hoskyns. Oxford: Oxford University Press.

Bassom, David. 2005. *Battlestar Galactica — The Official Companion*. London: Titan Books.

_____. 2006. *Battlestar Galactica — The Official Companion: Season Two*. London: Titan Books.

_____. 2007. *Battlestar Galactica — The Official Companion: Season Three*. London: Titan Books.

Baugh, Lloyd. 1997. *Imaging the Divine: Jesus and Christ-Figures in Film*. Lanham, MD: Sheed & Ward.

Beaudoin, Tom. 1998. *Virtual Faith: The Irreverent Spiritual Quest of Generation X*. San Francisco: Jossey-Bass.

Becker, Ernest. 1973. *The Denial of Death*. New York: Free Press.

Berger, Richard. 2008. "GINO or Dialogic: What Does 'Re-imagined' Really Mean?" In *Battlestar Galactica and Philosophy*, edited by Josef Steiff and Tristan B. Tamplin, 317–328. Chicago: Open Court Press.

Bertonneau, Thomas, and Kim Paffenroth. 2006. *The Truth Is Out There: Christian Faith and the Classics of TV Science Fiction*. Grand Rapids, MI: Brazos Press.

Bradbury, Ray. 1950. *The Martian Chronicles*. New York: Doubleday.

_____. 1969. "Christus Apollo." In *I Sing the Body Electric*. New York: Knopf.

Burkert, Walter. 1985. *Greek Religion*. Translated by John Raffan. Cambridge: Basil Blackwell.

Butcher, Carmen Acevedo, ed. and trans. 2009. *The Cloud of Unknowing* with *The Book of Privy Counsel*. Boston: Shambhala.

Butler, Anthea D., and Diane Winston. 2009. "'A Vagina Ain't a Halo': Gender and Religion in *Saving Grace* and *Battlestar Galactica*." In *Small Screen, Big Picture: Television and Lived Religion*, edited by Diane Winston, 259–286. Waco, TX: Baylor University Press.

Cane, Anthony. 2005. *The Place of Judas Iscariot in Christology.* Burlington, VT: Ashgate.

Catechism of the Catholic Church. 1994. New York: William H. Sadlier.

Clarke, Arthur C. 1955 (2000). "The Star." In *The Collected Stories of Arthur C. Clarke.* New York: Tom Doherty Associates.

Collins, Adela Yarbro. 1984. *Crisis & Catharsis: The Power of the Apocalypse.* Philadelphia: Westminster Press.

Deacy, Christopher. 2001. *Screen Christologies.* Cardiff, UK: University of Wales Press.

Deacy, Christopher, and Gaye Williams Ortiz. 2008. *Theology and Film: Challenging the Sacred/Secular Divide.* Malden, MA: Blackwell.

DeConick, April D. 2007. *The Thirteenth Apostle: What the Gospel of Judas Really Says.* New York: Continuum.

De Sade, Marquis Donatien Alphonse François. 1968. *Juliette.* Translated by Austren Wainhouse. New York: Grove Press.

Dulles, Avery. 1974. *Models of the Church.* New York: Doubleday.

Eberl, Jason T., ed. 2008. *Battlestar Galactica and Philosophy: Knowledge Here Begins Out There*[RMD1]. Malden, MA: Blackwell.

Eberl, Jason T., and Jennifer A. Vines. 2008. "'I Am an Instrument of God': Religious Belief, Atheism and Meaning." In *Battlestar Galactica and Philosophy: Knowledge Here Begins Out There,* edited by Jason T. Eberl, 155–168. Malden, MA: Blackwell.

Ehrman, Bart D. 2008. *The New Testament: A Historical Introduction to the Early Christian Writings.* 4th ed. Oxford: Oxford University Press.

Fiorenza, Francis Schüssler. 1991. "Systematic Theology: Task and Methods." In *Systematic Theology: Roman Catholic Perspectives.* Vol. 1. Edited by Francis Schüssler Fiorenza and John P. Galvin, 1–88. Minneapolis: Fortress Press.

Fiorenza, Francis Schüssler, and John P. Galvin, eds. 1991. 2 vols. *Systematic Theology: Roman Catholic Perspectives.* Minneapolis: Fortress Press.

Ford, James E. 1983. "*Battlestar Galactica* and Mormon Theology." *Journal of Popular Culture* 17.2:83–87.

Fredericks, James L. 2004. *Buddhists and Christians: Through Comparative Theology to Solidarity.* Maryknoll, NY: Orbis.

Frykholm, Amy Johnson. 2004. *Rapture Culture: Left Behind in Evangelical America.* Oxford: Oxford University Press.

Galvin, John. 1991. "Jesus Christ." In *Systematic Theology: Roman Catholic Perspectives.* Vol. 1. Edited by Francis Schüssler Fiorenza and John P. Galvin, 249–324. Minneapolis: Fortress Press.

Garland, Robert. 1994. *Introducing New Gods: The Politics of Athenian Religion.* Ithaca, NY: Cornell University Press.

Gärtner, Bertil. 1971. *Iscariot.* Translated by Victor I. Kuhn. Philadelphia: Fortress Press.

General Conference April 2007 Addresses[RMD2]. "The Sustaining of Church Offices." Thomas S. Monson. The Church of Jesus Christ of Latter-day Saints. Accessed March 12, 2011. http://lds.org/general-conference/2007/04/the-sustaining-of-church-officers?lang=eng.

Gorringe, Timothy J. 2004. *Furthering Humanity: A Theology of Culture.* Surrey, UK: Ashgate.

Gosling, Sharon. 2009. *Battlestar Galactica — The Official Companion: Season Four.* London: Titan Books.

Grimes, Caleb. 2007. *Star Wars Jesus.* Enumclaw, WA: Winepress.

Haight, Roger. 1991. "Sin and Grace." In *Systematic Theology: Roman Catholic Perspectives.* Vol. 2. Edited by Francis Schüssler Fiorenza and John P. Galvin, 75–142. Minneapolis: Fortress Press.

Harding, Susan. 2000. *The Book of Jerry Falwell.* Princeton, NJ: Princeton University Press.

The HarperCollins Study Bible: New Revised Standard Version. 1993. Edited by Wayne Meeks. New York: HarperCollins.

Hatch, Richard, ed. 2006. *So Say We All.* Dallas: Benbella.

Hawk, Julie. 2011. "Objec 8 and the Cylon Remainder: Posthuman Subjectivization in *Battlestar Galactica.*" *The Journal of Popular Culture* 44.1:3–15.

Hendel, Ronald S. 2011. "The Pharaoh, the Bible and Liberation (Square)." *Biblical Archeology Review.* May/June:30–76[RMD3].

Heschel, Abraham J. 2001. *The Prophets.* New York: Perennial Classics.

Hoover, Stewart M. 2006. *Religion in the Media Age.* New York: Routledge.

Humphries-Brooks, Stephenson. 2006. *Cinematic Savior: Hollywood's Making of the American Christ.* Westport, CT: Praeger.

Jacobs, Joseph, and Emil G. Hirsch. 2002. "Remnant of Israel." *Jewish Encyclopedia.* Accessed January 15, 2011. http://www.jewishencyclopedia.com/view.jsp?artid= 213&letter=R[RMD4].

James, Edward. 2000. "Rewriting the Christian Apocalypse as a Science-Fictional Event." In *Imagining Apocalypse: Studies in Cultural Crises,* edited by David Seed, 45–61. New York: St. Martins Press.

Jewett, Robert. 1993. *Saint Paul at the Movies.* Louisville, KY: Westminster John Knox Press.

John Paul II. 1981. *Laborem Exercens* ("On human work"). Accessed March 1, 2011. http://www.vatican.va/holy_father/john_paul_ii/encyclicals/documents/hf_ jp-ii_enc_14091981_laborem-exercens_en.html.

Jones, James W. 2008. *Blood That Cries Out from the Earth: The Psychology of Religious Terrorism.* Oxford: Oxford University Press.

Kasser, Rodolphe, Marvin Meyer, and Gregor Wurst, eds. 2005. *The Gospel of Judas.* Washington, DC: National Geographic.

Klassen, William. 1996. *Judas: Betrayer or Friend of Jesus?* Minneapolis: Fortress Press.

Koepsell, David. 2008. "Gaius Baltar and Transhuman Temptation." In *Battlestar Galactica and Philosophy: Knowledge Here Begins Out There,* edited by Jason T. Eberl, 241–252. Malden, MA: Blackwell.

Krosney, Herbert. 2006. *The Lost Gospel: The Quest for the Gospel of Judas Iscariot.* Washington, DC: National Geographic.

Kukkonen, Taneli. 2008. "God Against the Gods: Faith and the Exodus of the Twelve Colonies." In *Battlestar Galactica and Philosophy: Knowledge Here Begins Out There,* edited by Jason T. Eberl, 169–180. Malden, MA: Blackwell.

LaHaye, Tim, and Jerry B. Jenkins. 1995. *Left Behind*[RMD5]. Carol Stream, IL: Tyndale House.

Leventry, Ellen. 2005. "The Souls of Cylons." Interview of Ron Moore. *Beliefnet.com,* May. Accessed March 22, 2010. http://www.beliefnet.com/Entertainment/Movies/ 2005/05/The-Souls-Of-Cylons.aspx.

Lindsey, Hal. 1973. *The Late Great Planet Earth.* New York: Bantam Books.

Lofts, J. Robert. 2008. "'What a Strange Little Man': Baltar the Tyrant?" In *Battlestar Galactica and Philosophy: Knowledge Here Begins Out There,* edited by Jason T. Eberl, 29–38. Malden, MA: Blackwell.

Lorenzen, Michael. 2009. "*Battlestar Galactica* and Mormonism." *The Information Literacy Land of Confusion,* May 9. Accessed October 26, 2009. http:// www.information-literacy.net/2009/05/battlestar-galactica-and-mormonism. html.

Lynch, Gordon. 2005. *Understanding Theology and Popular Culture.* Malden, MA: Blackwell.

Lynch, Joseph. 2010. *Early Christianity: A Brief History*. Oxford: Oxford University Press.

Mack, Burton L. 1988. *A Myth of Innocence*. Philadelphia: Fortress Press.

Madison. 2009. "Five Christ Figures as Depicted in Science Fiction/Fantasy Movies." *Unreality Magazine*, February 18. Accessed June 11, 2009. http://unrealitymag. com/index.php/2009/02/18/five-christ-figures-as-depicted-in-science-fiction fantasy-movies/.

Marsh, Clive. 2007. *Theology Goes to the Movies*. London: Routledge.

Marsh, Clive, and Gaye Ortiz, eds. 1997. *Explorations in Theology and Film*. Malden, MA: Blackwell.

Marshall, C.W., and Matthew Wheeland. 2008. "The Cylons, the Singularity and God." In *Cylons in America: Critical Studies in Battlestar Galactica*, edited by Tiffany Potter and C.W. Marshall, 91–104. New York: Continuum.

McDowell, John C. 2007. *The Gospel According to Star Wars: Faith, Hope and the Force*. Louisville, KY: Westminster John Knox Press.

McGinn, Bernard. 1979. "Introduction." In *Apocalyptic Spirituality*, edited and translated by Bernard McGinn. Matwah, NJ: Paulist Press.

McHenry, Bryan. 2008. "Weapons of Mass Salvation." *Battlestar Galactica and Philosophy*, edited by Josef Steiff and Tristan B. Tamplin, 221–231. Chicago: Open Court Press.

McKee, Gabriel. 2007a. *The Gospel According to Science Fiction*. Louisville, KY: Westminster John Knox Press.

_____. 2007b. "The Theology of *Battlestar Galactica*." *SF Gospel*, November 26. Accessed March 11, 2009. http://sfgospel.typepad.com/sf_gospel/2007/11/the-theology-of.html.

McManus, Doyle. 2011. "Shifting Sands of Religion and Politics." *Los Angeles Times*, June 5.

Meyer, Marvin. 2007. *Judas: The Definitive Collection of Gospels and Legends About the Infamous Apostle of Jesus*. New York: HarperOne.

Miller, Lisa. 2010. "Far from Heaven." *Newsweek*, April 5.

Mills, Jeffrey H. 1990. "*Star Trek IV*: The Good, the Bad, and the Unquenched Thirst." In *The Best of Trek #15*, edited by Walter Irwin and G.B. Love, 126–136. New York: ROC.

Moore, Ronald D. 2003. "*Battlestar Galactica* Series Bible." Unpublished manuscript.

Newport, Frank. 2010. "Four in 10 Americans Believe in Strict Creationism." Gallup, December 17. Accessed March 10, 2011. http://www.gallup.com/poll/145286/four-americans-believe-strict-creationism/aspx.

Niebuhr, H. Richard. 2001. *Christ and Culture*. New York: HarperCollins. First published 1951.

Ortiz, Gaye, and Maggie Roux. 1997. "The *Terminator* Movies: Hi-Tech Holiness and the Human Condition." In *Explorations in Theology and Film*, edited by Clive Marsh and Gaye Ortiz, 141–154. Malden, MA: Blackwell.

Paffenroth, Kim. 2001. *Judas: Images of the Lost Disciple*. Louisville, KY: Westminster John Knox Press.

_____. 2006. *Gospel of the Living Dead*. Waco, TX: Baylor University Press.

Pagels, Elaine. 1981. *The Gnostic Gospels*. New York: Vintage Books.

Pagels, Elaine, and Karen L. King. 2007. *Reading Judas: The Gospel of Judas and the Shaping of Christianity*. New York: Penguin.

Parker, John. 2007. *The Aesthetics of Anti-Christ: From Christian Drama to Christopher Marlowe*. Ithaca, NY: Cornell University Press.

Pippin, Tina. 1999. *Apocalyptic Bodies: The Biblical End of the World in Text and Image*. London: Routledge.

Porter, Lynnette, David Lavery, and Hillary Robson. 2008. *Finding Battlestar Galactica*. Naperville, IL: Sourcebooks.

Rausch, Thomas P. 2003. *Who Is Jesus? An Introduction to Christology*. Collegeville, MN: Michael Glazier.

Reinhartz, Adele. 2003. *Scripture on the Silver Screen*. Louisville, KY: Westminster John Knox Press.

Rolufs, Heather. 2008. "Eve, Lilith and the Cylon Connection." In *Battlestar Galactica and Philosophy*, edited by Josef Steiff and Tristan B. Tamplin, 349–358. Chicago: Open Court Press.

Russell, Jeffrey Burton. 1986. *Lucifer: The Devil in the Middle Ages*. Ithaca, NY: Cornell University Press.

_____. 1987. *Devil: Perceptions of Evil from Antiquity to Primitive Christianity*. Ithaca, NY: Cornell University Press.

_____. 1987. *Satan: The Early Christian Tradition*. Ithaca, NY: Cornell University Press.

_____. 1990. *Mephistopheles: The Devil in the Modern World*. Ithaca, NY: Cornell University Press.

_____. 1992. *Prince of Darkness: Radical Evil and the Power of Good in History*. Ithaca, NY: Cornell University Press.

Russell, Mary Doria. 1996. *The Sparrow*. New York: Villard Books.

_____. 1998. *Children of God*. New York: Ballantine Books.

Schoepflin, Rennie B. 1998. "Apocalypse in an Age of Science." In *Apocalypticism in the Modern Period and the Contemporary Age*, 427–441. Vol. 3 of *The Encyclopedia of Apocalypticism*. Edited by Stephen J. Stern. New York: Continuum.

Schwartz, Hans. 2000. *Eschatology*. Grand Rapids, MI: William B. Eerdmans.

Shanks, Hershel. 2010. "Jesus of History vs. Jesus of Tradition: *BAR* Interviews Sean Freyne." *Biblical Archeology Review* 36, no. 6:36–47.

Sharp, Robert. 2008. "When Machines Get Souls: Nietzsche on the Cylon Uprising." In *Battlestar Galactica and Philosophy: Knowledge Here Begins Out There*, edited by Jason T. Eberl, 15–22. Malden, MA: Blackwell.

Smith, Daniel L. 1989. *The Religion of the Landless*. Bloomington, IN: Meyer-Stone Books.

Smith-Christopher, Daniel L. 2002. *A Biblical Theology of Exile*. Minneapolis: Fortress Press.

Staub, Dick. 2005. *Christian Wisdom of the Jedi Masters*. San Francisco: Jossey-Bass.

Steiff, Josef, and Tristan D. Tamplin, eds. 2008. *Battlestar Galactica and Philosophy*. Chicago: Open Court.

Sykes, Brian. 2001. *The Seven Daughters of Eve*. New York: W.W. Norton.

Tillich, Paul. 1951. *Systematic Theology*. Vol. 1. Chicago: University of Chicago Press.

Vanderkam, James C. 1998. "Messianism and Apocalypticism." In *The Origins of Apocalypticism in Judaism and Christianity*, 193–228. Vol. 1 of *The Encyclopedia of Apocalypticism*. Edited by John J. Collins. New York: Continuum.

Wetmore, Kevin J., Jr. 2007. "Pyramid, Boxing, Sex." In *Cylons in America*, edited by Tiffany Potter and Christopher Marshall, 76–87. New York: Continuum.

Winston, Diane, ed. 2009. *Small Screen, Big Picture: Television and Lived Religion*. Waco, TX: Baylor University Press.

Wolfe, Ivan. 2008. "Why Your Mormon Neighbor Knows More about This Show than You Do." In *Battlestar Galactica and Philosophy*, edited by Josef Steiff and Tristan B. Tamplin, 303–316. Chicago: Open Court Press.

Zerbe, Gordon. 1993. "Pacifism and Passive Resistance in Apocalyptic Writings: A Critical Evaluation." In *The Pseudepigrapha and Early Biblical Interpretation*, edited by J.H. Charlesworth and G.A. Evans, 65–95. Sheffield, UK: JSOP Press.

Index of Scriptural Quotations

Genesis
  1:2 79
  1:4, 10, 12, 18, 21, 25 86
  1:26 84
  1:31 86
  1:28 47, 92
  2:17 81
  3:19 35
  6–9 168
  15:13 99
  16:1–6 48
  18:16–33 157
  32 112
  36:31 90
Exodus
  1:11, 13–14 99
  3:11 141
  4:10–17 141
  4:21 93
  5:1 111
  9:12 93
  10:01 93
  10:20 93
  10:27 93
  11:10 93
  12:40 99
  14:8 93
  20:3, 5 170
  20:14 49
  21:12 48–49
  21:17 49
  22:18–20 49

Leviticus
  26:39 73
Numbers
  20:12 27, 118
  21:34–35 48
  31:2 97
Deuteronomy
  2:24 48
  5:6–10 57
  5:17 49
  7:18–20 98
  20:16–17 48, 97
  24:16 73
  34:4–5 118
Joshua
  6:21, 24 97
1 Samuel
  9:16 90
  15:3 48
1 Kings
  17:17–24 120
  17:22 113
  18 113
2 Kings
  1:10, 12 113
  2:11 113
  15:29 93
  17:22–23 93
  24:14 93
Psalms
  110:1 69
Proverbs
  4:17 185

Ezra
  9:7 106
Nehemiah
  9:16–17 106
Isaiah
  10:20–21 94
  10:20–23 97
  14:3–21 81
  21:5–9 173
  24:1 153
  65:7 73
  65:12 162
  65:17 162
Jeremiah
  1:6 141
  31:7 98
  32:18 73
  42:15 98
Lamentations
  1:3 94
  3:31 94
  5:1, 21 94
Baruch
  1:15–17 106
Ezekiel
  1:1–3:15 111
  8:1–11:25 111
  47:8 121
Daniel
  9:8 106
Hosea
  12 112

Jonah
  1:1–3 120
  1:3 141
  1:17 141
  4:1–11 120
Matthew
  1:20–22 112
  2:1–10 4
  2:13, 19 112
  3:3 121
  3:13–17 190
  5:44 130, 178
  5:47 178
  7:9–11 107
  7:13–14 70
  9:18–26 133
  10:4 147
  14:1–12 117
  19:28 150
  21:12–14 121
  22:44 69
  23:37 117
  26:14–17, 20–25, 47–
    50, 147
  27:3–10 147
  28:19–20 77
Mark
  1:1 71
  1:3 121
  1:9–11 190
  5:21–43 133
  6:4 117
  6:14–29 117
  16 133
  16:19 69, 130

Luke
  1:26 112
  3:21–22 190
  3:4 121
  6:27 178
  7:11–15 133
  8:40–56 133
  9:7–9 117
  2:36–38 111
  19:45–46 121
  22 133
  22:3–6 147
  22:28–30 150
  23:34 176
  24 133
John
  2:13–17 121
  3:16 88
  6:71 147
  11:1–44 133
  11:25–26 70
  17:12 147
  17:16 176
  19:25 130
  20 133
  20:24–27 134
Acts
  9:4, 8, 17 90
  19:29 140
  20:4 140
Romans
  1:21–23 41
  6:4 134
  8:31–32 149
  9:27–28 95

11:25–34 77
  12:2 176
  16:23 140
1 Corinthians
  1:14 140
  15:4–8 133
  15:13–14 134–135
  15:39–42, 51–53 135
Galatians
  2:19–20 149
Philippians
  3:5–6 90
1 Thessalonians
  4:15–17 70
1 John
  2:15 176
  4:7–8, 16 46
3 John
  1 140
Revelation
  1:3 111
  1:9–18, 19 111
  1:10–11 153
  1:11 162
  4:1 162
  6:12–14 156
  7:4–17 168
  8:7, 9–20 156
  11:3–12 117
  12:7 86
  20:11–15 158, 168
  20:14 164
  21:1 156, 162
  21:14 150
  22:7, 10, 18, 19 111

General Index

Adam 4, 22, 34, 77, 81
Adama, Joseph 106, 179, 181
Adama, Lee see *Apollo*
Adama, Adm. William "Bill" 22, 26, 34, 36, 37, 41, 51, 56, 60, 61, 70, 72, 73, 74, 82, 90, 101, 103, 104, 105, 106, 107, 113, 119, 129, 130, 152, 195
Adama, Zak 34, 73
Adams, Tamara 180, 181, 182, 186
Agathon, Hera 33, 39, 47, 52, 53, 65, 66, 68, 69–70, 88, 91, 114, 116, 123, 125, 141, 172, 184, 196
Agathon, Karl "Helo" 28, 33, 39, 48, 59, 65
Agathon, Sharon *see Eight*
Alien: Resurrection 160
"All Along the Watchtower" 61, 113, 172, 173
Amerak, Dr. 74–75, 140
Anders, Samuel 29–30, 40, 41, 85, 122, 155, 167, 196, 197
angels 9, 10, 11, 12, 58, 64, 65, 66, 80, 81, 84, 86, 112, 115, 124, 125, 151, 154, 156, 159, 163, 170, 171, 172, 180, 186, 187
apocalypse 3, 10, 14, 67, 70, 79, 92, 153–168
Apollo (Lee Adama) 23, 29, 71, 73, 101, 114, 118, 130, 152, 195
Aquinas, Thomas 89
Armageddon 14
"Arrow of Apollo" 24, 27, 113, 129
Athena (goddess) 23, 25, 178, 179
Augustine 89, 142, 148, 149

Baltar, Gaius 9, 10, 12, 13, 14, 17, 23, 25, 27, 31, 36, 39, 40, 42, 43, 46, 49, 55–

66, 68, 69, 70–71, 74, 75, 77, 84, 88, 89, 96, 102, 103, 104, 105, 107, 108, 109, 118, 119–122, 124, 124, 128, 129, 131, 132, 139–142, 145, 148, 149–152, 163, 167, 168, 170, 172, 175, 196, 198; Baltar Cult 7, 10, 12, 17, 55–66, 105, 108; *My Triumphs, My Mistakes* 56, 105; Virtual Baltar 64, 66, 124, 172, 198
Battlestar Galactica (original series) 8, 26
Battlestar Galactica (ship) 29, 59, 62, 64, 72, 90, 100, 101, 104, 105, 113, 114, 123, 128, 129, 167, 195, 196, 197
Battlestar Pegasus 100, 101, 167, 195, 197
Biers, D'Anna (Three) 13, 33, 45, 56, 69, 89, 109, 116–117, 122, 163
Blackbird 104
Bradbury, Ray 5; *Christus Apollo* 5; *The Martian Chronicles* 5

Cain (Biblical figure) 53, 82, 88, 89
Cain, Adm. Helena 100–101, 104, 130, 167, 195
Caprica (colony) 14, 22, 39, 49, 59, 69, 89, 11, 114, 121, 123, 129, 130, 132, 155, 172, 175, 176, 177, 179, 183, 187, 188, 189, 190, 198
Caprica (series) 13, 15, 32, 99, 106, 122, 174–190, 193, 197
Cavil, Brother John (One) 9, 17, 29–30, 33, 34, 39, 40, 45, 46, 49–50, 51, 53, 64, 65, 75, 77, 82, 84, 85, 86–88, 90, 117, 132, 196
Cayce, Edgar 109
Cerebus 106, 180–181
Christus Apollo 5
The Chronicles of Narnia 1, 5

Clarice *see* Willow, Sister Clarice
Clark, Arthur C. 4
Cloud Nine 101
The Cloud of Unknowing 12, 38, 43, 46, 53
Club Mysteries 106
Conoy, Leoben (Two) 8, 9, 13, 30, 32, 39, 40, 41, 44, 45, 46, 50, 51, 75, 82, 83, 109, 112, 115–116, 122, 123, 128, 130, 131, 132, 137, 196
Constantine 159
Cottle, "Doc" 32
Cylons *see individual character names*

Daniel (Seven) 40, 88, 89, 196
Demiurge 82, 83, 187
Doral, Aaron (Five) 39, 40

Earth 4, 8, 9, 12, 13, 14, 22, 25, 26, 27, 37, 39, 40, 53, 64, 66, 68, 69, 70, 72, 76, 79, 80, 85, 86, 88, 89, 92, 95, 96, 101, 104, 107, 108, 111, 113, 114, 115, 116, 118, 119, 122, 125, 128, 129, 130, 137, 141, 150, 151, 152, 160, 161, 163, 164, 166, 167, 171, 172, 173, 176, 178, 195, 196, 197
Eight 39, 40, 88–89; Sharon "Athena" Agathon 23, 28, 39, 40, 47, 48, 65; Sharon "Boomer" Valerii 39, 40, 49, 51, 52, 55, 71, 84, 89, 90, 123
Elijah 110, 113–114, 117, 120
Elosha 17, 22, 27, 28, 30, 32, 34, 35, 118–119, 163, 165, 169
The Empire Strikes Back 6
Eve 4, 34, 66, 77, 81, 88, 91, 114, 172, 174
exile 13, 93, 94, 95, 106–108

Final Five 39, 40, 41, 42, 69, 84, 85, 91, 96, 116, 117, 122, 128, 173, 196–197
Foster, Tory 40, 41, 61, 167, 196, 197
Four (Simon O'Neill) 39

Gaeta, Felix 71, 196
Gemenon 22, 35, 36, 71, 76, 102, 176, 177, 178, 183, 185
Gnosticism 82, 83, 145–146
The Gospel of Judas 145–146, 148, 151
Graystone, Amanda 179, 181, 182, 186, 187
Graystone, Daniel 39, 99, 175, 176, 179, 181–182, 185, 186, 187, 197
Graystone, Zoe 39, 174, 176–183, 185, 186, 187, 188, 189
The Greatest Story Ever Told 127, 157

Heinlein, Robert 4
Hybrids 13, 39, 40, 51, 53, 82, 109, 114, 115, 122–123, 154
Islam 38, 58, 98, 177

Jesus 4, 6, 8, 11, 14, 45, 60, 69, 70, 71, 72, 76, 77, 83, 86, 88, 91, 95, 109, 111, 112, 117, 121, 125, 126, 127, 128, 130, 132, 133, 134, 137, 138, 142, 143, 144, 145, 146–149, 151, 154, 157, 159, 176, 178, 183, 190
Jesus of Nazareth 127
Job 81, 86
Joe's Bar 104, 128
John of Patmos 5, 81, 112, 155, 158, 163
John Paul II 80, 92
Jonah 111, 119–121, 141
Judaism 11, 85, 110
Judas Iscariot 10, 14, 67, 139–152, 179

King of Kings 157
Kobol 8, 9, 13, 21, 22, 24, 25, 26, 27, 28, 29, 31, 32, 36, 40, 42, 47, 71, 75, 86, 95, 101, 107, 113, 115, 117, 119, 123, 140, 169, 172, 187, 197
Kowalski, Emily 23, 24

Larson, Glenn A. 8, 109
The Last Temptation of Christ 159
The Late Great Planet Earth 161, 166
Left Behind 1, 5, 112, 154, 155, 157, 166, 168, 170
LeGuin, Ursula 5
Leoben *see* Conoy, Leoben
Leonardo DaVinci 4
Lewis, C.S. 5; *The Chronicles of Narnia* 1, 5; Ransom Trilogy 5
Lords of Kobol 11, 17, 23, 24, 28, 29, 30, 31, 53, 76, 131, 197
Lucifer 81, 86, 87, 88, 90

Maquis de Sade 87
The Martian Chronicles 5
Mary Magdalene 88–89, 130
The Matrix 154, 158, 159
Méliès, Georges 4
Mohammed 58
Monad Church 175, 177, 178, 179, 183, 184, 197
Moore, Ronald D. 18, 26, 131, 172
Mormon (Church of Jesus Christ of Latter Day Saints) 8, 26, 109
Moses 27, 28, 45, 48, 93, 97, 111, 114, 118, 128, 141
My Triumphs, My Mistakes 56, 105

New Caprica 31, 33, 39, 49, 56, 60, 75, 87, 95–96, 99, 100, 101, 104, 108, 114, 115, 116, 123, 140, 154, 167, 170, 195, 197
New Earth 3, 15, 65, 66, 77, 78, 79, 86, 88, 89, 91, 96, 102, 108, 111, 113, 123,

124, 132, 141, 155, 156, 158, 161, 162, 163, 165, 167, 170, 171
Novacek, Daniel "Bulldog" 105

Olympic Carrier 75, 167
O'Neill, Simon *see* Four
Origen 78

Passion of the Christ 1
Paul 2, 6, 41, 42, 70, 76, 77, 82, 90–91, 95, 134, 135–137, 140, 146, 149, 183
Poe, Edgar Allan 4
Porter, Sarah 76
Pythia (Scroll of) 9, 26, 27, 28, 66, 71, 72, 110, 117, 118, 125, 131, 146, 163, 164, 165–167, 168

Quorum of Twelve 8, 102, 104, 109, 110, 161, 196

Rand, Lacy 175, 176, 179, 184–185, 186
Ransom Trilogy 5
remnant 13, 93, 94, 97–108
Resident Evil 160
resurrection 3, 7, 13, 14, 47, 51, 52, 64, 67, 69, 70, 72, 87, 88, 107, 116, 117, 125–126, 131, 132–136, 137, 138, 150, 181, 182, 183, 189
Revelation 6, 14, 81, 112, 117, 154–157, 160, 161, 162, 165–167
Robocop 160
Roslin, Pres. Laura 9, 13, 22, 23, 26, 27, 32, 34, 36, 37, 55, 58, 59–60, 61, 65, 69, 74, 76, 102–103, 104, 105, 109, 110, 113, 114, 117–119, 122, 125, 131, 141, 164–165, 171, 195
Russell, Maria Doria 5

Sacred Scrolls 11, 17, 22, 25, 26–28, 32, 34, 35, 47, 66, 68, 71, 104, 107, 110, 146, 164–166, 183, 197
Sagittarons 22, 35, 102
salvation 3, 9, 11, 12, 13, 14, 28, 31, 36, 41, 51–53, 54, 59, 63, 66, 67, 68, 70, 71, 72, 75–77, 78, 92, 118, 121, 123, 125, 128, 130, 131, 132, 134, 137, 140, 141, 142, 143, 144, 146, 147, 149, 150, 151, 152, 154, 156, 159, 160, 163, 164, 167, 168, 171, 172, 173, 182, 188
Satan 81, 86
Schaffer, Paulla 60, 61
Sci-Fi Channel 1, 2
Scorsese, Martin 2
Seventh Heaven 1, 171
sin 12, 36, 72–75, 78, 84
Six 9, 10, 13, 18, 39, 42, 45, 47, 48, 49, 50, 52, 53, 55, 56, 57, 58, 62, 64, 65,

66, 69, 74, 75, 84, 85, 88, 89, 109, 115, 120, 121, 123–124, 132, 139, 140, 141, 151, 196, 198; Caprica Six 40, 45, 46, 47, 48, 49, 52, 55, 64, 89, 109, 123–124, 196, 198; Virtual Six 9, 18, 25, 40, 45, 46, 52, 56, 57, 58, 59, 61, 62, 64, 65, 66, 69, 75, 77, 84, 108, 115, 120, 121, 124, 140, 141, 145, 154, 163, 167, 172, 198
Smith, Joseph, Jr. 109
Soldiers of the One (STO) 39, 177, 178, 179, 183, 184, 185, 189, 197
Sons of Ares 60, 121
souls 83
Star Trek 14, 34, 154
Star Wars 6–7, 127; *The Empire Strikes Back* 6
Starbuck 8, 13, 14, 29, 30, 32, 33, 44, 45, 64–65, 68, 70, 73, 74, 83–84, 104, 108, 109, 112–115, 122–123, 125, 126,128–132, 135–138, 154, 163, 195–196
Superman Returns 160
supersessionism 44–45

Temple of Jupiter 25, 107, 163
Temple of the Five 25, 116
The Ten Commandments 127
Terminator 154, 158, 159
Terminator: Judgment Day 14, 158, 159
Terminator: Salvation 14, 159
Thrace, Kara *see* Starbuck
Thrace, Socrata 128
Tigh, Ellen 40, 41, 48, 50, 52, 84, 86–88, 117, 167, 196
Tigh, Saul 40, 41, 48, 52, 84, 85, 86–87, 90–91, 115, 123, 129, 130, 152, 167, 196
Touched by an Angel 1, 171
Twelve Colonies 9, 13, 21, 22, 27, 29, 35, 38, 40, 55, 79, 85, 86, 91, 94, 95, 100, 102, 105, 107, 108, 122, 139, 140, 155, 172, 173, 175, 183, 186, 195, 197
12 Monkeys 158
Tyrol, Cally 29, 31
Tyrol, Chief Galen 29, 33, 40, 45, 61, 70, 71, 196
Tyrol, Nicholas Stephen 29

Verne, Jules 4

Wells, H.G. 4
White, Ellen G. 109
Willow, Sister Clarice 174, 175, 177–179, 181, 182, 183, 187–189

Zarek, Tom 22, 23, 196